CHARACTER AND ENVIRONMENT

CHARACTER
AND
ENVIRONMENT

A Virtue-Oriented Approach to
Environmental Ethics

Ronald L. Sandler

COLUMBIA UNIVERSITY PRESS
NEW YORK

Columbia University Press
Publishers Since 1893
New York   Chichester, West Sussex
Copyright © 2007 Columbia University Press
All rights reserved

Library of Congress Cataloging-in-Publication Data
Sandler, Ronald L.
   Character and environment : a virtue-oriented approach to environmental ethics /
Ronald L. Sandler.
      p.   cm.
   Includes bibliographical references and index.
   ISBN 978-0-231-14106-2 (cloth : alk. paper) — ISBN 978-0-231-51186-5 (electronic)
   1. Environmental ethics. 2. Environmental responsibility. 3. Virtue. I. Title.
GE42.S26 2008
179'.1—dc22

                                        2006100053

References to Internet Web sites (URLs) were accurate at the time of writing. Neither the
author nor Columbia University Press is responsible for URLs that may have expired or
changed since the manuscript was prepared.

To Emily Allison Mann

CONTENTS

PREFACE

This is a book on environmental ethics. My primary project is to develop and defend a virtue-oriented approach to environmental ethics. But it is also a book on virtue ethics. I defend a particular theory of virtue, virtue-oriented principle of right action, and virtue-oriented method of decision making. Moreover, the primary project has implications that extend beyond environmental ethics to moral philosophy more generally. It demonstrates the ways that an ethic of character can and should be informed by environmental considerations. It also helps to justify virtue-oriented ethical theory. Ethical theories must be assessed on their theoretical and practical adequacy with respect to all aspects of the human ethical situation: personal, interpersonal, and environmental. To the extent that virtue-oriented ethical theory in general, and the version defended here in particular, provides a superior environmental ethic to other ethical theories, it is to be preferred over them not just as an environmental ethic but also as an ethical theory.

ACKNOWLEDGMENTS

I began research for this book while at Southern Illinois University at Edwardsville. I thank all my colleagues in the Philosophy Department there for making it such an intellectually rich and supportive environment for doing philosophy. Special thanks are due to Skip Larkin, who helped me define and refine this project, and Judy Crane, whose work on philosophy of biology has influenced several aspects of this book. I am grateful to SIUE for a 2002 summer research fellowship to initiate research for this project.

I completed this book at Northeastern University, another wonderfully stimulating and supportive place for doing philosophy, and I thank all of my colleagues here for making it so. Special thanks are due to Steve Nathanson for his persistence in pushing me toward clarity of thought and presentation, and to Patricia Illingsworth and Susan Setta for their consistent encouragement and support. I am grateful to Northeastern University and the Department of Philosophy and Religion for a release from teaching during the spring 2005 semester to complete the first draft of the manuscript for this book.

All, or nearly all, of a draft of the manuscript was read by Phil Cafaro (at least twice), Steve Nathanson, Jason Kawall, Jennifer Welchman, Michael Meyer, Cynthia Townley, and students in my fall 2005 Environmental Philosophy Seminar. I am grateful to all of them for their many constructive comments, criticisms, and suggestions. I also thank Louke van Wensveen, Rosalind Hursthouse, Judy Crane, Chris Bosso, Rob Streiffer, Jim Anderson, Jeremy Bendik-Keymer, and John Danley for their helpful comments on either portions of the manuscript or papers containing material that appears in this book.

I am grateful to my graduate school advisors, Steve Nadler and Keith Yandel, for their instruction and guidance, as well as to Jim Anderson and Claudia Card for encouraging my interest in environmental ethics. Without their support this book would not have been written, and their influence permeates its subject matter, method, and style.

John Basl, Benjamin Miller, Emily Volkert, Thomas Lodwick, and William Currie provided valuable research assistance on this project. I am privileged to work with such motivated and capable undergraduate students. I also thank Jeff Sandler for his help editing and proofing the manuscript.

I am grateful to Wendy Lochner, my editor at Columbia University Press, for her support of this book and her patience as I completed it. I also thank Christine Mortlock and Leslie Kriesel for their help preparing the manuscript for publication.

Most of all, I thank my family. I am grateful to my parents, Karen and Howard, for their support; my brother, Jeff, for his companionship; and my children, Elijah and Ruth, for their love. This book is dedicated to my wife, Emily, a fabulous mother, scholar, and teacher, and beautiful person, who is my true love and closest friend. I thank her for sharing her life with me.

Some of the material in this book has appeared elsewhere in other forms. I thank the publishers and editors for permission to use material from each of the following articles:

Sandler, R. In press. "What Makes a Character Trait a Virtue?" *The Journal of Value Inquiry.*

Sandler, R. 2006. "A Theory of Environmental Virtue." *Environmental Ethics* 28 (3): 247–64.

Sandler, R. and J. Crane. 2006. "On the Moral Considerability of *Homo sapiens* and Other Species." *Environmental Values* 15 (1): 69–84.

Sandler, R. 2004. "Toward an Adequate Environmental Virtue Ethic." *Environmental Values* 13 (4): 477–95.

Sandler, R. 2004. "An Aretaic Objection to Agricultural Biotechnology." *Journal of Agricultural and Environmental Ethics* 17 (3): 301–17.

Sandler, R. 2003. "The External Goods Approach to Environmental Virtue Ethics." *Environmental Ethics* 25 (3): 279–93.

Sandler, R. 2002. "Environmental Ethics and the Need to Motivate Pro-Environmental Behavior." *Philosophy in the Contemporary World* 9 (2): 101–105.

CHARACTER AND ENVIRONMENT

Introduction

A Virtue-Oriented Alternative?

What is the good of drawing up, on paper, rules for social behavior, if we know that, in fact, our greed, cowardice, ill temper, and self-conceit are going to prevent us from keeping them? I do not mean for a moment that we ought not to think, and think hard, about improvements in our social and economic system. What I do mean is that all that thinking will be mere moonshine unless we realize that nothing but the courage and unselfishness of individuals is ever going to make any system work properly.... You cannot make men good by law: and without good men you cannot have a good society. That is why we must go on to think of the ... morality inside the individual.   —C. S. *Lewis*, Mere Christianity, 73

CHARACTER AND ENVIRONMENTAL ETHICS

Public discourse regarding the environment is framed almost exclusively in legislative and regulatory terms, so it is easy in environmental ethics to become fixated on what activities ought to be allowed or prohibited. After all, we legislate regarding behavior, not character; policy concerns actions, not attitudes; and the courts apply the standards accordingly. But it is always people, with character traits, attitudes, and dispositions, who perform actions, promote policies, and lobby for laws. So while we might condemn removing mountaintops, filling wetlands, and poisoning wolves, and make our case against these practices before lawmakers, courts, and the public, we must also consider the character of people responsible for them. How a person interacts with the environment is influenced by her attitudes toward it, and it seems to many that a central cause of reckless environmental exploitation is the attitude that nature is merely a resource for satisfying human wants and needs. As Aldo Leopold puts it in the foreword to *A Sand County Almanac*, "We abuse land because we regard it as a commodity belonging to us. When we see land as a community to which we belong, we may begin to use it with love and respect."[1] This is precisely the point, particularized to the environmental context, of the C. S. Lewis passage at the head of this chapter. Attempts to improve society, including its relations with the natural environment, will amount to mere moonshine if its citizens lack the character and commitment to make them work.

Good environmental character is not only valuable insofar as it leads to proper actions. It is also beneficial to those who possess it. Dispositions to appreciate, respect, wonder, and love nature enable people to find reward, satisfaction, and comfort from their relationship with nature. "Those who dwell, as scientists or laymen, among the beauties and mysteries of the earth are never alone or weary of life,"[2] observed Rachel Carson, and John Muir believed that "Everybody needs beauty as well as bread, places to play in and pray in, where nature may heal and give strength to body and soul alike."[3] For those who are receptive to it, nature can be a steady source of joy, peace, renewal, and knowledge.

These preliminary considerations intimate the multifariousness and richness of the relationship between human character and the environment. An adequate environmental ethic must have the descriptive and evaluative resources to accommodate this complexity, without homogenization or misrepresentation. The language of virtue and vice provides these resources. Louke van Wensveen, in her outstanding work on the history and progress of virtue language in environmental ethics, reports that she has "yet to come across a piece of ecologically sensitive philosophy, theology, or ethics that does not in some way incorporate virtue language."[4] Wensveen catalogues 189 virtue terms and 174 vice terms that have appeared in the contemporary environmental ethics literature, and she finds the use of virtue language to be integral, diverse, dialectic, dynamic, and visionary. It is not only everywhere in the discourse, it is indispensable to it. Virtue language, she concludes, puts us in touch with a powerful set of evaluative concepts and perspectives that, if afforded sufficient attention, can enhance our capacity to understand and respond to environmental issues. As she puts it, "One more language is one more chance."[5]

We could use one more chance. Our environmental problems are not simple, and they are not static. The wilderness and land use issues that dominated early environmentalism are still with us both in theory (e.g., conservation, preservation, and restoration paradigms) and in practice (e.g., off-road vehicle use and road building in national forests, fire suppression policy, wolf "management" programs, and species preservation). However, our pressing environmental problems go beyond issues concerning the use of the land and the treatment of flora and fauna "out there." In the 1960s and 1970s environmental issues came to us "here" in the form of pollution and chemicals, and brought their own theoretical disagreements (such as between cost-benefit analysis approaches to environmental decision making, free market approaches, distributive and procedural justice approaches, and environmental rights approaches) and practical issues (such as industrial zoning and permit issuance, manufacturing and consumer waste disposal, water privatization, and environmental justice). To these first- and second-generation problems have now been added third-generation problems that are not just "out there" or "right here" but "everywhere." Issues such as global warming, ozone depletion, and population growth offer unique theoretical and practical challenges because they are impersonal, distant (both spatially and temporally), collective action problems that involve the cumulative unintended effects of an enormous number of seemingly inconsequential decisions. Moreover, these three generations of environmental problems are interrelated. Energy policy, consumption patterns, trade policy, privatization of common goods, regulatory capacity, and corporate influence are implicated in each of them. Particular intergenerational problems also are often manifestations of the same process, from natural resources to consumer goods, at different stages (e.g., extraction of natural resources, transportation, refinement and manufacturing, consumption, and waste disposal). Furthermore, there is no reason to believe that a fourth generation of problems is not on the horizon. Genetic engineering and nanotechnology have the potential to realize environmental challenges that have previously been the stuff of science fiction.

Given the richness and complexity of our relationship with the natural environment and the diversity, dynamism, and interconnectedness of our environmental problems, it is somewhat surprising to find that many prominent approaches to environmental ethics are monistic. They emphasize one type of consideration as the basis for moral concern regarding the environment (for example, the inherent worth of living things, the interests of sentient beings, human preferences, human rights, or the integrity of ecosystems) and one type of responsiveness as justified on that basis (for example, respecting worth, minimizing suffering, maximizing preference satisfaction, respecting rights, or maintaining ecosystem integrity). Considering the variety of environmental entities to which we can be responsive and the forms of responsiveness possible, as well as the multiple dimensions of environmental issues, it seems unlikely that an adequate environmental ethic could be monistic in either of these ways. Evidence of this is that there are so many monistic approaches. Each gains some plausibility by capturing one of the many morally relevant aspects of our relationship with the natural environment. The natural environment provides humans with material goods. It contains values and individuals with worth independent of human beings. It allows for a variety of caring, aesthetic, recreational, and spiritual relationships and experiences. Attempts to accommodate these with a single moral basis or fit them into a single mode of moral responsiveness tend to distort them in the same way that the willingness to pay and contingent valuation method distort noneconomic goods when used to convert them into economic units. There is no distilling down all the bases and forms of moral responsiveness into one common moral currency.

I am, therefore, sympathetic with environmental pragmatists' claim that monistic environmental ethics are not sufficiently responsive to the diversity of environmental goods and values, the complexity of environmental issues, or the personal, social, cultural, political, and economic contexts in which they are embedded. But a pluralistic approach to environmental ethics is not necessarily a pragmatic approach. Pluralism in environmental goods and values does not imply that theoretical or foundational issues in environmental ethics are a distraction, are intractable, or should be set aside in favor of focusing on convergence among the practical and policy objectives of contrary monistic approaches. A theoretically grounded approach to environmental ethics that can accommodate pluralism in the justification for, bases of, and forms of environmental responsiveness would provide an alternative to both environmental monism and environmental pragmatism.

The virtue-oriented approach to environmental ethics that I advocate is pluralistic in each of these ways: with respect to the types of goods and values that make character traits environmental virtues—the justification for moral responsiveness; with respect to the types of objects, events, and entities for which environmental virtues are operative—the bases of moral responsiveness; and with respect to the types of reactions and behaviors that environmental virtues involve—the forms of moral responsiveness. An ethic of character is indispensable for a complete environmental ethic. It also can be the basis for an inclusive environmental ethic that accommodates the richness and complexity of human relationships and interactions with the natural environment and provides guidance on concrete environmental issues and problems. Establishing this is the primary project in this book.

OVERVIEW

The questions central to any environmental character ethic, and the questions that motivate and orient this book, are:

1. What makes a character trait an environmental virtue or vice?
2. What are the particular attitudes and dispositions that constitute environmental virtues and vices?
3. What is the proper role of an ethic of character in an environmental ethic?
4. How can an ethic of character help us understand and respond appropriately to the environmental challenges that we face?

What makes a character trait an environmental virtue or vice? In chapter 1 I defend a naturalistic, teleological, and pluralistic account of what makes a character trait a virtue or vice. It is naturalistic because it is consistent with and motivated by scientific naturalism. It is teleological because what makes a character trait a virtue is its conduciveness to promoting certain ends, and what makes a character trait a vice is its being detrimental to realizing those ends. It is pluralistic because the ends are both agent-relative (of which there is a plurality) and agent-independent (plural as well). This general account can be applied to particular areas or types of human activity, including human interactions and relationships with the natural environment, to identify virtues and vices that pertain to them.

What are the particular attitudes and dispositions that constitute environmental virtues and vices? In chapter 2 I apply the account of what makes a character trait a virtue to provide substantive specifications of environmental virtues and vices that emerge from the relationship between the environment and human flourishing. Among the virtues are dispositions that promote the integrity of ecosystems so that they can produce the goods necessary for human health (virtues of sustainability), dispositions that allow people to enjoy and be benefited by the natural environment (virtues of communion with nature), and dispositions conducive to maintaining opportunities for those goods and benefits (virtues of environmental stewardship and virtues of environmental activism). Environmental virtue is not limited to character traits that enhance our experience in environmental contexts—for example, openness, appreciation, receptivity, love, and wonder. Traits such as temperance, fortitude, commitment, optimism, and cooperativeness, which are favorable to effective efforts for securing environmental goods, resources, and opportunities, are also environmental virtues. Environmental vices discussed in this chapter include dispositions that are detrimental to maintaining environmental health at the levels needed to provide the goods necessary for human flourishing (e.g., greed, intemperance, and profligacy), dispositions that prevent us from realizing benefits that the natural environment can provide (e.g., arrogance, hubris, and intolerance), and dispositions that are detrimental to the protection and maintenance of environmental goods (e.g., apathy, pessimism, and misanthropy).

In chapter 3 I consider whether nature or natural entities have value independent of their relationship to human flourishing that informs the content of environmental virtues and vices. I argue that living organisms and some sufficiently cohesive and organized environmental collectives have a good of their own that we ought to be concerned about for their sake. This inherent worth justifies dispositions of care, considerateness, and compassion toward them (virtues of respect for nature), and establishes callousness, indifference, and cruelty toward them as vices. I also argue that although ecosystems and species are not among the environmental collectives that have a good of their own, they are appropriately included in the fields of many environmental virtues (land virtues).

What is the proper role of an ethic of character in an environmental ethic? In chapter 4 the focus shifts to environmental decision making. I defend a virtue-oriented principle of right action and a virtue-oriented approach to decision making. I argue that an action is right to the extent that it best accomplishes the target of the operative virtues for a particular agent in a particular situation. Because the virtues, informed by situational and agent particularity, provide the standard of rightness, action guidance is accomplished through their application to a concrete situation. This is done by first identifying which virtues are relevant and then determining what course of action those virtues favor in that situation. This can involve the use of virtue rules—rules that embody the substance of the virtues—collaborative discourse with others, the counsel of mentors, the study of role models, and moral wisdom. I advocate applying this approach in environmental contexts and to environmentally related issues.

In chapter 5 I present the argument, outlined earlier in this introduction, in favor of the virtue-oriented approach as an environmental ethic, and reply to several specific objections to the possibility of an adequate virtue-oriented approach to environmental ethics. I discuss the ways the approach is objective/relative and anthropocentric/nonanthropocentric, enumerate the many respects in which it is pluralistic, and reflect on commonalities and differences between the virtue-oriented approach and pragmatic approaches to environmental ethics.

How can an ethic of character help us understand and respond appropriately to the environmental challenges that we face? In chapter 6 I apply the virtue-oriented method of environmental decision making to the issue of genetically modified crops, thereby demonstrating "in practice" what is argued for "in theory" in the previous chapters: the virtue-oriented approach provides effective and nuanced action guidance on concrete environmental issues. The approach favors a position of selective endorsement of genetically modified crops. It establishes a general presumption against their use as the primary method of responding to our growing agricultural challenges. However, if a particular genetically modified crop is to be adopted as part of a comprehensive response that also addresses the social, institutional, and ecological components of some compelling agricultural challenge, such as preventing widespread malnutrition, and there is strong evidence that the technology will not compromise the capacity of ecosystems (both agricultural and nonagricultural) to produce the goods necessary for human and nonhuman flourishing, then the crop should be supported.

In the concluding chapter I review what I take to be the implications of the main themes of this book for environmental ethics and moral philosophy more generally. I also indicate some of the work pertaining to virtue-oriented environmental ethics and the relationship between human character and the natural environment that remains to be done.

I

What Makes a Character Trait a Virtue?

Men need virtues as bees need stings. An individual bee may perish by stinging, all the same bees need stings; an individual man may perish by being brave or just, all the same men need courage and justice. —*Peter Geach*, The Virtues, *17*

Good character, from the agent's point of view is not so much character that is seen to be biologically necessary or desirable as it is character that one wants in the choices one must make between persons and between possible selves.
—*Edmund Pincoffs*, Quandaries and Virtues, *68*

IDENTIFYING ENVIRONMENTAL VIRTUE

If claims about which character traits are environmental virtues and vices are to be more than rhetoric, there must be some basis or standard for their evaluation. Moreover, disagreements about which traits are environmental virtues or vices often arise from different conceptions of what makes a character trait a virtue or vice generally. A person who believes that virtues are character traits conducive to maximizing material benefits for herself will endorse a different set of dispositions toward the environment than a person who believes that virtues are character traits conducive to living in harmony with all living things. The central project of this chapter is to defend a general account of what makes a character trait a virtue or vice, which can be applied to environmentally related interactions, relationships, and activities to generate substantive accounts of environmental virtues and vices.

This *virtue theory approach* to identifying environmental virtues and vices is not the approach most often employed by environmental ethicists. One common alternative is the *environmental exemplar approach,* which is grounded in firm beliefs about who is environmentally virtuous. It proceeds by examining the character of those exemplars to derive substantive accounts of particular environmental virtues, as well as a general account of what makes a character trait an environmental virtue. For example, on the basis of careful study of the lives and characters of Aldo Leopold, Rachel Carson, and Henry David Thoreau, Philip Cafaro concludes:

> Any environmental virtue ethics worthy of the name must...include: (1) A desire to put economic life in its proper place—that is, as a support for comfortable and decent human lives, rather than as an engine powering endlessly more acquisition and consumption...; (2) A commitment to science, combined with an appreciation of its limits...; (3) Nonanthropocentrism; (4) An appreciation of the wild and support for wilderness protection...; [and] (5) A bedrock belief that life is good: both human and nonhuman.[1]

The environmental exemplar approach has two significant limitations that arise from the privilege it affords obtaining beliefs about who is environmentally virtuous. First, to the extent that those beliefs can be distorted, narrow, or otherwise inadequate, the approach can result in mistaken assessments of some character traits and an inaccurate account of what makes a trait an environmental virtue. Second, the approach does not provide resources for adjudicating between competing beliefs about who is environmentally virtuous. The lives and characters of the heroes of North American environmentalists may differ substantially from those of the environmental heroes of North American sportsmen, ranchers, loggers, or developers, as well as from those of people in other parts of the world. Therefore, the fact that some of us, or even quite a lot of us, find a particular person to be environmentally admirable is not sufficient to establish that the traits she exemplifies are environmental virtues. This is not to dismiss the importance of the study of exemplars; rather, it is to recognize that obtaining beliefs about who is environmentally virtuous can be only one among several considerations that must be taken into account when identifying environmental virtues and developing a theory of what makes a character trait an environmental virtue. It is also to recognize that our regarding a particular trait as an environmental virtue does not make it an environmental virtue.

Another common alternative is the *extensionist approach,* which begins with a character trait considered to be a virtue in interpersonal interactions or relationships and then proceeds by arguing that the virtue ought to be operative in environmental interactions or relationships as well. For example, Geoffrey Frasz defends friendship with the land as an environmental virtue on the grounds that a person's relationship with the land can provide enrichment and benefits analogous to those attending healthy interpersonal friendships. Natural communities and ecosystems, he argues, have intrinsic value and interests in the same sense that humans do, and "one can gain more in the long run for one's life by being a friend to the natural world than by merely focusing on the short-term gains one can selfishly attain."[2] Therefore, just as we ought to cultivate friendship with other people, we ought to cultivate friendship with the land. The extensionist approach is also employed by Jennifer Welchman in her defense of benevolence and loyalty as environmental virtues. An environmentally virtuous person, she argues, is a capable and constant steward of nature, and the character traits that make for a competent steward of nature are the same as those that make for a competent steward in interpersonal matters.[3] Principal among these are benevolence and loyalty, so benevolence and loyalty are environmental virtues. It is indicative of the extensionist approach's prevalence that both Frasz and Welchman employ it despite holding contrary views on what is necessary for an adequate environmental ethic. Welchman is concerned with developing an enlightened anthropocentric approach to environmental ethics, whereas Frasz is committed to defending a nonanthropocentric ethic.

Like the study of exemplars, thinking in terms of extension from interpersonal virtues can be useful as part of an approach to identifying environmental virtues and vices, but is inadequate on its own. Whether a particular interpersonal virtue is appropriately extended to some environmental or environmentally related context, activity, or relationship must be determined case by case, virtue by virtue. The crucial issue in each case is whether the bases of responsiveness of the virtue and the considerations that justify it as a virtue in interpersonal contexts are present also in some environmental contexts. Take, for example, Frasz's extensionist argument that friendship with the land is an environmental virtue. If the argument is sound, the features that make friendship a virtue in certain interpersonal contexts and the conditions for its operation in those contexts must obtain as well for at least some people's relationship with the land. They do not. Friendship involves mutual concern for the welfare of the other. However, the land is not concerned with our or anything else's welfare, since it lacks the necessary psychological capacities. There may be certain parts of the biotic community—i.e., sufficiently psychologically complex individuals—that are capable of concern for people such that if they had the right sort of relationship with them, one with a history of mutual benefit and reciprocal concern, friendship might be both possible and justified. So we may be able to speak literally of friendship with certain individuals within ecosystems, but we can speak only metaphorically of the virtue of friendship with the land. It does not, however, follow from this that no virtues are appropriately extended to the land. For example, a full account of gratitude might reveal that a history of benefit, but not mutual concern, is necessary for the virtue to be operative. If so, that the land does not care about us does not preclude gratitude toward it from being an environmental virtue. The appropriateness of the extension would then depend upon whether the considerations that justify gratitude as a virtue in interpersonal contexts are present also in some environmental contexts. These examples illustrate that it is not possible to employ the extensionist strategy without a background account of what makes a character trait a virtue, since claims about a virtue's justification and operation presuppose such an account.

Another reason that extensionism cannot be an exhaustive approach to identifying environmental virtues and vices is that there may be virtues specific to environmental entities, interactions, or relationships that might be justified through distinctive environmental values. If there are such values, then environmental virtue may involve dispositions to appropriately acknowledge and respond to them, whether or not they are implicated in human flourishing or have a ready analogue in interpersonal ethics.

Thus, while the environmental exemplar and extensionist approaches can contribute to identifying environmental virtues and vices, neither is an adequate alternative to the virtue theory approach. With respect to the environmental exemplar approach, a background theory about what makes a character trait a virtue is necessary as a remedy against the possibility of distorted, biased, or otherwise limited beliefs about who is an environmental exemplar, as well as for adjudicating among conflicting claims about who is environmentally virtuous. With respect to the extensionist approach, assessing a candidate extension involves determining whether the justification for the virtue and its bases of responsiveness really are present in the environmental context. This requires a background account of what makes the character trait a virtue. Moreover, neither approach tracks what actually makes a character trait an environmental virtue.

THE NATURALISTIC ASSUMPTION

Character traits are dispositions to take certain kinds of considerations to have normative or motivational force with respect to actions, emotions, and desires, under certain circumstances.[4] People exhibit different character traits when they standardly take the same consideration to be a reason, either justifying or motivating, for responding in different ways. This is the basis of Aristotle's claim that "the coward, the rash person, and the brave person are all concerned with the same things, but have different states related to them."[5]

The following discussion of what makes a character trait a virtue or vice begins from the naturalistic premise that human beings are essentially biological beings. Like all other living organisms, we are composed of matter, live and die, depend upon our environment for survival, are subject to the laws of nature, and have our "nature" in our genes. We are, like them, the product of evolutionary processes that have no goal, no teleology. If this naturalistic premise is violated in what follows—if, for example, there is an implicit appeal to the "teleology of nature"—then the argument will have gone awry. To embrace this form of naturalism is not to claim that human beings are the same as individuals of other species. We are different in our physiological makeup, psychological capacities, and way of going about the world. But being unique is nothing unique to us. Individuals of every species differ in these ways from individuals of all other species. If they did not, they would not be of a different species. There is thus quite a lot of sameness and quite a lot of difference between human beings and individuals of other species. Central to any attempt to understand our relationship with the natural world and the nonhuman individuals that populate it is sorting out which of these similarities and differences are ethically significant. A perennial question along this theme is: What difference does our rationality make? I will argue that in specifying the dispositions constitutive of human virtue, including environmental virtue, it makes a considerable difference.

However, I do take it as a corollary to the naturalistic premise that questions about ethics—i.e., questions about how we should live—are questions about how we should live as the biological beings that we are, given the particular world we are in. They are not questions about how we should live as rational beings or moral agents independent of the facts about human beings and our environment. Doing ethics involves reflecting on ourselves, a distinctive kind of living, social, sentient, rational animal, and our world in an attempt to determine how a creature like us ought to go about in a world like ours. Approaching ethics in this way does not eliminate room for disagreement about what makes a character trait a virtue or vice. There have been quite a few recent attempts to provide a theory of virtue consistent with scientific and ethical naturalism. In the next section I consider one of these attempts in some detail, both because I believe it gets quite a lot right about what makes a character trait a virtue and because it functions as a convenient foil against which to develop the account that I advocate.

THE NATURAL GOODNESS APPROACH

A widely held view of what makes a character trait a virtue is that virtues are character traits that a person needs to flourish or live well.[6] Let us accept, provisionally, this eudaimonistic account. In an attempt to provide content to this general account, Rosalind Hursthouse, building on work by Philippa Foot, argues that the evaluative structure of claims about good human beings is analogous to that of claims about good individuals of other species, so that "when we talk about ethically good human beings, we have not suddenly started to use the word 'good' in a totally new 'moral' or 'evaluative' way."[7] According to this *natural goodness approach*, scientific naturalism provides a distinctive evaluative structure for assessing the goodness of a living thing as a living thing, as well as the premise that humans are to be evaluated as a type of living thing. Foot summarizes the view as follows:

Judgments of goodness and badness...[have]...a special "grammar" when the subject belongs to a living thing, whether plant, animal, or human being.... "Natural" goodness...which is attributable only to living things themselves and to their parts, characteristics, and operations, is intrinsic or "autonomous" goodness in that it depends directly on the relation of an individual to the "life form" of its species.[8]

What, then, do we mean by "good" when we ascribe it to a living thing as a living thing? Hursthouse proposes that when it comes to plants, evaluations of goodness are made according to how well their parts (for example, leaves, roots, and flowers) and operations (for example, drawing up water, flowering, and dropping leaves) serve the ends of survival and continuance of their species, in the way characteristic of their species. An oak with shallow roots and a rhododendron that never flowers are defective. They are, in those respects, poor specimens of their kind. But when it comes to species whose members have greater psychological sophistication, there is often more to living well than mere survival and contributing to species continuance. For species whose members are sentient, there is avoidance of pain and experience of pleasure. For species whose members are social, there is being a member of a well-functioning social group. Moreover, how adept an individual is at realizing the (now four) ends often depends upon more than its bare physiological parts and operations. Individuals of some species perform actions and have desires and emotions. Therefore, according to Hursthouse, the goodness of psychologically sophisticated social animals is evaluated as follows:

A good social animal...is one that is well fitted or endowed with respect to (i) its parts, (ii) its operations, (iii) its actions, and (iv) its desires and emotions; whether it is thus well fitted or endowed is determined by whether these four aspects well serve (1) its individual survival, (2) the continuance of its species, (3) its characteristic freedom from pain and characteristic enjoyment, and (4) the good functioning of its social group—in the ways characteristic of the species.[9]

Just like an oak with shallow roots and a rhododendron that never flowers, a free-riding wolf, an antisocial bonobo, and a brittle-hoofed moose are defective. They are, in those respects, poor specimens of their kind.

Claims such as these do not go far, if at all, beyond the kind of evaluations that botanists, ethologists, and zoologists regularly make. Because there is a fact of the matter about how the parts, processes, emotions, and actions of individuals of a particular species standardly function in the form of life of that species (i.e., its members' characteristic ways of pursuing and accomplishing the relevant ends), there is a standard for judging the goodness of individuals as a member of their species.[10]

Natural goodness assessments are not always clean and easy to make, especially when it comes to making overall judgments of individuals, as opposed to judging a single aspect in light of a single end. Species boundaries can be hard to define, and often there is significant variation in how individuals of a species characteristically go about pursuing the relevant ends. This is particularly true for different sexes of some species, for some species with distinct life stages, for some species that range over diverse habitats, and for species in which different types of individuals play different social roles. Such variations often require contextualizing claims about what is characteristic for the species. Moreover, natural goodness judgments are, as Hursthouse puts it, "true only 'for the most part.'"[11] It is important to be mindful of this indeterminacy and complexity when making judgments of the natural goodness of individuals. However, this does not undermine the legitimacy of such judgments. Although some cases will be difficult or even inscrutable, others will be quite clear, even if contextualized—that a particular individual is a good or bad specimen, in certain respects, given its environment, age, and so on. Moreover, it is not a shortcoming of natural goodness evaluations that they can be messy in this way. The imprecision is built into the subject matter. It is in the evaluations of natural goodness because it is in the science, and it is in the science because it is in the world. Finally, it is important to recognize that being a good specimen of one's kind does not guarantee a long, enjoyable, reproductively successful, or otherwise flourishing life. The world is a place of chance and peril. To be a good specimen of one's kind is not to be outside the reach of circumstance and fortune. A panther that fails to find a mate because all other panthers in the area have been killed by poachers is not a defective panther. It is an unfortunate one.

What does all this have to do with us? Recall that according to proponents of the natural goodness approach, we should not expect the structure of evaluative judgments of goodness and badness to be transformed as we move from assessments of plants to assessments of nonhuman animals to assessments of human beings. Therefore, they advocate applying the natural goodness form of evaluation to us, not only with respect to strictly biological evaluations (assessments of health) but also with respect to character evaluations (assessments of virtue and vice), which involve evaluating what remains after the bare biological parts and processes are separated out: emotions, desires, and actions (from both reason and inclination).[12] Doing so generates the following *natural goodness thesis*:

> A human being is ethically good (i.e., virtuous) insofar as she is well fitted with respect to her (i) emotions, (ii) desires, and (iii) actions (from reason and inclination); whether she is thus well fitted is determined by whether these aspects well serve (1) her survival, (2) the continuance of the species, (3) her characteristic freedom from pain and characteristic enjoyment, and (4) the good functioning of her social groups—in the way characteristic of human beings.[13]

Although Hursthouse and Foot believe evaluations of human character have the same structure as evaluations of the goodness of other species, they both also recognize that our rationality makes a difference in at least two important and interconnected ways. First, there is no single way that human beings "characteristically" pursue or realize the naturalistic ends.[14] Our biology constrains us to some extent. For example, human infants cannot survive on their own and we require some interpersonal relationships. But even so, human social systems, ways of taking pleasure and avoiding pain, and approaches to raising children have varied widely over time, among cultures, and between individuals.[15] Furthermore, we might go about doing these things quite differently in the future than we do right now or have done in the past. Our capacities to conceive, execute, and propagate the alternatives, which require theoretical and practical rationality as well as imagination and particular forms of social learning, make this variation possible.[16] We imagine a way of going about or realizing something, judge it as good, and then devise ways to attempt to accomplish it.[17] If it works out well, then we might pass it on to others either actively or passively. Therefore, although human beings do not have a characteristic way of going about the world in the same sense as do other species, we do characteristically go about the world in a rational way, where, as Hursthouse puts it, "A 'rational way' is any way that we can rightly see as good, as something we have reason to do."[18] Furthermore, that there are a variety of character traits we might have and that our characteristic way of going about the world is "rationally" provide the basis for evaluating character traits in light of their conduciveness to promoting endorsable (or rightly seen as good) realizations of the naturalistic ends. Therefore, ethics is not "just a branch of biology or ethology."[19] Enabling this normative ethical naturalism is the second way proponents of the natural goodness approach believe our rationality makes a significant difference.[20]

The natural goodness approach to evaluating character traits is attractive in several respects. It is informed and motivated by scientific naturalism, including a naturalistic understanding of human beings. The aspects of human beings that are evaluated (desires, emotions, and actions from reason and inclination) are those standardly associated with ethical character. The criteria against which these aspects are assessed cohere well with common beliefs about the role that virtues play in our lives. The approach fits with familiar eudaimonistic views about what makes a character trait a virtue. Moreover, it is able to accommodate crucial ways our rationality makes a difference in evaluating our goodness, as opposed to evaluating the goodness of nonrational, nonhuman living things. For these reasons, I believe that the natural goodness approach provides a generally accurate account of how a naturalistic evaluation of character traits ought to be structured: character traits ought to be evaluated according to how conducive they are to promoting certain ends; those ends must be informed by the sort of living, sentient, social, rational animals that we are; and what are subject to evaluation are our dispositions regarding actions, desires, and emotions. However, there are some problems with how scientific naturalism is used to justify the natural goodness approach. There are also differences that our rationality makes when evaluating our goodness that are not reflected in the thesis. Our rationality gives rise to additional ends that are part of our flourishing and enables us to modify our life form in ways that can alter the ends that are part of our flourishing. It also allows us to recognize noneudaimonistic ends—ends independent of our own flourishing—as making a claim on us. The upshot of these considerations (discussed below) is that we must move to a teleological, pluralistic account of what makes a character trait a virtue.

THE LIFE FORM OF THE SPECIES PERSPECTIVE

Proponents of the natural goodness approach place too much justificatory burden on scientific naturalism. The approach is thought to follow from a naturalistic understanding of human beings and that "good" has a distinctive evaluative, grammatical, or logical structure when attributed to a living thing as a living thing. However, for this to be the case there must be a single naturalistic or scientific perspective for evaluating a living thing as a living thing, something like the model in botany and ethology, on which an individual is evaluated according to how well fitted it is for fulfilling the life form of its species—i.e., the characteristic way individuals of the species go about the world and realize the relevant ends. However, there are quite a lot of ways to divide up the natural world into kinds other than by species. Why not model our ethical evaluations on evaluations of a living thing as a member of a genus, a bearer of a particular genotype, or a member of a local group or population? Moreover, there are many ways to evaluate individuals scientifically other than as ethologists and botanists do. For example, an evolutionary biologist might evaluate living individuals according to how well adapted they are for promulgating their genes through future generations, while an ecologist might evaluate them according to how well they promote the integrity of the ecosystems of which they are part. Such evaluations are as naturalistic and scientific as those made by ethologists and botanists. Why, then, model our ethical evaluations of humans on one rather than the other?[21] Appeals to a distinctive evaluative, grammatical, or logical structure of "goodness" attributions will not be any help here, since it is the distinctiveness and content of that structure that is at issue. There are several naturalistic and scientific ways to evaluate the "goodness" of a living thing as a living thing, none of which is privileged for modeling ethical evaluations when viewed from the perspective of scientific naturalism.

Scientific naturalism and the attributive nature of "goodness," therefore, cannot justify evaluating character traits as virtues according to their conduciveness to fulfilling the life form of our species. There are other equally scientific and naturalistic ways of evaluating a human being as a living thing—for example, as a member of some category other than *Homo sapiens* or by standards not grounded in our life form. However, it does not follow that there is no justification for making ethical evaluations at the level of human moral agent in this world and from the perspective of our life form. The justification comes from the ethical side of ethical naturalism, from a generality commitment in ethics to norms at the level of human moral agents, and a commitment to human flourishing being understood from the perspective of an individual's physical, emotional, social, environmental, and psychological experience (i.e., her life form), not the perspective of her genes or her ecosystem.[22] These commitments do not undermine the legitimacy of adopting the "life form of the individual as a member of a species perspective" when making ethical evaluations. They show, perhaps unsurprisingly, that there are substantive ethical commitments involved in ethical naturalism, which scientific naturalism does not justify. These commitments orient ethical naturalism by validating a particular naturalistic perspective, the ethological or botanical perspective, for modeling ethical evaluations. Thus, the level of generality and perspective of character trait evaluation advocated by proponents of the natural goodness approach are preserved, albeit not without conceding that scientific naturalism does not fully justify them. The theoretical underpinnings of the structure of evaluations of human goodness are thus somewhat different than advocates of the natural goodness approach propose.

THE ASPECTS EVALUATED

Scientific naturalism does not fully justify beliefs, desires, and actions as the aspects of ourselves to be evaluated in ethical naturalism. This is not only because scientific naturalism does not fully justify the ethological model for ethical evaluation but also because nothing in scientific naturalism directs ethical evaluation toward those aspects and away from, for example, an individual's biological parts and operations.

However, we need not look for some scientific or naturalistic justification for focusing on these aspects of ourselves when evaluating character traits. Our conception of ethical character concerns beliefs, desires, reasons, and actions. A virtuous person is disposed to desire appropriate things for appropriate reasons, do the right thing for the right reasons, and do so with proper emotions.[23] For example, a compassionate person is appropriately disposed with regard to the suffering of others. A person fails to be compassionate if she is not disposed to help people who are suffering when she is well positioned to do so with little cost to herself (is not well disposed in regard to actions), if she helps in such situations only because she wants others to feel indebted to her (is not well disposed in regard to desires and reasons), or if she is contemptuous and resentful of those she helps (is not well disposed in regard to emotions). A courageous person is well disposed in actions, reasons, and emotions with regard to physical and psychological dangers. A person who sacrifices herself or exposes herself to risks for bad reasons or for ends or by means that are not justifiable, or desires to do so, is poorly disposed in those respects.[24]

Dispositions regarding desires, emotions, reasons, and actions are the aspects of people that are standardly associated with virtue. They are justified as the proper objects of ethical evaluation by our pre- and post-theoretical beliefs about ethical character, not because they find privilege within scientific naturalism. Once again, a feature of the natural goodness approach is preserved, although scientific naturalism alone provides insufficient justification for it.

THE ENDS CONSTITUTIVE OF HUMAN FLOURISHING

Scientific naturalism does not fully justify the ends constitutive of human flourishing. This is not only because it does not fully justify the ethological model for ethical evaluation but also because those ends are not fixed by the biological or anthropological facts about human beings. It is not merely, as proponents of the natural goodness approach emphasize, that how we can realize the ends constitutive of human flourishing in a form rightly seen as good is left unsettled by our evolutionary history, the biological functioning of our parts and systems, and how we have realized the ends in the past. What the ends are is also left unsettled.

Because we are a species of biological being and the life form perspective is appropriate for ethical evaluation, the type of naturalistic ends included in the natural goodness thesis are the proper place to begin developing an account of human flourishing. Because we are living beings, our ends include survival and species continuance. Because we are sentient beings, they include enjoyment and the avoidance of pain. Because we are social beings, they include the well-functioning of our relationships and social groups. Moreover, because our rationality makes a difference in the ways discussed earlier, the realizations of these ends must be endorsable or properly seen as good. There is certainly room for discussion about the details of the naturalistic ends appropriate to us as living, social, sentient animals. For example, a proper understanding of the ends for a living individual does not include mere continuance of its species, but rather promulgation of its genetic material through future generations.[25] Nevertheless, something close to the natural goodness thesis' account of the ends appropriate to the living, sentient, social beings we are is going to be correct.

However, our rationality, culture, and technology enable us to develop our form of life in ways that have implications for the relative weight afforded to the ends and make possible the emergence of additional ends. As a result, we cannot look only at our evolutionary history or the biological functions of our parts or systems to settle the ends constitutive of human flourishing. We must also consider, critically of course, common beliefs about what constitutes human flourishing, as well as the ways rationality, culture, and technology shape and provide novel possibilities for our life form. Specifying the ends is thus a process of wide reflective equilibrium that incorporates, in addition to facts about our evolutionary past, our anthropological history, and the functions of our biological parts and systems, possibilities that our rationality opens to us both in itself and through culture, social practice, and technology, and common beliefs about human flourishing.

The ends appropriate to us as living, sentient, social animals gain further support because they cohere well with commonly held pre- and post-theoretical beliefs about the role that the virtues play in our lives, as well as with beliefs about what makes a character trait a virtue.[26] For example, honesty and compassion are thought to contribute to the good functioning of a person's social group and the formation of relationships that provide both enjoyment and assistance when needed. Temperance is thought to contribute to a person's physical and psychological well-being. Tolerance and charity are thought to contribute to social stability. Moreover, if a character trait were typically detrimental or thought to be detrimental to a person's social groups, longevity, and enjoyment and avoidance of pain, it likely would not be considered a virtue. Thus, the naturalistic argument for these being components of our flourishing is buttressed by common beliefs about what makes character traits virtues or vices.

However, these ends do not exhaust the constituents of human flourishing. Our rationality gives rise to additional eudaimonistic ends, beyond those appropriate to us as living, sentient, social animals. Hursthouse, when articulating the set of naturalistic ends that are part of her natural goodness account, raises the issue of whether there are ends that are appropriate to us in virtue of our rationality. She briefly considers and rejects two—"preparation of our soul for the life hereafter" and "contemplation"—and claims that no other alternatives present themselves.[27] However, there are at least three promising candidates for components of human flourishing that are not appropriate to nonrational (or significantly less or differently rational) social animals: meaningfulness, knowledge, and autonomy.[28]

We have the rational, cognitive, and psychological capacities to be concerned about the meaningfulness of our lives in a way that bears, pigeons, squid, and gophers cannot be about theirs. It is a consideration that we often appeal to when making evaluations of people, including ourselves. Moreover, it is intelligible to say that fortitude, perseverance, and optimism are virtues in part because they are conducive to people living meaningful lives. The considerations in favor of including meaningfulness as an end are thus similar to those for including the other naturalistic ends. Scientific naturalism constrains what can be endorsed as "a meaningful life" or "a life with meaning," but it does not render untenable the possibility of a meaningful life. Even if a conception of meaningfulness concerned with transcendental explanations for why *Homo sapiens* or a particular person exists is not consistent with scientific naturalism, a meaningful life can be understood through what goes on in this world: our projects, endeavors, and relationships, and our efforts and accomplishments regarding them.[29] Given that including meaningfulness as an end constitutive of human flourishing finds strong support within common beliefs about human flourishing and that scientific naturalism does not justify excluding it, it should be included as an end against which our dispositions regarding actions, desires, emotions, and reasons are evaluated. Thus, there is at least one end appropriate to us as rational animals, above and beyond those appropriate to us as living, sentient, social animals.

The case for including knowledge as an end is the role that the accumulation of knowledge, both individual and communal, plays in human life and the fact that possessing knowledge is commonly considered to be a human good. Just as we are social, emotional, and sentient, so too we are knowers. We continually process data and information, and form, sort out, choose among, deliberate upon, and accept and reject beliefs. This is not to claim that no nonhumans hold beliefs or have knowledge. Nor is it to claim that humans have no innate, instinctual, or genetic knowledge. But the accumulation and transmission of acquired knowledge between people and over generations is among the most striking and distinctive features of the way human beings go about the world. It is what enables our complex cultures and technologies, which distinguish us from other species.[30] People across all cultures spend considerable time and effort on knowledge creation, accumulation, and transmission. Beliefs, and getting them right and building upon them, are central to human activity. There are exceptions: some beliefs may be justified for their survival value or the contribution they make to the believer's psychological well-being or the good functioning of her community. Moreover, there may be some trivial knowledge, such as the number of blades of grass in my backyard, that cannot plausibly be seen as constitutive of human flourishing. Nevertheless, in general and under most circumstances, more knowledge is preferable to less knowledge, and a belief that is true is preferable to a belief that is false. Furthermore, many character traits, such as studiousness, openness, innovativeness, articulateness, patience, and humility, are considered virtues in part because of their conduciveness to the production, transmission, and reception of knowledge. For all these reasons, the accumulation of knowledge is among the ends constitutive of human flourishing.

The case for including autonomy as an end is that, because there are multiple forms of realizing the ends and multiple ways of pursuing them, it is possible for an individual to realize them in a way that is endorsable without it being a way that she has endorsed. However, such a life is missing something crucially human, something that is a part of our living well because of what our rationality makes possible, and something that is commonly thought to be relevant to the quality of our lives. Autonomy, then, concerns a person's capability to identify for herself the projects that orient her life and how she would realize the ends constitutive of human flourishing, as well as the capabilities (social, material, and psychological) to pursue them in the manner of her choosing.[31] Crucial to autonomy are understanding, freedom, and control. Understanding is a person's basic practical knowledge of her social, political, technological, and ecological environment. It is a functional knowledge of what is going on around her, why it is happening that way, and where she fits in. Freedom and control are the social context and internal capabilities of a person to reflect upon and choose her desired realization of the ends, as well as the social and material resources to pursue them.

Including meaningfulness, knowledge, and autonomy as constituents of human flourishing that emerge from our rationality does not imply that a person cannot flourish at all if these are not fully realized in her life. A person might live well in this or that way, or to a considerable extent overall, even as she fails to substantially realize one or more of the constituents of human flourishing. Enjoyment, well-functioning social groups, and a long, healthy life can be goods, even if they are not accompanied by full autonomy or meaningfulness in the senses described above. Moreover, there is no hierarchical ordering of the importance of each of the ends. Their prominence in people's lives is variable.

Incorporating the ends appropriate to us as rational beings into the natural goodness thesis generates the following thesis, which has the same teleological structure, life form of the individual perspective, and aspects evaluated as the natural goodness account, but different theoretical underpinnings:

> A human being is ethically good (i.e., virtuous) insofar as she is well fitted with respect to her (i) emotions, (ii) desires, and (iii) actions (from reason and inclination); whether she is thus well fitted is determined by whether these aspects well serve (1) her survival, (2) the continuance of the species, (3) her characteristic freedom from pain and characteristic enjoyment, (4) the good functioning of her social groups, (5) her autonomy, (6) the accumulation of knowledge, and (7) a meaningful life—in the way characteristic of human beings (i.e., in a way that can rightly be seen as good).

The arguments for including these additional ends have been brief. As with the ends appropriate to us as living, sentient, social animals, there is room for discussion about the ends appropriate to us as rational animals, and the thesis above can be modified easily to accommodate changes should they be warranted.[32] The thesis can also be modified as necessary to accommodate ends that go beyond a strictly naturalistic conception of human flourishing. For example, the U.S. National Science Foundation is supporting a research program that explores the possibilities for people

and society at the intersection of nanotechnology, biotechnology, information technology, and computer science.[33] The expectation is that "converging technologies integrated from the nanoscale would achieve tremendous
improvements in human abilities, and enhance social achievement."[34] According to Mihail Roco, who is Senior Advisor for Nanotechnology at the
National Science Foundation:

> Accelerated improvement of human performance has become possible
> at the individual and collective levels. We have arrived at the moment
> when we can measure signals from and interact with human cells and
> the nervous system, begin to replace and regenerate body parts, and
> build machines and other products with finesse suitable for direct inter-
> action with human tissue and the nervous system.[35]

Among the "key visionary ideas" of the program are "expanding human cognition and communication" and "improving human health and
physical capabilities" with products placed both inside and outside the
human body.[36] If it is successful, someday a description of the sort of beings we are might not be strictly naturalistic, and an account of the constituents of our flourishing might not be a strictly naturalistic account.[37]

It remains to be seen whether the development and widespread
implementation of technologies—such as synaptic knowledge access
ports, integrated human/machine intelligences, and digitally engineered personalities—that would challenge a strictly naturalistic conception of human flourishing are science fiction or science in progress.[38] But they are possible, and as such illustrate again that scientific
naturalism does not settle the ends constitutive of human flourishing.
Beyond giving rise to additional naturalistic ends, our rationality may
enable us to develop technologies that alter our life form in ways that
require de-emphasizing some naturalistic ends or recognizing some
artifactual ones.[39] Someday human beings might be living, sentient,
social, rational, networked animals.

THE PLURALISTIC TELEOLOGICAL ACCOUNT

It is time to reconsider the eudaimonistic assumption that has been operating since early in this chapter. According to eudaimonism, ethics is

about flourishing or living well, and a person is ethically successful or virtuous if she is well disposed to do so. But if How should I live? is the fundamental ethical question, then What kind of person should I be? is the fundamental question concerning character. This question has a broader scope than does What character traits are conducive to my flourishing? Moreover, our rational and psychological capacities enable us to value things in themselves and acknowledge that this value makes a claim on us to respond, independent of whether doing so (or being disposed to do so) promotes or is constitutive of our own flourishing.[40] Therefore, although it may turn out that eudaimonistic considerations are the only relevant ones when assessing character traits, it is presumptuous to rule out the possibility of other types of reason giving considerations from the beginning. The bare possibility that "What *makes* traits of character virtues is not just one feature (such as the promotion of good states of affairs or benefiting the agent), but several" requires moving to a more inclusive or pluralistic account of what makes a character trait a virtue, one that can accommodate both eudaimonistic and noneudaimonistic ends, should there be any.[41] For example, if living things or sentient animals have a good of their own that justifies concern for them for their own sake, then some character traits might be virtues at least in part because they promote, or do not hinder, the realization of their good. We certainly tend to think that something like this is the case with regard to benevolence toward other humans. This is not (yet) to claim that living things or sentient animals have such value. Moreover, it does not immediately follow from something's having agent-independent value what appropriate responsiveness to its value would involve. However, given that we can recognize such noneudaimonistic considerations, we must inquire whether there are any and, if there are, whether they justify some forms of responsiveness or character traits over others.

A committed eudaimonist might reply that she can accommodate these sorts of considerations either by subsuming them under the eudaimonistic ends already discussed or by including additional eudaimonistic ends. However, these responses fail to appreciate the nature of these additional considerations, which are distinguished from eudaimonistic considerations precisely because they directly concern ends or values independent of the agent's own flourishing. A eudaimonist might try to provide an argument that noneudaimonistic ends are not relevant to the

substantive specification of the virtues, but she cannot expect to sub-
sume agent-independent ends under agent-relative ends. Moreover, to
add them as ends on the grounds that acknowledging them is part of
agent flourishing is to give up the distinctive content of eudaimonism
and grant pluralism in what makes a trait a virtue. A eudaimonistic account of virtue that allows considerations unrelated to agent flourishing
to justify character traits as virtues is not really eudaimonism.

Amending the previous thesis on what makes a character trait a virtue
to accommodate the possibility of noneudaimonistic considerations in
the assessment of character traits generates the following *pluralistic teleological account* of what makes a character trait a virtue:

> A human being is ethically good (i.e., virtuous) insofar as she is well fit-
> ted with respect to her (i) emotions, (ii) desires, and (iii) actions (from
> reason and inclination); whether she is thus well fitted is determined by
> whether these aspects well serve (1) her survival, (2) the continuance of
> the species, (3) her characteristic freedom from pain and characteristic
> enjoyment, (4) the good functioning of her social group, (5) her autono-
> my, (6) the accumulation of knowledge, (7) a meaningful life, and (8) the
> realization of any noneudaimonistic ends (grounded in noneudaimonis-
> tic goods or values)—in the way characteristic of human beings (i.e., in
> a way that can rightly be seen as good).

This is the account of what makes a character trait a virtue that I endorse.
It is naturalistic, teleological, and pluralistic. It is naturalistic because it is
consistent with and motivated by scientific naturalism. It is teleological
because character traits are evaluated according to their conduciveness
to promoting certain ends. It is pluralistic because those ends are both
agent relative (of which there is a plurality) and agent independent (of
which there may be a plurality).

Some virtue theorists have argued that there are also nonteleological
considerations that make a character trait a virtue. The historical patron
of this view is David Hume, who considered the basis for the virtues to
be both usefulness and agreeableness.[42] A contemporary proponent of
the view is Michael Slote, who argues that character traits are justified by
their admirability.[43] Christine Swanton also advocates for nonteleological
justification on the Humean grounds that a "generally disutile trait can
be approved in virtue of its 'dazzling' qualities, or its ability to 'seize the

heart' by 'its noble elevation' or 'engaging tenderness.'"[44] Such traits are virtues, she argues, because they express fine inner states.

However, as discussed earlier, we cannot identify the virtues by merely reading off what human beings are like now or have been like in the past. The mere descriptive claim that some people find some traits to be admirable or agreeable does not imply that we ought to respond to them in that way or cultivate them. We must ask whether finding them agreeable and useful can be endorsed upon reflection, which is determined by whether they serve well the eudaimonistic and noneudaimonistic ends or whether a virtuous person or otherwise qualified observer would find them agreeable. The former involves evaluating them teleologically, while the latter requires an account of a virtuous person or qualified observer. In neither case does a trait's being admirable or agreeable provide an independent basis for its being a virtue, even if our finding it agreeable or admirable is a reliable indication that it is a virtue.[45]

Moreover, while it is true that the virtues are expressive, since they often have conative and affective profiles as well as evaluative and practical ones, to claim that certain character traits are virtues because they express fine inner states is to put the cart before the horse. They are expressive of fine inner states because they are expressive dimensions of inner states that are virtues. Evaluations of which character traits are virtues includes evaluations of which expressive dispositions are virtues. What makes a particular expressive disposition a virtue is not merely that it expresses a fine inner state, but that it does so in a way that tends to promote worthwhile ends. Expressive dispositions that tend to undermine social cohesion, people's health, or other ends are not virtues.

Advocates of nonteleological evaluation might respond by arguing that what makes a particular inner state fine, and thereby a virtue, is not itself teleological but something internal to the state, such as harmony among beliefs, desires, and emotions. However, the plausibility of this depends on the fact that high levels of dissonance among our beliefs, desires, and emotions are often detrimental to our well-being and, in some cases, the well-being of others. If the opposite were true, if harmonious inner states tended to compromise our capacity to live well and respond appropriately to other goods and values, we would not count them as fine. The same will hold for any internal relations among our beliefs, desires, and emotions that might be offered. The justification for their being fine will be based on their being conducive to our flourishing or realizing noneudaimonistic ends.

For these reasons, the pluralistic teleological account need not be amended to accommodate nonteleological evaluations of character traits. However, it does not follow from a strictly teleological account of what makes a character trait a virtue that all virtues are dispositions to promote certain ends. There is a difference between what makes a particular character trait a virtue and the substantive dispositional content of that virtue. On the pluralistic teleological account, all the considerations relevant to what makes a particular trait a virtue are teleological. But they might justify expressive or appreciative dispositions that are not targeted at promoting the ends. For example, a disposition to express gratitude when benefited by the efforts of another person may be a virtue because it is conducive to social cohesion and helps maintain beneficial relationships. But a grateful person does not aim at these things. She is responsive to what has been done for her, and aims at appropriate acknowledgment of it, not at benefiting herself or her social group in the long run. Therefore, although the pluralistic teleological account does not admit nonteleological considerations at the level of virtue justification, it does allow that some of the substantive dispositions constitutive of virtue are expressive rather than productive.

The remainder of this section consists of responses to several potential questions regarding the pluralistic teleological account. The aim is to clarify aspects that are significant in later chapters, as well as to help locate the account within the terrain of contemporary theories of virtue.

Is Virtue Constitutive of Human Flourishing?

On the pluralistic teleological account, the virtues are constitutive of human moral goodness. They are also conducive to promoting and maintaining agent flourishing and ends grounded in agent-independent goods and values. One important way virtues promote agent flourishing is by shaping their possessor's ethical outlook. A virtuous person accurately perceives what flourishing consists in and what agent-independent goods and values there are. This is reflected in her understanding of reward, benefit, gain, sacrifice, harm, and loss, for example, as well as in her conative, affective, and practical dispositions. As a result, she is well positioned to find meaning, reward, pleasure, and satisfaction in meeting well the demands of the world, eudaimonistic and noneudaimonistic. This is not to claim either that virtue is necessary for flourishing or that it is sufficient for flourishing. The demands of the world are too diverse and extensive, the role of luck and fortune in determining life outcomes is too great, and we are too physically, cognitively, and psychologically limited for these to be the case.[46] Nevertheless, one crucial way virtue promotes both agent flourishing and agent-independent ends is by shaping a person's ethical outlook to reflect what things are actually worth, and thereby substantially integrating her flourishing with the promotion of the ends. In this sense, virtue is also "constitutive" of human flourishing.

Are Actions Evaluated According to How Well They Promote the Ends?

The objects of evaluation of the pluralistic teleological account are not actions. The account does not claim that we should evaluate particular instances of assisting others, disclosing the truth, or hunting wild animals, for example, according to how well they promote the ends. In fact, it allows that an act of courage, compassion, generosity, or gratitude may be detrimental to realizing the ends, and yet be virtuous and even right. Nor is the approach concerned with evaluating practices, such as meat eating.[47] If meat eating is wrong, it is not because it is detrimental to the agent, her social relationships, or the continuance of the human species, but because it is contrary to virtue (e.g., compassion, temperance, or justice) in the form it takes under the circumstances (e.g., how the animal was treated, the ecological costs of its production and transportation, the available alternatives, and the social context of the meal), and there may be other forms of meat eating or other circumstances in which it would not be contrary to virtue. The virtue-oriented approach to environmental ethics is two-tiered. Tier 1 is concerned with identifying character traits that are virtues and vices. Tier 2 is concerned with assessing particular practices, behaviors, policies, or actions, under particular circumstances, according to the virtues. The pluralistic teleological account applies only to tier 1 assessments.

Is This a Consequentialist Theory of Virtue?

The pluralistic teleological account resembles some consequentialist theories of virtue in several significant respects. For example, as with

Julia Driver's consequentialist account, "a virtue is a character trait that systematically produces a preponderance of good."[48] Moreover, on both the pluralistic teleological account and Driver's account, human flourishing is a basic good, and it is not reducible to biological flourishing.[49] However, there are also several dissimilarities between the two accounts. For example, there are differences in the role that naturalism plays in justifying them, the significance of nonhuman goods and values,[50] and what they recognize as constituents of human flourishing.[51]

There are also significant differences between Driver's view and the virtue-oriented approach regarding the relationship between virtue and action. The virtue-oriented approach is two-tiered. Character traits are evaluated as described in the pluralistic teleological account, while actions, practices, and policies are evaluated according to the virtues. On Driver's view, both character traits and actions are evaluated according to their consequences.[52] Due to its two-tiered structure, the virtue-oriented approach more closely resembles rule consequentialism, and Brad Hooker's rule internalization version of it in particular, than act consequentialism.[53]

How Determinate a Specification of the Virtuous Life Does the Account Provide?

The pluralistic teleological account allows that there are innumerable ways for people to make their way in the world virtuously. Some projects and life courses will be ruled out—for example, the life of a gangster or grifter. The reason is that there is no way to be a gangster or grifter without being dishonest, disaffected, and otherwise vicious. But this will not be the case with the vast majority of life courses, careers, roles, and projects. Carpenters, school teachers, clergy, farmers, nurses, computer programmers, political leaders, talk radio hosts, and stay-at-home fathers, for example, may be virtuous or not, and the account does not imply that there is a hierarchical ordering of their ethical value. The account also underdetermines how a virtuous school teacher or farmer (or whatever) will behave. There may be multiple ways of responding virtuously in a particular situation, and there are variables relevant to the expression of virtue that will differ among individuals—for example, cultural context, status, bonds, skills, knowledge, commitments, and available resources. Moreover, the pluralistic teleological account is consistent with there being role- (e.g., parent), position- (e.g., leader), life stage- (e.g., elder), or context- (e.g., workplace) specific virtues, and with there being virtues that involve partiality toward those near and dear (e.g., children and close friends).

Furthermore, there will not always be coincidence among the character traits justified by eudaimonistic ends and those justified by noneudaimonistic ends. For example, the sort of fortitude, commitment, and focused devotion that may be most conducive to success in promoting environmental protections may not be the character traits most conducive to a person's own flourishing. But it would be a mistake to conclude from this that a person with those traits is not well disposed to meet the demands of the world. She is virtuous, though her virtue is substantially different from that of a person who is better disposed toward her own flourishing.[54] Therefore, the pluralistic teleological account allows that noneudaimonistic considerations can favor character traits that are not maximally conducive to promoting agent flourishing, and vice versa. This is not a weakness of the account. It reflects the facts about our situation. We are finite and complex beings, the demands of the world are ubiquitous and various, and there is no evolutionary necessity that eudaimonistic and noneudaimonistic ends always coincide. Moreover, a single, complete, harmonious, and unified specification of human virtue would not fit well with the vagaries and complexities that exist in the rest of the natural world. Given the naturalistic premise, there is reason to think that we should not be any different.

The pluralistic teleological account is a general account of what makes a character trait a virtue that can be employed to identify particular dispositions constitutive of human virtues. However, for all the reasons discussed above, not all virtuous lives are the same, and virtuous people do not always do the same thing under the same circumstances.

Is the Account Too Accommodating of What Can Be Considered a Virtue?

Given the previous response, one concern regarding the pluralistic teleological account might be that it does not adequately constrain what can be counted as a virtue. After all, almost every character trait is conducive to realizing at least one of the ends in at least some form under at least some circumstances. However, we are not without biological constraints and tendencies. For example, we are physically, intellectually, and psychologically limited, we depend on our environmental for survival, we must invest substantial resources in our young if they are to survive, and we have innate emotional and psychological predispositions.[55] There will be significant variation in how conducive character traits are to promoting the ends overall—as a whole and across contexts—as a result of their differential sensitivity to the facts about our life form and our world.

Furthermore, not all realizations of the ends are equally endorsable. As discussed earlier, accounts of the meaningfulness of life that are inconsistent with scientific naturalism are not endorsable, since they are contrary to the best information about ourselves and the world. Moreover, realizations of one end that are detrimental to accomplishing others, or the same end in the future, are less endorsable than those with greater fecundity. For example, recreational methamphetamine use can be pleasurable, but it undermines realizing most of the ends in the long run, so realizing pleasure in that way is unendorsable. Similarly, social groups that stymie the autonomy and intellectual development of their members, such as some college fraternities, are unendorsable for that reason, even if they function well. Other realizations of the ends may be unendorsable because they are detrimental to the flourishing of others or are premised on false beliefs. For example, the Ku Klux Klan and other racially motivated hate groups are socially disruptive, detrimental to those outside of the group, and premised on false beliefs about human biology and the moral significance of skin color and ethnicity. Therefore, even (or, more to the point, particularly) when these types of social groups function well, they are not endorsable.

However, the strongest argument that the pluralistic teleological account provides sufficient guidance on which character traits to cultivate is its effectiveness in application, which will be illustrated when it is employed to identify several environmental virtues and vices. To the extent that those identifications are successful, the concern that the account fails to provide standards that adequately discriminate which character traits are reasonably counted as virtues is misplaced.

Does the Account Violate the Naturalistic Premise That Nature Has No Teleology?

According to the pluralistic teleological account, character traits are assessed against several eudaimonistic and noneudaimonistic ends. But

part of the naturalistic premise is that there are no goals or ends of nature. How can nature both have ends and not have ends? The ends appealed to in the pluralistic teleological account are not "ends of nature"
in the sense ruled out by the naturalistic premise. What the naturalistic
premise denies are ends from the perspective of nature: any plan or goals
for nature as a whole. One implication of this denial is that ends for
individual organisms cannot be made sense of from that perspective.[56]
However, this does not rule out that individual organisms have strivings
of their own, which make intelligible ends for the organisms in and of
themselves.[57] As Elliot Sober has put it,

> Darwinism has not banished the idea that parts of the natural world are
> goal-directed systems, but has furnished this idea with a natural mecha-
> nism. We properly conceive of organisms (or genes, sometimes) as being
> in the business of maximizing their chances of survival and reproduc-
> tion. We describe characteristics as adaptations—as devices that exist for
> the furtherance of these ends. Natural selection makes this perspective
> intelligible.[58]

This is central to Paul Taylor's conception of living things as teleological
centers of life that have a good of their own.

> A living plant or animal...is, independently of anything else in the uni-
> verse, itself a center of goal-oriented activity. What is good or bad for it
> can be understood by reference to its own survival, health, and well-be-
> ing.... It is in terms of *its* goals that we can give teleological explanations
> of why it does what it does.[59]

This sense of "ends of nature"— ends from the perspective of the individual—does not require a teleology of nature, and this is the sense
operative in the pluralistic teleological account.[60]

To What Extent Is the Account Naturalistic?

On the pluralistic teleological account, evaluations of character traits are
not merely biological appraisals. The account is not fully justified by scientific naturalism. The ends constitutive of human flourishing are not
fixed by the biological facts about us. Human goodness (virtue) is not

reducible to good biological functioning. However, the account is consistent with scientific naturalism and the naturalistic premise. Its justification, content, and application do not involve non-natural properties or supernatural phenomena. Moreover, scientific naturalism informs the structure of the account and the ends constitutive of human flourishing. Evaluations of our goodness are modeled on a type of naturalistic evaluation (ethological) of individuals of other species. Furthermore, evaluations of character traits are empirically grounded, since they depend on the extent to which the traits are conducive or detrimental to our realizing eudaimonistic and noneudaimonistic ends in a world like ours. So although the account does not involve a complete naturalizing or biological reduction of human flourishing and virtue, it is naturalistic in several significant respects.

An objection commonly raised against naturalistic theories of virtue is that they fail to show why a person has reason to be, or should want to be, a good biological specimen of *Homo sapiens*. There are frequently situations in which being an imperfect biological specimen of *Homo sapiens* (e.g., infertility during normal reproductive years) is not detrimental, or may even be conducive, to a person's well-being. Moreover, people often have what seem worthwhile goals or projects (e.g., artistic achievement) other than, and sometimes detrimental to, being a good specimen of *Homo sapiens* or flourishing biologically. Why, then, should human flourishing be identified with biological flourishing, or being a good specimen of *Homo sapiens* or flourishing biologically be taken as making ultimate normative claims on us?

For several reasons, the pluralistic teleological account is not open to this objection, in any of its forms. It does not identify human flourishing with biological flourishing; nor does it claim that human flourishing is fully determined by scientific naturalism. The ends constitutive of human flourishing are informed by the biological facts about us, as well as by common beliefs about human flourishing and the possibilities provided by culture and technology. Moreover, the account does not claim that a person's only or primary goal should be to flourish, let alone to flourish biologically. It allows that noneudaimonistic goods and values can make a claim on us, and that those claims can be in tension with individual flourishing. Furthermore, the account does not claim that being a good specimen of *Homo sapiens* is always good for a person or that a person's being virtuous ensures that she will flourish (biologically or otherwise). It allows that circumstances and chance can prevent even a virtuous person from flourishing. Finally, the account does not claim that a person should perform the actions most conducive to her flourishing (biologically or otherwise). It evaluates character traits, not actions, policies, or practices.

The pluralistic teleological account is a theory of what makes a character trait a virtue. It specifies the considerations that constitute reasons for cultivating one character trait rather than another. It does not provide justification beyond this for why we ought to be virtuous; and it should not be expected to. The considerations that make one character trait more justified than another are the reasons for cultivating that character trait rather than the other. The point of ethical inquiry is to identify what being a virtuous person or acting well involves, not winning over a committed amoralist or moral skeptic. The place where justification in ethics comes to an end is the place where ethical inquiry begins.

CONCLUSION

A character trait is a virtue to the extent that it is conducive to promoting eudaimonistic and noneudaimonistic ends grounded in agent-relative and agent-independent goods and values. This general account can be applied to particular areas or aspects of human activity to identify the virtues and vices that pertain to them. In the next two chapters, I do this for our relationships and interactions with the natural environment and the nonhuman individuals that populate it. That is, I employ the pluralistic teleological account to specify the dispositions constitutive of several environmental virtues and vices.

2

The Environment and
Human Flourishing

But what is the good life? Is all this glut of power to be used for only bread-and-butter ends? Man cannot live by bread, or fords, alone. Are we too poor in purse or spirit to apply some of it to keep the land pleasant to see, and good to live in?

—*Aldo Leopold*, Game Management, *xxxi*

My sole concern is that we should do nothing which will reduce [people's] freedom of thought and action, whether by destroying the natural world which makes that freedom possible or the social traditions which permit and encourage it.

—*John Passmore*, Man's Responsibility for Nature, *195*

Mankind is a part of nature and life depends on the uninterrupted functioning of natural systems which ensure the supply of energy and nutrients.... Civilization is rooted in nature, which has shaped human culture and influenced all artistic and scientific achievement, and living in harmony with nature gives man the best opportunities for the development of his creativity, and for rest and recreation.

—*General Assembly of the United Nations,*
"World Charter for Nature," Preamble

MORAL CONSIDERABILITY

One of the central preoccupations of environmental ethicists is determining the extent to which we ought to enlarge the scope of our moral community. The issue is often conceptualized in terms of concentric circles emanating out from the agent, with each circle representing a different possibility. Should the circle of moral considerability encompass only oneself (egoism)? Only one's family (nepotism)? Only one's fellow citizens (patriotism)? All of humanity (anthropocentrism)? All sentient beings (sentientism)? All living individuals (biocentric individualism)? All ecosystems (ecocentrism)? Or some other class? There is an extensive literature concerned with identifying the properties of an individual or collective that are necessary and sufficient for moral considerability and thereby define the proper circle. On many of the prominent views in this literature, moral considerability does not come in degrees or in kinds. (However, an epistemological "gray area" where it is difficult to tell where to place some individuals is often acknowledged.) Either an individual is an experiencing subject of a life and has intrinsic value and rights, or it is not an experiencing subject of a life and it has no rights;[1] either an individual is sentient and its suffering must be considered as much as the comparable suffering of any other sentient being, or it is not sentient and has no morally considerable interests;[2] either an individual is a teleological center of life and has inherent worth equal to any other teleological center of life, or it is not a teleological center of life and has no inherent worth;[3] either an individual is rational and an end in itself, or it is not rational and is a mere thing.[4]

The concentric circle approach to depicting the ethical landscape does not comport well with our actual, lived experience. The morally significant relationships, individuals, and features in our lives do not appear monistic in any of the ways described above, and attempts to explain all of our moral relations by reducing them to any one tend to be forced and open to compelling counterexamples. It is not that we have not yet found the right circle—it is that there is no single correct one. Pluralism in moral considerability recognizes that there is not one set of considerations that defines the extension of moral responsiveness, but rather several that ground some concentric, some overlapping, and some independent fields of moral concern. One reason there are so many popular forms of monism is that they each identify something with distinctive ethical significance.

On the virtue-oriented approach, pluralism in moral considerability is accommodated within the purview of different virtues, which are differentiated by the types of objects, events, and properties to which they are responsive (their *bases of responsiveness*) and the types of reactions and activities that they involve (their *forms of responsiveness*). For example, the basis of responsiveness for compassion is the suffering of others, and the forms of responsiveness are concern for others, desiring to assist others, and acting to diminish the suffering of others. The basis of responsiveness for gratitude is being benefited by another, and the forms of responsiveness are recognition of the benefit, a desire to acknowledge it, and actions that acknowledge it.[5] The bases of responsiveness and the forms of responsiveness that define moral considerability are always relative to a particular virtue. Different virtues are responsive to different things in different ways. An individual, event, or community might be an appropriate object of gratitude but not compassion, wonder but not loyalty, or respect but not generosity. Moreover, as the examples above indicate, the extension of the fields of some virtues (e.g., compassion) are defined by intrinsic properties (e.g., the capacity to suffer), whereas the fields of other virtues (e.g., gratitude) are defined by relational properties (e.g., being benefited). Therefore, both intrinsic and relational properties can be morally significant.

Because there are numerous virtues that involve responsiveness to some aspect of the natural environment, the virtue-oriented approach to environmental ethics is pluralistic with respect to both the types of environmental entities (e.g., individual organisms, landscapes, ecosystems) that are morally considerable and the types of responsiveness that are appropriate to them. The approach is also nonreductive and nonhierarchical with respect to the varieties of moral considerability. Each virtue is justified according to the pluralistic teleological account of what makes a character trait a virtue. Therefore, variety in moral considerability is not multiple manifestations of or derivations from one basic type of moral standing. Moreover, there is no mechanism within the pluralistic teleological account for establishing one type of moral considerability as superordinate to another in principle, abstracted from particular contexts. When virtues conflict, which takes precedence is dependent upon contextual factors, such as what is at stake, what other virtues are operative, the agent's relationship to the situation, and the agent's particular abilities. Although some virtues may frequently take precedence over others in practice, this is the result of the features of the concrete situations in which the virtues conflict, not a principled superiority of one form of moral considerability over another.

Another significant feature of the virtue-oriented account of moral considerability is that there is a distinction between the goods and values that provide the ends against which character traits are evaluated and moral considerability. Which character traits are virtues, and thereby which entities are morally considerable and how they are to be considered, is determined by which dispositions are conducive to promoting the ends. This, in turn, is determined by the goods and values that there are, as well as by facts about us and the world. As a result, what makes a trait a virtue is in some cases quite different from that virtue's basis of responsiveness. For example, I argue later in this chapter that there are anthropocentric and agent-relative considerations that justify cultivating dispositions of responsiveness to environmental entities. Thus, there is human-oriented justification for the moral considerability of environmental entities.

One objection to this might be that it undermines a virtuous person's environmental commitment: she will not really be concerned about the environment and the individuals that comprise it; she will be concerned about humans and only derivatively concerned about the environment. This objection confuses doing virtue theory with living virtuously, and conflates what makes a trait a virtue with a virtuous person's reasons for actions. Actions, behaviors, and practices are evaluated in terms of the virtues, and a virtuous person is responsive to the morally relevant features of a situation, not to what makes a character trait a virtue.[6] Even if what makes a trait a virtue is anthropocentric, the considerations that a person who possesses the virtue takes as reasons for acting might be nonanthropocentric.

ENVIRONMENTAL VIRTUE

On the virtue-oriented approach, moral considerability is relative to each virtue and is defined by the bases to which a virtue (or, more accurately, the person who possesses the virtue) is responsive, as well as the modes or forms of that responsiveness. An *environmentally responsive virtue* is any virtue that involves responsiveness to some environmental entities—i.e., for which some environmental entities are morally considerable. Many environmental virtues are environmentally responsive virtues, but not all are. Some virtues might serve environmental ends or be justified by environmental considerations, even though they do not involve responsiveness to environmental entities. An *environmentally justified virtue* is any virtue that is in part justified by environmental considerations (e.g., the worth of living organisms, beneficial relationships with environmental entities, or environmental resources). An *environmentally productive virtue* is any virtue that promotes or maintains environmental goods or values (e.g., ecological integrity or the flourishing of living organisms). There is thus a plurality of ways environmental considerations are implicated in the virtues, including and beyond environmental entities being morally considerable. In what follows, the term "environmental virtue" is used inclusively. Environmentally responsive virtues, environmentally justified virtues, and environmentally productive virtues are all environmental virtues.

In the remainder of this chapter I discuss several ways the relationship between the environment and human flourishing informs the dispositions constitutive of environmental virtues and vices. In the next chapter I focus on whether there are environmental entities with value or worth independent of human flourishing that make character traits environmental virtues or vices. The point is to identify the considerations that play a role in making character traits environmental virtues and vices, provide substantive accounts of some prominent environmental virtues and vices, and differentiate several varieties of environmental virtues and vices. It is not to provide a complete specification of all environmentally responsive virtues, environmentally justified virtues, environmentally productive virtues, and their corresponding vices.

AGENT FLOURISHING

We are biological beings whose survival and good functioning depend upon the intake of certain materials (e.g., food, water, and oxygen) and avoiding the intake of others (e.g., lead, mercury, and asbestos). These goods are basic because they are necessary for life and health, and are preconditions for the other components of human flourishing. As long as we depend on the natural environment for them, dispositions that maintain access to them in sufficiently unpolluted states are justified, whereas dispositions that undermine their quality and accessibility are unjustified. This general line of argument is sound and is widely regarded as such by environmental ethicists. However, there is substantial disagreement about the strength of environmental considerateness that it establishes and how it informs environmental virtues and vices.

Louke van Wensveen has argued that these considerations help establish that any "genuine virtue includes the goal of ensuring ecosystem sustainability."[7] Her core argument for this view is as follows: ecosystem sustainability is a necessary condition for the cultivation of a virtue; a genuine virtue includes the goal of ensuring the necessary conditions for its cultivation; therefore, a genuine virtue includes the goal of ensuring ecosystem sustainability.[8] She believes that the first premise of the argument is justified by basic goods considerations:

> The cultivation of a virtue involves a person's ability to feel, think, and act in certain ways. Any feeling, thought, or action is made possible thanks to physical conditions that sustain the person as a living being. Many of these essential physical conditions—such as oxygen, water, food, and fiber—derive from ecosystems. (By contrast, many of the physical conditions that may impede virtuousness, such as pollution and lack of food, can be linked to ecosystem stress.) The cultivation of a virtue also requires that a person can *continue* to feel, think, and act in certain ways over an indefinite period of time. Therefore, it implies that the supporting ecosystem must also endure over time, which is exactly what the notion of ecosystem sustainability conveys.[9]

According to Wensveen, environmental goods are necessary for virtue because they are necessary for life and agency. Virtues are dispositions concerning choice, reasons, actions, and emotions, so we can be virtuous only if the structures and processes that make these possible are functional. Due to the longevity involved in moral development and the achievement and maintenance of virtue, the supply of goods that supports those structures and processes must be sustained over time. Therefore, a disposition to maintain, and dispositions that tend to maintain, reliable availability of basic goods over the course of one's lifetime are justified, whereas dispositions that undermine their availability are unjustified. This portion of Wensveen's argument is unproblematic. It is essentially an application of the pluralistic teleological account, on which character traits conducive to their possessor's flourishing (including longevity and autonomy) are virtues and character traits detrimental to their possessor's flourishing are vices.

However, it does not follow that a disposition to promote ecosystem sustainability is a precondition of virtue. Food, water, and oxygen are derived from ecosystems, and without these and other basic goods we would not be able to live as healthy moral agents, but a sustainable ecosystem is not required to provide these for the duration of a person's moral development. An unhealthy ecosystem may be able to supply the goods and opportunities requisite for life, health, and cultivating and maintaining virtue for several human lifetimes before it becomes so degraded that it cannot do so. Assuming a person enjoys the goods that a healthy ecosystem provides—imagine an ecosystem that is early in its decline or in which the goods are provided by artificial means[10]—why should she be incapable of cultivating virtue just because after she is dead some ecosystems will no longer be able to provide them? Moreover, if ecosystem sustainability is a necessary condition for virtue, then it is impossible for those who live in environmentally unsustainable societies to be virtuous. This is implausible, and indicates that setting a realistic environmental minimum for the cultivation of virtue and setting a robust environmental standard pull in opposite directions. The more substantial the environmental minimum, the less plausible it will be that those who do not live in an environment or society that meets the minimum cannot be virtuous or flourish. The less substantial the environmental minimum, the less demanding the sustainability requirement. This problem persists, albeit in a less severe form, even if the ecosystem sustainability condition is formulated probabilistically—if it is harder or less likely, though still possible, for a person to be virtuous in the absence of ecosystem sustainability. An ecosystem in early decline or artificial alternatives may provide as reliable a source of basic goods for an agent's lifetime as a sustainable ecosystem, and the probability of a person flourishing is the same regardless of the source of the goods.

One response to these limitations might be to emphasize the social context of agent flourishing. Environmental degradation is often detrimental to social stability. It can create shortages of essential goods and result in environmental refugees, each of which produce social and political unrest. So perhaps ecosystem sustainability, or some other robust and longitudinal measure of environmental health, such as "ecosystem integrity,"[11] is a precondition for social stability and thus for a person's flourishing. However, this version of the basic goods approach is subject to the same problems as Wensveen's precondition of life, agency, and virtue argument. It either sets the conditions for agent flourishing too high or is subject to technological and artificial alternatives objections. The more robust the level of social stability required for human flourishing, the more improbable the standard. It is implausible that a person cannot flourish now if her society uses natural resources in a way that will undermine social stability for those who will come later, or even for some of her contemporaries. But the less robust the standard, the less stringent the environmental minimum necessary to meet it and the greater the possibility that technological alternatives or slowly degrading ecosystems can provide the requisite goods. The relationships between a person's flourishing, her social context, and basic environmental goods can establish the need for a certain amount of those goods for some time, but does not require global, long-term, or strong ecosystem sustainability.

Given the limitations of these basic environmental goods arguments, establishing ecosystem sustainability as a necessary condition for a person's flourishing would seem to require a constituent of flourishing that persists postmortem. One possibility might be that a person's flourishing now involves the prospect of her children and even her children's children having the resources to flourish later, and that unsustainable practices and dependence on unreliable or unproven artificial alternatives threaten their prospects. After all, it will be part of their flourishing that their children and their children's children are able to flourish. However, the idea that the quality of our lives could be affected at all by posthumous events does not comport well with many people's conception of human flourishing. The belief that the extent of a person's flourishing is entirely determined during her own lifetime is favored by contemporary materialism and individualism. Moreover, these evaluative attitudes, along with other factors (such as high geographic mobility), encourage people to take on "ground" projects—projects around which we orient our lives—that are disconnected from the land or any particular place and do not require considering what living conditions will be like for those who come later. Against such attitudes and projects, many environmental ethicists have appealed to obligations to future generations. However, other environmental ethicists have argued that our flourishing is often informed by the actions of future generations, just as the flourishing of individuals of past generations is informed by our actions. Here is John O'Neill on this point:

Consider the hedgerows of Britain: these are the product of the skilled work of labourers that stretches back for centuries. If a succeeding generation with no sense of the skill embodied in the hedgerows and no appreciation of their value destroys them as mere impediments to more profitable agriculture, then that generation harms not only itself, but also the past. The disappearance of the hedgerows is more than 'just' an act of environmental vandalism. This is not to say that respect for past generations and a desire to do well by them entails that we leave all embodiments of their activities untouched. It does mean, however, that such concerns should form an important component of our practical deliberations.[12]

If our flourishing is implicated in the attitudes and actions of future generations in this way, then we have an interest in future generations being able to appreciate, maintain, and, when necessary, continue or culminate our projects. Therefore, because it contributes to the fulfillment of our projects and the meaningfulness and validation of our own lives, we ought to be disposed to promote and maintain environmental goods necessary for individuals in future generations to achieve intellectual and moral maturity and be healthy and productive. If we deplete environmental resources or degrade ecosystems to the point that those goods are not available to them, we diminish ourselves.

There is, however, a limit to how much longevity this line of argument can support. It seems implausible that the extent of a person's flourishing is unsettled for indefinite generations after her own death or that it depends on the life outcomes of her very distant progeny. One must set a reasonable standard—one's grandchildren or great-grandchildren, perhaps—but that gets only so far in terms of longevity, and the specter of slowly degrading ecosystems and artificial alternatives looms once again. As with the other basic goods arguments, this one seems to be right as far as it goes. It justifies dispositions that tend to maintain at least a minimum level of environmental resources for some duration into the future. But there will be a limit to how abundant the resources must be for future generations to appreciate and continue people's projects, as well as a limit on how far into the future they must be sustained. There is also no reason that artificial alternatives, as they become available, cannot provide the requisite resources. Therefore, while this version of the basic goods argument will justify dispositions that promote some level of environmental goods for some duration, it will not justify as longitudinal and robust a level of environmental concern as many would like.

One response to these limitations might be to argue that it is part of a person's good that she have a justified belief, or something else suitably cognitive or psychological, that her distant progeny will flourish or her other ground projects will be appreciated or sustained after her death. That belief would in turn only be justified if she had reason to believe that the requisite external goods for flourishing would be present in later generations, and perhaps that belief might only be justified if there were ecosystem sustainability. In this way, a disposition to promote ecosystem sustainability would be constitutive of virtue, but the extent of a person's flourishing would not depend upon how things turn out for her distant progeny or her other longitudinal ground projects. However, this response remains open to the artificial alternatives objection. One might have a justified belief that artificial alternatives will be available to distant generations on the basis of current technological capabilities or the probable rate of technological advancement. Moreover, the response does not address the implausibility of a person's flourishing being dependent upon the prospects for her very distant progeny or her other longitudinal ground projects being appreciated or sustained by distant generations.

The agent-oriented basic environmental goods argument for ecosystem sustainability has several incarnations: as a precondition of a life, health, agency, and virtue argument; as a precondition for social stability argument; and as a fulfillment of ground projects argument. However, regarding each we can ask: How much of the environmental good is really required? For how long? And why must it be supplied by a sustainable ecosystem? In each case the answers that would justify strong ecosystem sustainability are not particularly plausible. In order to flourish, an agent must have, for example, sufficiently clean air and opportunities to cultivate virtue. But when we inquire why those basic goods must be provided by a nondegrading ecosystem, no satisfactory answer is forthcoming. This does not imply that the relationship between basic environmental goods and agent flourishing is not at all relevant to determining the substantive dispositions constitutive of virtue. Taken together, the agent-oriented basic goods arguments do justify *virtues of (weak) sustainability*—i.e., character traits that under most conditions (so long as there is not a sufficiently stable artificial alternative) dispose their possessor to maintain or promote a limited-term sustainability (one that extends for at least a few generations) at a weakly sustainable level (one concerned with the production of certain kinds of goods rather than with maintaining the multifarious bases for their production).

In addition, some character traits will be justified as *virtues of environmental activism* on the basis of their conduciveness to success in social and political domains in securing environmental goods at the levels described above. Due to the regulatory, legal, social, political, cultural, and economic dimensions of many environmental issues, environmental gains are rarely achieved quickly or easily. Moreover, they are rarely fully secure, since zoning laws, permit issuances, land protections, and pollution regulations can always be challenged or changed, and individuals can easily slip into environmentally degradative practices or lifestyles. Those who wish to protect basic environmental goods for themselves and their communities must be alert for all manner of possible threats, such as ruin (e.g., chemical contamination of public water resources), removal (e.g., water privatization and bulk water sales), or frivolous use (e.g., watering golf courses in the desert). Character traits such as commitment, astuteness, discipline, attentiveness, discernment, fortitude, creativity, courage, self-control, cooperativeness, patience, solidarity, perseverance, and optimism are, therefore, crucial to efforts to achieve and maintain protection of environmental goods.

Virtues of environmental activism have been somewhat overlooked and underappreciated by environmental ethicists in comparison with other environmental virtues.[13] For those of us raised on North American environmentalism in particular, it is tempting to contemplate our environmental heroes as walkers in the woods or hikers of the mountains. The image is of an individual with personal excellence flourishing in harmony with and appreciation of wild (or near wild) environments. So when we think about environmental virtue, it is easy to become focused on virtues that are operative in those contexts—e.g., wonder, love, openness, receptivity, humility, and mindfulness. However, these provide only a partial picture of what makes our environmental heroes environmentally virtuous. Thoreau walked in the Walden woods and wrote, spoke, and acted for change. John Muir explored the Sierra Nevadas and founded the Sierra Club. Rachel Carson meticulously observed and recorded the behavior of barnacles and stirred social conscience. A loving, caring, compassionate, wondering, humble, open person will lack important environmental virtues if she is not also engaged, committed, and cooperative. She does not respond well to considerations that call for support of environmental ends if she is inactive or incompetent. Virtues of environmental activism are therefore environmental virtues as much as virtues that are operative in the context of wilderness experience.[14]

In addition to basic goods, the environment also provides aesthetic goods, recreational goods, and a location to exercise and develop physically, intellectually, morally, and spiritually. This straightforwardly justifies dispositions conducive to conserving and, when appropriate, preserving these goods and opportunities. It also justifies cultivating *virtues of communion with nature*, character traits that enable an individual to enjoy and take advantage of them. An individual who is unable to appreciate the beauty of the sunset or the call of a songbird literally misses out on the experience: "Though we travel the world over to find the beautiful, we must carry it with us, or we find it not."[15] Ralph Waldo Emerson's point here is as applicable to intellectual engagement as it is to aesthetic encounter. The natural environment provides the opportunity for intellectual challenge and reward, but those benefits come only to those who are disposed first to wonder and then to try to understand. Leopold, Thoreau, and Muir certainly exemplified tireless enthusiasm for understanding nature, as well as the joy that process and accomplishment can involve, and Carson casts wonder as a preeminent virtue:

> It is our misfortune that for most of us that clear-eyed vision, that true instinct for what is beautiful and awe-inspiring, is dimmed and even lost before we reach adulthood. If I had influence with the good fairy who is supposed to preside over the christening of all children I should ask that her gift to each child in the world be a sense of wonder so indestructible that it would last throughout life, as an unfailing antidote against the boredom and disenchantments of later years, the sterile preoccupation with things that are artificial, and alienation from the sources of our strength.[16]

The benefits of wonder to its possessor are many: challenge, exhilaration, joy, and satisfaction.[17] So too, Carson believed, are the benefits of wonder for the natural world. Wonder is a gateway to love, gratitude, appreciation, and care for that which is found wonderful. "Wonder and humility are wholesome emotions, and they do not exist side by side with a lust for destruction." Therefore, "the more clearly we can focus our attention on the wonders and realities of the universe about us, the less taste we will have for the destruction of our race."[18] Wonder is, thus, environmentally informed, environmentally responsive, and environmentally productive. It is a virtue because of what it enables in us and for our community, quite apart from (though perhaps in addition to) its promoting or maintaining any worth natural entities might have in themselves.[19]

Nature also provides opportunities for renewal of energy and spirit. "There is something infinitely healing in the repeated refrains of nature," writes Carson. "Those who dwell...among the beauties and mysteries of the earth are never alone or weary of life. Whatever the vexations or concerns of their personal lives, their thoughts can find paths that lead to inner contentment and to renewed excitement in living."[20] But, once again, these benefits are not available to everyone. A person must be willing to put forth the effort required, if only to go outdoors and pay attention, to cultivate genuine engagement with and openness toward nature.[21] If you are receptive, then, Muir exhorts, "Climb the mountains and get their good tidings. Nature's peace will flow into you as sunshine flows into trees. The winds will blow their own freshness into you, and the storms their energy, while cares will drop off like autumn leaves."[22] For those who are open to it, nature can be a source of nurturing, renewal, knowledge, and joy.[23]

Each of these varieties of enrichment requires engagement with the natural environment, albeit with different forms of intimacy, duration, familiarity, faculty, and investment. They indicate the bounty of opportunity, which extends well beyond what has been discussed, for meaningful and beneficial relationships with the land and its denizens. Moreover, these personal benefits are attached to ecological ones, since those who are familiar with the land tend to care for it and are less likely than others to exploit and degrade it.[24] The implication of these aspects of the human-environment relationship is not that we ought to tend to the environment and natural entities with the idea that doing so will benefit us, and that a welcome by-product is that it is also good for the biotic community. For the benefits to accrue, we must be committed to the engagements or natural entities themselves, in just the same way that the full benefits of friendship can be realized only upon sincere concern for the welfare of the other. O'Neill believes that this is crucial to environmental ethics:

An environmental ethic should proceed on similar lines [as the case for friendship]. For a large number, although not all, of individual living things and biological collectives, we should recognize and promote their flourishing as an end itself. Such care for the natural world is constitutive of a flourishing human life. The best human life is one that includes an awareness of and practical concern with the goods of entities in the nonhuman world....

The claim that care for the natural world for its own sake is a part of the best life for humans requires detailed defense. The most promising general strategy would be to appeal to the claim that a good human life requires a breadth of goods. Part of the problem with egoism is the very narrowness of the goods it involves. The ethical life is one that incorporates a far richer set of goods and relationships than egoism would allow. This form of argument can be made for a connection of care for the natural world with human flourishing: the recognition and promotion of natural goods as ends in themselves involves just such an enrichment.[25]

The "richer set of goods" that fills out O'Neill's argument is just the sort discussed above and enabled by love, wonder, humility, care, receptivity, attentiveness, and other virtues of communion with nature. The point is not that nature alone provides these goods—certainly meaningfulness, joy, recreation, and beauty can be found in the personal, interpersonal and artificial—or even that it is in all cases a superior source.[26] The point is that they are goods, and that nature and natural entities often provide a rich and unique form or realization of them. To the extent that interactions and relationships with nature can be pleasurable, rewarding, and beneficial, there is reason to be disposed to preserve the opportunities for them and to open oneself up to them.[27]

HUMAN FLOURISHING

It is widely accepted that we ought to be benevolent toward other people. Given the pluralistic teleological account of what makes a character trait a virtue, this general acceptance is justified either if interpersonal benevolence is conducive to promoting the eudaimonistic ends or if other human beings have worth or value that we have reason to be responsive to in this way. I believe that both are the case. Each person has a good of her own that there are strong reasons to care about, and this justifies

virtues of passive benevolence, such as considerateness and nonmaleficence. Virtues of active benevolence, such as helpfulness, compassion,
and charitableness, are justified, and virtues of negative benevolence
are further justified, because the dispositions constitutive of them are
conducive to realizing endorsable forms of social cooperation, having
children with the opportunity to live well, and other eudaimonistic
ends. However, defending these claims is beyond the scope of this book.
Therefore, in what follows, I simply assume that among the virtues are
those character traits commonly recognized as comprising interpersonal benevolence—e.g., assisting people in need (helpfulness), attempting
to reduce people's suffering (compassion), and sharing excess resources
with others (charitableness).

Since all people depend upon basic environmental goods for survival
and health, a benevolent person will be concerned that they are available to as many people as possible. Interpersonal benevolence therefore
increase dramatically the longevity and coverage of basic environmental
goods to be promoted and maintained by virtues of sustainability and
virtues of environmental activism. This is so even if active benevolence is
justified only toward some subset of people, as would be the case if universal active benevolence were less conducive than more restricted forms
to realizing the eudaimonistic ends, since passive benevolence extends
to all people. Nonmaleficence requires not compromising the ecological
conditions and goods on which other people depend for their well-being,
and restitutive justice often requires actively promoting those conditions
and goods when they have been wrongfully compromised. Therefore,
passive benevolence alone substantially expands the level of environmental commitment embodied in virtues of sustainability and virtues of environmental activism beyond what is justified by considerations related
to agent flourishing.[28]

This does not imply that environmental virtue involves equal concern about all people's access to basic environmental goods. Virtues
of interpersonal benevolence are not always ultimate or overriding.
Moreover, interpersonal benevolence does not preclude role- and posi-
tion-specific virtues pertaining to areas such as parenting and leadership, or virtues that are sensitive to historical and geographical contingencies, such as gratitude, loyalty, reciprocal justice, and friendship.
These often involve a special commitment to securing environmental
goods for people or groups of people with whom one stands in certain

relations—e.g., friends, neighbors, children, or compatriots. Therefore, although considerations of interpersonal benevolence justify dispositions conducive to promoting or maintaining the availability of basic environmental goods for people whose flourishing is not germane to one's own or with whom one does not stand in some special relation, a virtuous person will often prioritize securing environmental goods for some people over others.

There are many other ways, in addition to increasing the robustness of virtues of sustainability and virtues of environmental activism, that a commitment to interpersonal benevolence informs the substantive content of environmental virtues and vices. For example, dispositions conducive to peace and opposed to violent conflict are environmentally productive and justified virtues, since warfare and violence generally compromise the availability of environmental goods. They often involve the destruction of wilderness, wildlife, and farmlands, as well as the contamination of air and water. They disrupt food production even when agricultural lands are not spoiled, dislocate people from land that they know how to steward, and create refugees who must degrade the environment in order to survive. Ecological violence—doing harm to others by intentionally compromising the environmental resources they depend upon—is and historically has been common. For these reasons, the "World Charter for Nature," the "Rio Declaration on Environment and Development," and "The Earth Charter" each emphasize the importance of nonviolence and peace as well as political, social, and economic justice and stability as crucial components of a comprehensive environmental ethic. It is also for these reasons that Wangari Maathai, a Kenyan environmentalist and human rights activist, was awarded the 2004 Nobel Peace Prize.[29] Dispositions conducive to promoting and maintaining social stability and avoiding violent conflict are virtues, and those detrimental to them are vices, in part because of their relationship to environmental goods.

Dispositions conducive to social stability are not only environmentally justified and environmentally productive, they can also be environmentally responsive. A source of both international and domestic tensions is dwindling or compromised environmental resources. When resources become scarce, nations, states, and communities can be brought into conflict over what remains; examples include disputes over fishing rights and fresh water access.[30] So, not only are peace and social stability good for the environment, environmental sustainability is conducive to peace and social stability. Considerations of good social functioning therefore justify dispositions that tend to maintain levels of environmental goods such that conflict and instability are not fostered.

Considerations of interpersonal benevolence and good social functioning can also underwrite dispositions of respect for the status of particular natural entities. Many natural objects, areas, and events have cultural, historical, or religious significance within a community. Respecting their status can be important to maintaining the integrity and well-functioning of the community or advancing its worthwhile projects. Therefore, dispositions of concern and care for environmental entities that are sacred sites, components of a culture's history or imaginary, or vital to a community's way of life are environmental virtues. For example, visitors ought to be respectful of Uluru—a sacred site to the Anangu people in central Australia that is among the largest freestanding rock monoliths in the world—because of the status and role it has within the Anangu culture and practice.

Considerations of interpersonal benevolence also justify virtues pertaining to the maintenance and distribution of environmental "public goods," which range from basic and economic goods to aesthetic, recreational, and cultural goods. These *virtues of environmental stewardship*, as Jennifer Welchman calls them, involve dispositions to appreciate the various ways environments function as public goods, dispositions to maintain them as public goods, and dispositions to see that the goods are justly distributed. Welchman identifies diligence, trustworthiness, justice, loyalty, and honesty as particularly salient for those who have a special role, position, or responsibility, official or unofficial, pertaining to environmental public goods—e.g., regulators, conservation biologists, and leaders in environmental organizations.[31] However, considerations of benevolence and good social functioning, which make claims on all of us, imply that virtues of environmental stewardship are not reserved for them.

CONSUMPTIVE DISPOSITIONS

In the previous sections, I provided an overview of the ways the relationship between the environment and human flourishing informs the content of virtues and vices, and developed a typology of environmental virtue on the basis of different considerations that make character traits environmental virtues. In this section, I demonstrate in more detail what character trait evaluation involves in a particular case by focusing on one set of traits. Consumptive dispositions consist of: 1) materialistic evaluative dispositions—i.e., prioritizing possession and accumulation of material goods in evaluations of people, relationships, careers, and so on; 2) affective dispositions toward the possession or accumulation of material goods—i.e., being desirous of possessing or accumulating material goods; 3) emotional dispositions oriented around the presence or absence of material goods—e.g., distress, anxiety, or sadness regarding their absence; and 4) practical dispositions toward possessing and accumulating material goods—i.e., prioritizing doing that which is considered conducive to amassing those goods. These dispositions are doubly detrimental. Those who possess them are less likely to be happy than those with alternative dispositions, and they also undermine the availability and quality of many environmental goods. These dispositions are, for both of these reasons, vices.[32]

Recent research on the psychology of consumption has found that those with materialistic value orientations report lower levels of well-being than those with more social and self-realization value orientations.[33] In *The High Price of Materialism*, Tim Kasser summarizes these findings:

> People who are highly focused on materialistic values have lower personal well-being and psychological health than those who believe that materialist pursuits are relatively unimportant. These relationships have been documented in samples of people ranging from the wealthy to the poor, from teenagers to the elderly, and from Australians to South Koreans. Several investigators have reported similar results using a variety of ways of measuring materialism. The studies document that strong materialistic values are associated with a pervasive undermining of people's well-being, from low life satisfaction and happiness, to depression and anxiety, to physical problems such as headaches, and to personality disorders, narcissism, and antisocial behavior.[34]

It is easier to establish that there is a relationship between materialistic dispositions and subjective well-being than it is to determine why the relationship obtains. The research indicates that "needs for security and safety, competence and self-esteem, connectedness to others, and autonomy and authenticity are relatively unsatisfied when materialistic values are prominent in people's value systems."[35] When these needs are inadequately met, people tend to be unhappy, yielding the relationship between materialistic dispositions and (un)happiness. But why are these needs relatively unmet for people who are materialistically oriented? It is tempting to infer that what causes them to go unsatisfied is somehow related to their possessors' being materialistic. However, while it might be that materialism is part of the explanation for why those needs are not met, it might also be that people embrace materialistic values because their other needs are unsatisfied, or there might be a common cause for both materialism and need frustration. Kasser is quick to point out that more research is required to sort out these and other possibilities,[36] but reports that the research conducted so far suggests that the causal relationship between materialism and need frustration runs both ways.

> Materialistic values become prominent in the lives of some individuals who have a history of not having their needs well met. Thus, one reason these values are associated with a low quality of life is that they are symptoms or signs that some needs remain unfulfilled. But materialistic values are not just expressions of unhappiness. Instead, they lead people to organize their lives in ways that do a poor job of satisfying their needs, and thus contribute even more to people's misery.[37]

Research further suggests that materialistic value orientations are particularly detrimental to social relationships.

> The effects of materialism on SWB [subjective well-being] are at least partly mediated by relationship quality. Materialists tended to have relationships of lower quality (as assessed by their family and friends). Furthermore, with relationship quality controlled, the relations between materialism and SWB decline. These results suggest that a materialist can be happy if he or she is able to preserve the quality of his or her relationships. However, the inverse relationship between materialism and relationship quality suggests that there are built-in trade-offs that tend to undermine the quality of materialists' relationships.[38]

That consumptive dispositions encourage people to organize their lives in ways that compromise their relationships is evidenced by several trends in the paradigmatic consumer society: the United States.[39] For example, commute times are increasing in part because people desire larger homes that can accommodate more consumer goods, and these can only be afforded by moving farther away from city centers.[40] But an increase of 10 minutes of daily commute time is associated with a 10 percent decrease in civic involvement. Furthermore, increased commute time and the need to work longer hours because of material "demands" can also detract from time spent with family and friends.[41] So too can larger houses, which allow and encourage family members to spend time apart even when at home, and the proliferation of goods that enable nonsocial forms of recreation.[42] Thus, materialistic dispositions are not conducive to living well. Greed is not good. Frugality, appreciation, and temperance are more conducive to a person flourishing, at least to the extent that they are less likely to undermine healthy interpersonal relationships.

Consumptive dispositions are also detrimental to living well insofar as they promote the degradation of environmental goods on which people depend. There is, of course, no way to avoid an economic relationship with the natural world. Humans are biological beings who depend upon the environment for their material needs. But the amount of goods taken to satisfy people's needs and wants, as well as the ways they are taken, affect how much and how rapidly the goods are expended and the capacity for them to be renewed. Consumptive dispositions foster rapid and unsustainable diminishment of basic and nonbasic environmental goods.

Consumption requires energy. It takes energy to extract natural resources, refine them, manufacture consumer goods, use the goods (in many cases), dispose of them and the manufacturing by-products upon use, and provide transport along each step of the process. The larger people's homes, the more appliances they have, the more vehicles they drive, the less fuel-efficient those vehicles, and the more cities sprawl, the more energy used.[43] The bulk of it comes from fossil fuels, the burning of which produces airborne pollutants (e.g., mercury, sulfur dioxide, ozone, and particulates) that cause illnesses such as asthma, cardiovascular disease, and cancer, as well as developmental defects.[44] Therefore, the more energy consumed, given obtaining energy source and method-of-generation distributions, the more people get sick and die from airborne pollutant-related illnesses.

The burning of fossil fuels for energy is also the primary anthropogenic cause of global warming.[45] Carbon dioxide is the most prevalent greenhouse gas (others include methane, nitrous oxide, hydrofluorocarbons, perfluorocarbons, and sulfurhexafluoride), and fossil fuel use is the main anthropogenic source of atmospheric carbon dioxide.[46] Therefore, the more energy used, given obtaining energy source and method-of-generation distributions, the more accelerated and exacerbated are the negative consequences of global warming. These include increases in displacements of people, outbreaks of diseases, uncertainty in food production, and frequency and intensity of severe weather.[47] Again, the more consumed, the more the air, in this case the atmosphere, is compromised.

Consumption also requires water. The amount of water on this planet is finite. There are approximately 1.4 billion cubic kilometers of water on Earth. But only 2.5 to 2.6 percent of it is fresh water, and only about .77 percent circulates quickly enough to be considered part of the hydrological cycle.[48] At present, people are using and polluting the accessible fresh water faster than it can be replenished or cleansed. Over one billion people lack reliable access to safe drinking water and over two billion people lack access to basic sanitation.[49] The choices people make about consumption affect the availability of usable water. Industry accounts for 22 percent of water use worldwide, and the more people consume, the more water industry uses. But the effects of consumer choices on the availability of water are most significant when it comes to food. Agriculture accounts for 70 percent of water use worldwide. (Towns and municipalities account for the remaining 8 percent.)[50] Producing 500 calories of beef requires 4,902 liters of water, whereas 500 calories of poultry requires only 1,515 liters, 500 calories of beans only 421 liters, and 500 calories of potatoes only 89 liters. Ten grams of protein from eggs can be produced with only 244 liters of water, whereas 10 grams of protein from beef requires 1,000 liters, and 10 grams of protein from corn requires only 130 liters.[51] Thus, the fresh water available at a particular time can be used more or less efficiently in the production of food. This is significant, since every year there is less water available. For example, the Ogallala aquifer, the largest in North America at around 190,000 square miles stretching from Texas to South Dakota and the source of irrigation for one fifth of the farmland in the United States, is being depleted at 15 times the rate it is replenished. It has been dropping an average of 3 feet per year since 1991.[52]

The depletion of water resources is a result of both population growth and consumption. Growing population increases demand even if per capita water usage remains constant, and the populations in the United States and the world are both on the rise.[53] But per capita consumption is going up as well. Seventy percent of the world's water goes to agriculture. If Americans are eating to the point of obesity—which we are[54]—then we are using more water for agriculture per capita. Twenty-two percent of water is used in industry. If Americans are consuming more goods per capita—which we are[55]—then we are using more water per capita. Furthermore, usable water can be lost or compromised. This happens, for example, through contamination from run-off from agriculture and waste streams from manufacturing and mining, slurrying fossil fuels for transportation, pollution from the combustion of fossil fuels, inundation from rising sea levels, and changes in climate patterns.[56] Moreover, as supplies decrease and demands increase, fresh water becomes an increasingly attractive commodity. Trade in bottled and bulk water is already part of the globalized economy, as are water management services, and transnational corporations are increasingly seeking to secure rights to water supplies.[57] Therefore, water availability is not a localized issue. Profligate water usage in one part of the world can have an effect on the accessibility, affordability, and security of fresh water in other parts of the world. Finally, even if insufficient fresh water availability were just a matter of population growth, which it is not, it would still be necessary to curb consumption to ensure that people have an accessible, affordable, and secure supply. Dispositions that tend to increase consumption would still be unjustified, while those conducive to conservation of basic goods through limited consumption would be justified.

Consumptive dispositions are bad for people. Greed, intemperance, profligacy, and envy are vices. They tend to be detrimental to their possessor's well-being, and they favor practices that compromise the environment's ability to provide environmental goods. Moderation, self-control, simplicity, frugality, and other character traits that oppose materialism and consumerism are environmental virtues, inasmuch as they favor practices and lifestyles that promote the availability of environmental goods.[58]

CONCLUSION

The relationship between the environment and human flourishing is relevant to the specification of virtue and vice in two interrelated ways. First, some dispositions are more conducive than others to maintaining the quality, quantity, and accessibility of environmental goods (both basic and nonbasic). Second, many of the benefits that the environment provides are only available to those who are disposed to seek or receive them. Given the pluralistic teleological account of what makes a character trait a virtue, these considerations justify virtues of sustainability, virtues of environmental activism, virtues of environmental stewardship, and virtues of communion with nature. In the next chapter, the focus shifts from the relationship between the environment and human flourishing to environmental entities themselves. I argue that there are environmental values that justify incorporating human-independent ends into the pluralistic teleological account and thereby inform the substantive content of virtues and vices.

3

The Environment Itself

Respect Earth and life in all its diversity.
—Earth Charter International,
"The Earth Charter," Principle 1

Take any demand, however slight, which any creature, however
weak, may make. Ought it not, for its own sole sake to be satisfied? If not, prove why not.
—William James, Essays in Pragmatism, 73

RESPECT FOR NATURE?

In 1992, the United Nations Conference on Environment and Development (UNCED) was convened in Rio de Janeiro, Brazil. A significant
outcome was the development of the "Rio Declaration on Environment
and Development," the first principle of which is: "Human beings are at
the center of concerns for sustainable development. They are entitled to
a healthy and productive life in harmony with nature." The declaration
emphasizes the importance of environmental sustainability to human
well-being, as well as the obligation to consider the welfare of future
generations. Nevertheless, its anthropocentric conceptualization of environmental issues, and the absence of any recognition of the worth of
nature independent from humans, were disappointing to many who are
environmentally concerned. From their perspective, the declaration constituted a retreat from the "World Charter for Nature," adopted by the
United Nations General Assembly in 1982, which affirmed: "Every form

of life is unique, warranting respect regardless of its worth to man, and, to accord other organisms such recognition, man must be guided by a moral code of action." The first principle of the World Charter is: "Nature shall be respected and its essential processes shall not be impaired." As valuable as the Rio Declaration might be, it is not the clarification, operationalization, and expansion of the World Charter that many had hoped and worked for.[1]

In 1994, a group named the Earth Council, working independently of national and United Nations political affiliation, began the process of formulating an updated charter that would provide a more encompassing vision of shared environmental values than those represented in the Rio declaration. Developing and drafting the charter involved thousands of people from hundreds of organizations in dozens of countries. There was a resolute effort to include a variety of cultures and represent diverse sectors of societies. The resultant document, The Earth Charter, was finalized in 2000. Its stated aim is to join people "together to bring forth a sustainable global society founded on respect for nature, universal human rights, economic justice, and a culture of peace." In contrast with the Rio Declaration, The Earth Charter makes concern for nature foundational to its ethic. The first two principles are "Respect Earth and life in all its diversity" and "Care for the community of life with understanding, compassion, and love." Moreover, echoing the sentiments of Leopold, Muir, and Lewis, the charter argues that in the absence of these character traits, all the vision and prescription in the world will not move people to do what they ought regarding the environment. The Earth Charter has been endorsed by thousands of organizations, hundreds of city governments, several national governments, and the United Nations Educational, Scientific, and Cultural Organization (UNESCO).[2] There is, it seems, widespread support for the view that an adequate environmental ethic requires recognition of the worth of nature and natural entities, which grounds virtues of care, love, and respect toward them.

I have already argued that many of these character traits are virtues for reasons pertaining to the relationship between human flourishing and the environment. For example, whether or not nature is intrinsically valuable or nonhuman organisms have inherent worth, care and love for them open people to rewarding and enjoyable experiences and relationships and are conducive to promoting and maintaining environmental goods. But are they further justified, and do they garner further normative force, on the bases emphasized in The Earth Charter and by many advocates of respect for nature—that the Earth, the community of life, and every living organism have value independent of their relationship to human flourishing?[3] Moreover, are there additional environmental virtues that are justified by the value of nature or the worth of environmental entities themselves? This chapter addresses these questions.

INDIVIDUAL ORGANISMS

Among environmental ethicists, Paul Taylor has been a prominent and influential advocate of respect for nature. According to Taylor, "Actions are right and character traits are morally good in virtue of their expressing or embodying a certain ultimate moral attitude...respect for nature."[4] This ultimate moral attitude has evaluative, conative, practical, and affective dimensions. "The valuation dimension of the attitude of respect for nature is the disposition to regard all wild living things in the Earth's natural ecosystem as possessing inherent worth."[5] An individual possesses inherent worth if it has a good of its own—"we can say, truly or falsely, that something is good for [it] or bad for it, without reference to any *other* entity"[6]—and it is better, all other things being equal, that its good is realized than that it is not. We have reason to be concerned about the welfare or interests of individuals with inherent worth, and not because we value them, caring for them is constitutive of or conducive to our flourishing, or they are instrumental to realizing some end that we desire (though they may have those sorts of value as well).[7] The conative dimension of the attitude of respect for nature "is the disposition to aim at certain ends and to pursue certain purposes.... [In particular,] avoiding doing harm to or interfering with the natural status of wild living things, and...preserving their existence as part of the order of nature."[8] The practical dimension of the attitude is to be disposed to effectively reason through, decide upon, and execute courses of action that promote the ends that a person with respect for nature values, desires, and aims to realize. The affective dimension is to be "disposed *to feel pleased about* any occurrence that is expected to maintain in existence the Earth's wild communities of life, their constituent species-populations, or their individual members ... [and] disposed *to feel displeased about* any occurrence that does harm to living things in the Earth's natural ecosystems."[9] Taylor considers the evaluative dimension to be the attitude of respect for nature's central component. The others are thought to follow from it through the premise that a comprehensive moral attitude involves substantial integration among a person's evaluative, conative, practical, and affective dispositions. The evaluative dimension is also what most people, including those who developed "The Earth Charter," appear to have principally in mind when they advocate an attitude of respect toward nature. Thus, it is the focus in what follows.

Taylor regards the attitude of respect for nature as "the most fundamental kind of moral commitment that one can make."[10] By this he means that it represents entry into a particular moral outlook, not a position justified by some already legitimated outlook. It is justified instead by a "*belief-system* that underlies and supports the attitude" and shows "that it is acceptable to all who are rational, factually informed, and have a developed capacity of reality-awareness."[11] Taylor's argument for the attitude of respect for nature therefore proceeds in two stages: establishing that any rational, factually informed, and open-minded person would accept the belief system that he calls the "biocentric outlook," and showing that given the biocentric outlook, the only (or, at least, most) rational attitude for a person to have involves acknowledging the worth of all living things.[12] It is thus "the biocentric outlook [that] provides the explanatory and justificatory background that makes sense of and gives point to a person's taking" the attitude of respect for nature.[13]

The biocentric outlook consists largely of scientific naturalism and a naturalistic understanding of human beings. Adopting it involves embracing these four claims: 1) humans are members of the earth's community of life in the same sense and same way as individuals of other species;[14] 2) the natural world is an interconnected and interdependent system on which humans are dependent; 3) all individual living organisms are teleological centers of life in the same way and same sense as humans; and 4) there is no nonquestion-begging justification for maintaining the superiority of humans over members of other species.[15] The first two of these claims are based on evolutionary, ecological, and biological science. They should be uncontroversial insofar as scientific naturalism is correct. The third claim requires some clarification, and the fourth claim requires some defense.

The third claim, that living organisms are teleological centers of life, was touched upon earlier during the discussion of "ends" in nature. A teleological center of life is a living thing that is internally organized toward its own ends or good, understood in terms of the biological functioning and form of life of the organism.[16] That individual organisms are teleological centers of life is, like the first two aspects of the biocentric outlook, a matter of naturalistic fact. It is clear that living organisms have a good of their own. Sulfuric acid is harmful to red spruce and poachers are harmful to panthers in straightforward ways that are independent of our interests and desires. Poachers are harmful to panthers even if we do not like panthers, do not value them, do not need them, and caring about them is not part of our flourishing. It is intelligible to talk about the good of living organisms and their being benefited or harmed only because they are organized or strive toward certain ends, such as survival, health, and reproduction. Therefore, living organisms are teleological centers of life.

The fourth claim constitutive of the biocentric outlook is that there is no nonquestion-begging standpoint from which to justify claims about the superior worth of humans. The type of worth at issue here is associated with being a moral subject, not with moral agency and moral responsibility. A moral agent is an individual who possesses the capacities in virtue of which they can act morally or immorally, be praiseworthy or blameworthy, or have duties or obligations. Nonhuman living organisms lack these capacities. They are not able to understand moral concepts, formulate principles employing those concepts, deliberate about the truth of those principles, apply them to make judgments in concrete situations, or act on the basis of those judgments.[17] For these reasons, their actions do not have moral worth and they are not morally responsible for them. However, this does not preclude nonhuman living organisms from being moral subjects. A moral subject is an individual whose good or interests are to be considered in moral deliberations and who can be treated rightly or wrongly. Being a moral agent is not a necessary condition for being a moral subject. There are commonly recognized duties to refrain from harming infants, severally mentally retarded people, and senile people, even though they are not moral agents. Therefore, that nonhuman living organisms are not moral agents does not settle the issue of whether they have inherent worth in the sense relevant to being a moral subject.[18]

That we evolved through the same natural processes as every other species, are composed of the same sorts of materials as all other living things, and are not connected to any transcendental reality or divine (or otherwise cosmic) plan rule out metaphysical bases for our being inherently superior or having greater inherent worth than members of other species. We do not have a special soul, location on the great chain of being, or role in the scheme of the universe.[19] If we are inherently superior or have more inherent worth, it must be due to something that distinguishes us from members of other species in this immanent and material world. But once this is acknowledged, establishing our superior worth becomes exceedingly difficult. There are all sorts of capacities and abilities that humans have that individuals of other species lack or possess to a lesser degree. We are quite good mathematicians, moral philosophers, information managers, and technological innovators in comparison with other living organisms. We modify our environment, how we go about the world, and ourselves in considerably more complex and diverse ways than members of other species, which enables us to thrive across environments in a manner unavailable to them. However, there are also capacities and abilities that individuals of other species have that we lack. We are poor photosynthesizers in comparison with oak trees and poor silk spinners in comparison with orb spiders. Moreover, it is just a contingent outcome of evolution that there are no other species with psychological and cognitive capacities (and all that comes with them) that meet or exceed ours. If evolution did give rise to a species with greater psychological or cognitive capacities than ours, or we discovered that there are already some out there, presumably we would not conclude that they have greater worth than we do. There is no reason to think that worth is a function of cognitive and psychological capacity, which is why we ought not to use it as a basis for making distinctions among people according to inherent worth.[20] Furthermore, although there are innumerable genetic, phenotypic, and historical differences between humans and members of other species, there is nothing special about this. Each species is unique in these ways, otherwise it would not be a distinct species. Moreover, there is no reason to believe that inherent worth is dependent upon uniqueness. Each person has the same inherent worth regardless of how similar her traits, history, and genetic makeup are to those of other people. Identical twins do not have less inherent worth than other people because they are so similar to each other in these regards. It is also difficult to establish human superiority by appealing to our genetic or phenotypic complexity. The metamorphosis of butterflies is more remarkable than puberty or any other transformation that we undergo. Our eyes are not as sophisticated as many mammals', we have only one nervous system whereas cephalopods have two, and amphibians can draw oxygen from both air and water. There is nothing especially remarkable about our genome.[21] It is 98 percent shared with chimpanzees, and the rat genome is roughly the same size (about 25,000 genes). Moreover, even if it were true that humans were genetically or phenotypically more complex than other species, it is not obvious why that would imply our being superior in any sense other than "more genetically (or phenotypically) complex." What does comparative genomic or phenotypic complexity have to do with inherent worth?

The basic difficulty with asserting the superior worth of individuals of one species over another within a naturalistic framework is that there is no ready standard by which to justify the claim. We might think that rationality, moral agency, and creative capacity are highly valuable, more so than the capacity to photosynthesize or spin silk, and we would be correct, as long as by "valuable" we mean "valuable to creatures like us that make their way in the world as we do." In the form of life of individuals of other species, these capacities are not merely less valuable, they are irrelevant. In the form of life of sockeye salmon, the capacity to maintain tight buoyancy control is crucial, and the capacities for complex language and understanding quantum physics play no role at all. Nor does it make sense to claim that sockeye salmon would be better off with cognitive and psychological capacities like ours. A "sockeye salmon" that had those capacities would not be a sockeye salmon, it would be a different species, in which those capacities did play a crucial role in its form of life. There is thus no neutral standpoint, independent from the context of the life form of a particular species, from which to establish that one species' set of capacities or way of going about the world should be the standard for measuring the inherent worth of individuals of other species.[22] Therefore, there is no nonquestion-begging basis for the claim that we have greater inherent worth than individuals of other species.

Moreover, the view that humans possess greater inherent worth than individuals of other species does not cohere with the other beliefs that make up the biocentric outlook. Everything in scientific naturalism favors the conclusion that we are just another variety of biological organism.[23] So there are positive considerations, in addition to the arguments against the superior worth of humans, in support of the *principle of species impartiality*:

> This is the principle that every species counts as having the same value in the sense that, regardless of what species a living thing belongs to, it is deemed to be prima facie deserving of equal concern and consideration on the part of moral agents. Its good is judged to be worthy of being preserved and protected as an end in itself and for the sake of the entity whose good it is. Subscribing to the principle of species-impartiality, we now see, means regarding every entity that has a good of its own as possessing inherent worth—the *same* inherent worth, since none is superior to another.[24]

The principle of species impartiality describes the evaluative component of the attitude of respect for nature. Taylor believes that if it is justified, so too is the attitude of respect for nature.

RECASTING RESPECT

There are some problems with how the concept of inherent worth and the principle of species impartiality function within the ethic of respect for nature that Taylor advocates. David Schmidtz has described well one of them:

> It will not do to defend species egalitarianism by singling out a property that all living things possess, arguing that this property is morally important, then concluding that all living things are therefore of equal moral importance. The problem with this sort of argument is that, where there is one property that provides the basis for moral standing, there might be others. Other properties might provide bases for different kinds or degrees of moral standing.[25]

The problem here is not with Taylor's argument for the inherent worth of all living organisms. It concerns the role that Taylor would have that worth play in his ethic. He takes recognition of the inherent worth of living organisms to be the central evaluative component of the attitude of respect for nature, which is the basic moral attitude that grounds the rest of the environmental ethic. Respect for nature is not one moral attitude or one virtue among others. It is the moral attitude. This leaves no room in the ethic for other types of moral standing, justified on different grounds and involving different bases and forms of responsiveness. So, for example, Norway maples and bottlenose dolphins are equally morally considerable, for the same reasons and in the same way. Dolphins' sentience, intelligence, sociability, and caring capacities are not taken to be relevant to how and why they are to be considered in practical deliberations.

A second and related problem with Taylor's ethic concerns its practical implications. Because the attitude of respect for nature is its basic moral attitude, the principle of species impartiality seems to imply that there is no basis for favoring the life and interests of a panda over the life and interests of a bamboo stand, or for preferring the life and interests of a human to the life and interests of an apple tree. So, if there is a choice between saving a human or an apple tree, it is a toss-up. But this would seem to constitute a *reductio ad absurdum* of the view.[26] To forestall this objection, Taylor defends a series of priority principles intended to show the practical implications to be other than what they seem.[27] Some of these principles describe conditions when it is permissible for humans to aggress against harmless nonhuman living organisms. But if all living organisms have equal inherent worth and that is the ultimate moral consideration, how could aggression against another living thing be justified? It is difficult to imagine that a person who accepted the principle of species impartiality could endorse such principles. James Sterba, who advocates a modified version of Taylor's view, responds to this problem by arguing that we simply cannot "require people to be saints" and must therefore avoid "imposing an unreasonable sacrifice on the members of our own species."[28] He then goes on to endorse an even less demanding set of priority principles than Taylor's. This response concedes that the practical implications of having the attitude of respect for nature ground the rest of the ethical system are unrealistic and unacceptable. Yet, rather than taking this as a reason to reconsider the theory, Sterba takes it as a reason to change the practical principles, effectively detaching them from their theoretical justification.

This difficulty with Taylor's view, like the previous one, is not the result of any problem with his argument for the inherent worth of living things. It concerns the roles that Taylor has the inherent worth of living things and the attitude of respect for nature play in his environmental ethic. Both difficulties are mitigated when his monistic commitments are jettisoned and his arguments are properly contextualized within the virtue-oriented approach. The inherent worth of living things establishes the good of living organisms as a noneudaimonistic end to be incorporated into the pluralistic teleological account of what makes a character trait a virtue. *Virtues of respect for nature*, then, are character traits that are virtues largely because they are conducive to promoting the good of living things. However, because the inherent worth of living things provides only one end against which character traits are evaluated, the dispositions constitutive of the virtues of respect for nature will be informed also by the other ends. Moreover, there will be other virtues, including some environmental virtues, that may in some cases favor aggressing against nonhuman living things even when they pose no threat to people. Therefore, recasting the arguments for the inherent worth of living things and the attitude of respect for nature in this way, within the context of the virtue-oriented approach, retains what is insightful about them while avoiding the difficulties associated with having an ultimate, foundational, and encompassing moral attitude based on a single type of value orient an entire environmental ethic.

To see this more clearly, consider the common objection to biocentric individualist and biocentric egalitarian environmental ethics (including Taylor's) that they are hopelessly detached from the facts about our form of life. We cannot exist without killing a large number of living organisms, since many aspects of our basic biological functioning (e.g., our immune system) involve killing other living things, and our survival (e.g., collecting food) requires that we appropriate other living things. Thus, any ethic that advocates, even as an ideal, noninterference with nature or not causing harm to other living organisms is inappropriate for our life form. J. Claude Evans puts this point as follows: "The fact that living things are teleological centers of life cannot be separated, even in thought, from the fact that all life is caught up in a system of interdependence.... Any ethical theory that does not recognize *and affirm* this fundamental fact is not a serious candidate for an environmental ethic, no matter how many principles it contains for *overriding* our supposed *prima facie* obligation *not* to appropriate."[29] It also is often argued that, as a result of their insensitivity to the facts about our form of life, biocentric individualist and biocentric egalitarian ethics are "wildly out of line with most people's intuitions and with common-sense morality."[30] As Victoria

Davion has pointed out, most people are not concerned about "the morality of swatting pesky flies, mowing the lawn, building patios, and finally itch scratching,"[31] because they do not care about the good of the living things killed during these activities.

There are some radical biocentric egalitarian views, such as Albert Schweitzer's ethic of reverence for life, for which these criticisms are justified.[32] However, the role of the inherent worth of living things (and thereby biocentric egalitarianism) in the virtue-oriented approach is such that these criticisms are not applicable to it. The virtues of respect for nature are informed by their conduciveness to enabling other living things to flourish as well as their conduciveness to promoting the eudaimonistic ends. Character traits that are insensitive to our form of life are not conducive to promoting the eudaimonistic ends. Thus, dispositions constitutive of virtues of respect for nature will be informed by our form of life.[33] Care toward other living organisms—i.e., dispositions not to kill them, impede their biological functioning, or undermine the conditions that they need to flourish—cannot extend to bacteria and viruses. If it did, we literally could not live with it. Moreover, it cannot involve opposition to all appropriation of living things. We must appropriate to survive. Not all appropriation is caring, compassionate, ecologically sensitive, and nonmaleficent, but neither is all appropriation inconsiderate, ecological insensitive, or otherwise disrespectful. To assert that it is would be to endorse a set of character traits highly detrimental to a person's meeting well the ends. The same is true of other virtues of respect for nature, such as compassion and distributive and restitutive justice. Although they are justified in large part because they are respectful of the inherent worth of living things, the dispositions constitutive of them are shaped by the other ends as well. They are, therefore, appropriate to our form of life.[34]

In addition to justifying virtues of respect for nature, inclusion of the good of living organisms as an end against which character traits are evaluated reinforces many other environmental virtues. For example, given the environmental costs of war and social instability, the good of living organisms justifies dispositions that promote peace, justice, and social stability. It also supports the case against consumptive dispositions, since they contribute to environmental degradation and the destruction of living things. Whether or not virtues of respect for nature take precedence when they conflict with other virtues, including other environmental virtues, is determined contextually. Virtues of respect for nature do not have special status within the virtue-oriented approach to environmental ethics.

DIFFERENTIAL COMPASSION

That considerations in addition to the inherent worth of nonhuman organisms inform the dispositions constitutive of virtues of respect for nature has implications for the commonly recognized virtue of compassion toward sentient nonhumans. The predominant approach to defending compassion toward nonhumans is to argue by extension from compassion toward people.[35] The extensionist argument is strongest if pain is intrinsically bad (and pleasure intrinsically good), and this establishes sentience (i.e., the capacity to experience pleasure and pain) as the criterion for the moral considerability of an individual. If this is the basis and order of justification, then there is no morally relevant difference between the pain of humans and the pain of nonhumans (or between humans and sentient nonhumans) that would justify differential consideration of or responsiveness to their pain. However, this is not the proper order of justification. Concern for the well-being of individuals is primary. If we should be responsive to the suffering of sentient individuals, the reason is that we should be concerned about their well-being and avoiding suffering and experiencing pleasure are part of their flourishing. How we should be disposed to respond to their suffering is, therefore, determined by how we should be responsive to their good. Should we be disposed to assertively promote their flourishing (active benevolence)? To refrain from interfering with them (restraint)? To avoid harming them (passive benevolence)? And so on.

A familiar objection to environmental ethics based on active compassion or benevolence is that the practical implications are unacceptable. If we ought to minimize all animal suffering so far as we are able, we will have to expend our resources to prevent lions from eating antelopes and to feed squirrels during lean times, for example.[36] But such activities, even if they would efficiently reduce overall suffering, seem absurd. On the virtue-oriented approach, the "absurdity" of a disposition of active, assertive compassion toward all animals (including all wild ones) is that it is not conducive to an agent flourishing or meeting well the other demands of the world—i.e., it is not sensitive to our form of life. Moreover, as discussed above, the justification for such a disposition overplays the moral significance of pain. Since concern for individuals is primary, all living things have equal inherent worth, and when we help one living organism we harm another,[37] we ought to be disposed more toward not impeding flourishing, which for sentient animals includes not causing them pain, than (more narrowly) toward reducing pain. Furthermore, because concern for individuals is primary, not all pain is equally a characteristic part of the form of life of an individual, and not all forms of appropriation have the same ethical profile, not all animal pain should be regarded in the same way. For example, the pain of a mink caught in a steel-jaw trap should be regarded differently than the pain of the mink when giving birth, and the pain of an antelope caused by a trophy hunter should be regarded differently than the pain of an antelope caused by a subsistence hunter. For these reasons, evaluative, conative, practical, and affective dispositions (appropriately shaped by our form of life) against causing nonhuman animals to suffer unnecessarily or excessively by either harming them directly or compromising their habitat are strongly justified, whereas dispositions to actively and assertively reduce any and all suffering of sentient animals are not well justified. This is not to claim that it is never compassionate to alleviate nonanthropogenic suffering of nonhuman animals. For example, although compassion toward nonhumans need not involve dispositions to actively seek out opportunities to prevent the suffering of wild animals, it may, particularly given our biological predispositions regarding the present suffering of others, involve dispositions to assist wild animals when appropriate opportunities present themselves—e.g., when dolphins become beached nearby.

As described above, compassion toward nonhuman animals more closely resembles restraint and nonmaleficence than it does the active compassion commonly believed to be appropriate toward other people. However, in many cases the practical implications of this *differential compassion* toward sentient nonhumans are similar to the practical implications of standard *extensionist compassion*. The two largely converge, for example, with respect to anthropogenic harm to nonhuman animals. On both differential and extensionist compassion, most factory farming, animal experimentation, and trapping are cruel, since they involve causing unnecessary and excessive animal suffering. Moreover, differential compassion often involves actively assisting domestic animals, particularly when doing so also expresses other virtues, such as gratitude, loyalty, fidelity, and restitutive justice. Promoting the well-being of companion animals, work animals, animals that have been used in experimentation, and animals that have been harmed by human activity is therefore strongly justified.[38] Where the practical implications of differential compassion and extensionist compassion primarily come apart is on cases where extensionist compassion favors actively promoting the well-being of animals for which the relational considerations of the sorts described above do not obtain.

ENVIRONMENTAL COLLECTIVES

What about species, ecosystems, and other environmental collectives? Do they have inherent worth distinct from that of the individual organisms that comprise them, which informs the ends against which character traits are evaluated? Taylor argues that they do not. His view is that they are merely classes or collections, and that to talk of the good of a species population or an ecosystem is really only to speak statistically about "the medium distribution point of the good of its individual members."[39] Sterba, however, believes that

> Species are unlike abstract classes in that they evolve, split, bud off new species, become endangered, go extinct, and have interests distinct from the interests of their members. For example, a particular species of deer, but not individual members of that species, can have an interest in being preyed upon. Hence, species can be benefited and harmed and have a good of their own, and so should qualify in Taylor's view as moral subjects. So too, in Taylor's view, ecosystems should qualify as moral subjects since they can be benefited and harmed and have a good of their own, having features and interests not shared by their components.[40]

At issue between Sterba and Taylor is how organized and cohesive these collectives are, and how organized and cohesive a collective must be to have a good of its own. Sterba bases his view on the work of Lawrence Johnson, who has argued that species and ecosystems are sufficiently organized and cohesive that they are best conceived of as living individuals.[41] However, the best chance for fitting species (or ecosystems or other environmental collectives) under some characterization of life starts by recognizing that being a living thing may be a matter of degree.[42] If a compelling case can be made that species are living entities, they are less so than organisms. The question then becomes whether particular environmental collectives are living to an extent and in those ways that ground a good of their own. There might be a sense in which ant colonies, corporations, zoos, prison systems, and the Catholic Church are living entities, for example, but it may not be a sense that grounds a good of their own, let alone inherent worth, distinct from that of their organism parts. This reveals that the status of species or ecosystems as "living" under some suitably liberal definition actually does little if any work toward establishing that they have a good of their own and inherent worth. The real issue is whether something as loosely aggregated, in terms of cohesion and organization, as a species or ecosystem can have a good of its own that makes intelligible respect for it.[43] But this is just to get back to the original issues above.

The cohesiveness and organization required for an environmental collective to have a good of its own and inherent worth are substantially more than mere spatiotemporal proximity or even causal interconnectedness. For something to have a good of its own, it must be goal- or end-directed, otherwise there is no standard for substantiating claims about its being harmed or benefited. Moreover, the collective's directedness must not be a mere accident or unintended consequence of the relations among its parts. The parts must be coordinated toward the ends, rather than merely productive of them, and the explanation for why the parts are organized or function as they do must include that such organization or functioning promotes the ends. Furthermore, the ends must not be derivative upon the wants, desires, or good of others, including the good of the collective's parts. If they are, then the collective will not have its own good or interests. This is the case, for example, with most artifacts. The explanation for their organization is intelligible only by reference to human interests or desires. Such artifacts may have a good—i.e., a state (or range of states) conducive to accomplishing the ends toward which it is directed—but the ends are not their own, so the good is not their own.

Some environmental collectives are organized in ways that satisfy these criteria. For example, in ant colonies the parts of the collective (the individual ants) are organized and behave in ways that promote the continuance and propagation (the good) of the collective (the colony), even when it is contrary to their own survival. Moreover, the good of the colony is not derivative upon the good of others, including the colony's own members. Instead, the well-functioning of the individual ants is derivative on the colony's ends. Furthermore, the individuals behave as they do because sacrificial behavior is beneficial to the colony (evolutionarily and functionally).[44] Thus, some environmental collectives have a good of their own. But is their good something we should care about—do they have inherent worth? I argued earlier, following Taylor, that all living organisms with a good of their own have inherent worth. However, as discussed above, the issue of whether an entity is living is really a diversion. What matters are the actual properties that the entity (organism or collective) has. So, if nonliving nonorganisms have a good of their own, then it would be a bias in favor of either living things or organisms (or both) not to ascribe inherent worth to them, unless there are nonquestion-begging reasons for not doing so—reasons that do not rely on the mere fact that they are not living or not organisms. Given this, if the beliefs constitutive of the biocentric outlook are, *mutatis mutandis,* as appropriate to environmental collectives with a good of their own as they are to humans and other living organisms, which they are, then they have inherent worth as well.

That some environmental collectives have inherent worth does not imply that they all do. Ecosystems are not nearly as tightly organized and cohesive as either living organisms or ant colonies. It is difficult to define the limits of an ecosystem, which is a contested concept even among ecologists, and to identify what the goal or end of an ecosystem would be. It is sometimes suggested that the goal is to maintain integrity and stability, understood in terms of the capacity to respond to stress, maintain certain ratios among constituent populations, or maintain certain levels and patterns of energy flows. But these measures are too static to be used to characterize the ends of ecosystems, given the dynamism of those systems. They are not really constrained to a range of states defined by certain patterns of energy flows or species populations. Moreover, the states of ecosystems are not the product of any central organization. They are the outcome of many individual living things making their way through a landscape created by, for example, other living things, geological events, and climactic conditions, and populated by, for example, predators, mates, obstacles, and food sources. When ecosystems appear to be goal-directed systems that maintain or repair themselves or that tend toward some stability or equilibrium, this is only a by-product of the behavior of the individuals pursuing their own good and the natural features that comprise the ecosystem.[45] The explanation why individual organisms that are part of an ecosystem do what they do is independent of the health of the ecosystem (or any other ecosystem "ends"), and individual organisms can flourish to the detriment of the ecosystem's stability or equilibrium. For all of these reasons, ecosystems are not goal-directed systems with their own good, and therefore do not have inherent worth. This is not to deny that we can talk meaningfully about the health of an ecosystem—e.g., in terms of its stability or resilience to stresses.[46] Nor is it to deny that we can formulate general principles or generate models regarding ecosystem processes—e.g., concerning population dynamics or vegetation succession. Ecology is a legitimate science. However, this does not establish that ecosystems are goal-directed systems with their own good in the sense necessary for their having inherent worth.

The situation is similar with respect to species. At any time a species consists of a number of organisms bearing certain biological relations to each other (e.g., parent/offspring, potential mate, competitor), and there is a certain distribution of genetic and phenotypic traits across its populations. The organisms that comprise a species, the distribution of traits, and the population size change from one generation to the next. The resilience, longevity, adaptability, and population size of a particular species are in some sense measures of its health. Functioning well for a species would seem to involve maintaining populations of interbreeding organisms, propagating itself, and adapting to environmental pressures. Moreover, as Sterba emphasizes, what is detrimental to particular individuals of a species might be conducive to greater longevity, pliability, and so on for the species. Nevertheless, this falls short of establishing that species have a good of their own in the sense necessary for inherent worth. As with ecosystems, a static conception of species must be resisted. Over time, a species can change in indefinitely and unpredictably many ways. It is not in the interest of a species that it maintain a constant character understood as a particular distribution of genetic and phenotypic traits, population size, or even ecological niche. To avoid going extinct, it must adapt to environmental changes, and this may require a substantial modification in character understood in any of these ways. Also, like ecosystems, species are less definitely defined than living organisms and some other environmental collectives. It is often difficult to identify the limits of a species, and the concept is unsettled both biologically and metaphysically.[47] Moreover, the explanation why individual organisms do what they do is independent of the longevity, adaptability, and other characteristics of the species. As with ecosystems, the apparent ends or goals of a species are only a by-product of the behavior of the individuals comprising the species pursuing their own ends. Conspecific individuals are not coordinated or organized in ways or for reasons pertaining to ends that are distinctly the species'. As a result, neither the well-functioning nor the flourishing of the parts (the individual organisms) that comprise the collective (the species) is determined by the extent to which they promote the good of the species.[48] So, while some collectives of members of some species are sufficiently organized and cohesive that the collective has its own ends and good (e.g., ant colonies), species as a whole are not. Therefore, species, like ecosystems, do not have inherent worth. Within the context of the virtue-oriented approach, this means that conduciveness to promoting their good is not among the considerations that make a character trait a virtue.

However, it does not follow from ecosystems and species lacking inherent worth that dispositions conducive to maintaining ecosystem health and biodiversity are not virtues. Virtues of sustainability, for example, are justified because human flourishing and the flourishing of living organisms (as well as some environmental collectives) depend upon the availability of basic and nonbasic goods, conditions, and opportunities that sufficiently intact and unpolluted ecosystems provide. Similarly, dispositions that favor preserving species and biodiversity are virtues to the extent that they are conducive to the flourishing of both humans and nonhumans. Moreover, environmental collectives often have historical, cultural, scientific, or aesthetic value, and being attentive and responsive to those values can be beneficial and enriching as well as respectful to those who care about them. In these ways, species, ecosystems, and other environmental collectives are often morally considerable, even though they lack inherent worth.

LAND VIRTUES

Many environmental philosophers have argued that an appropriately naturalistic understanding of human beings will locate us not only socially as members of human communities but also ecologically as members of biotic communities.[49] This is one of the central themes of Aldo Leopold's *A Sand County Almanac*:

> All ethics so far evolved rest upon a single premise: that the individual is a member of a community of interdependent parts. His instincts prompt him to compete for his place in that community, but his ethics prompt him also to co-operate (perhaps in order that there may be a place to compete for).
>
> The land ethic simply enlarges the boundaries of the community to include soils, waters, plants, and animals, or collectively: the land....
>
> In short, a land ethic changes the role of *Homo sapiens* from conqueror of the land-community to plain member and citizen of it. It implies respect for his fellow-members, and also respect for the community as such.[50]

According to Leopold, we should regard ourselves as citizens of the land community because we are biological beings whose flourishing is dependent upon our relationships to the community and the goods and opportunities, both economic and noneconomic, that it provides.[51] Leopold further believes that "when we see land as a community to which we belong, we may begin to use it with love and respect."[52] There is thus a substantial character ethic dimension to Leopold's "Land Ethic"— an action is right insofar as it tends to promote the integrity, stability, and beauty of the biotic community and is wrong insofar as it tends otherwise[53]—which Bill Shaw summarizes as follows: "Beginning with the notion that it is the community rather than the individual community member that takes precedence in 'The Land Ethic,' and that the 'good' of the community consists of its harmony of elements—integrity, stability, and beauty—the 'land virtues' should be those character traits (habits) that foster the 'good.'"[54]

One objection to this community-oriented approach to justifying environmental virtues is that the biotic community and the individuals that comprise it do not have (with rare exception) the capacities to participate in cooperative arrangements and deliberative discourse, which are often considered distinctive of moral communities. Moreover, as John Passmore points out, "the philosopher has to learn to live with the 'strangeness' of nature, with the fact that natural processes are entirely indifferent to our

TABLE 1

A TYPOLOGY OF
ENVIRONMENTAL VIRTUE

		Environmentally Responsive, Environmentally Justified, Environmentally Productive			
Land Virtues	Virtues of Sustainability	Virtues of Communion with Nature	Virtues of Respect for Nature	Virtues of Environmental Activism	Virtues of Environmental Stewardship
love	temperance	wonder	care	cooperativeness	benevolence
considerateness	frugality	openness	compassion	perseverance	loyalty
attunement	farsightedness	aesthetic sensibility	restitutive justice	commitment	justice
ecological sensitivity	attunement	attentiveness	nonmaleficence	optimism	honesty
gratitude	humility	love	ecological sensitivity	creativity	diligence

This table organizes the typology of environmental virtue develop in chapters 2 and 3. Environmental virtue includes environmentally responsive virtues, environmentally justified virtues, and environmentally productive virtues. Varieties of environmental virtue are distinguished by different considerations that make character traits environmental virtues. A particular environmental virtue need not be exclusive to one variety.

existence and welfare—not *positively* indifferent, of course, but *incapable* of caring about us."[55] This objection highlights that the sense of "community" proposed by Leopold is not a community of moral agents or a political community distinguished by, for example, cooperative practices or mutual obligations. For this reason, it is perhaps better not to characterize it as a community at all. Nevertheless, we are dependent upon and benefited by the ecological systems in which we are inextricably embedded, as are the nonhuman individuals toward which we should be caring and compassionate. Therefore, whether or not we can participate in deliberations or reciprocal concern with other "members" of the "community," character traits that favor considerate "community" interactions (those that promote rather than undermine the land's ecological health and integrity) are virtues. Many of the virtues of sustainability, virtues of communion with nature, and virtues of respect for nature, such as love, wonder, attunement, care, temperance, ecological sensitivity, receptivity, and appreciation, are thus also *land virtues*, since they make for good "citizens" of the biotic "community."

CONCLUSION

Living organisms and some environmental collectives have inherent worth, which is the basis for a noneudaimonistic end that is part of the pluralistic teleological account of what makes a character trait a virtue. This end justifies virtues of respect for nature, including care, compassion, and restitutive justice, and reinforces several virtues of sustainability, virtues of environmental activism, and virtues of environmental stewardship. The land virtues are those character traits that make human beings good "citizens" of the biotic "community." Ecosystems and species do not have inherent worth.

4

Environmental Decision Making

> By virtue I mean virtue of character; for this is about feelings
> and actions.... We can be afraid, for instance, or be confident, or
> have appetites, or get angry, or feel pity, and in general have plea-
> sure or pain, both too much and too little, and in both ways not
> well. But having these feelings at the right times, about the right
> things, toward the right people, for the right end, and in the
> right way, is the...best condition, and this is proper to virtue.
> —*Aristotle*, Nicomachean Ethics, 1106b17–24

VIRTUE-ORIENTED PRINCIPLES OF RIGHT ACTION

There are two central components to the virtue-oriented approach to environmental ethics: a theory of environmental virtue and an approach
to environmental decision making. The previous chapters focused on
the former; this chapter concerns the latter. A virtue-oriented approach
to decision making is one in which the virtues are the primary evaluative concepts. Actions, practices, and policies are assessed in terms of
them, and what makes one more justified than another is that it better
accords with, expresses, or hits the target of virtue. It is the virtues that
are action guiding, and that some action does or does not accord with
virtue that is reason giving, rather than, for example, its consequences
or its compliance with deontological rules or contractual constraints.
So, while character traits are evaluated teleologically, actions, practices,
and policies are not. This is significant, since a particular action or

policy might have the consequences in its favor, yet be cruel, arrogant, or dishonest.

There is not anything particularly "environmental" about the virtue-oriented principle of right action and method of decision making that I advocate. They simply comprise a virtue-oriented approach that can be applied in environmental contexts and in which environmental virtues are operative. This is appropriate, since the separation of an interpersonal ethical sphere from an environmental ethical sphere is spurious. Moreover, environmental ethics that employ a separate ethic approach have notorious difficulty adjudicating between the two ethics on the ubiquitous occasions when they overlap or conflict.

The standard for contemporary virtue-oriented principles of right action is Rosalind Hursthouse's: "An action is right if and only if it is what a virtuous agent would do in the circumstances."[1] This principle functions within virtue-oriented ethical theory in the same way that principles of right action function within consequentialist and deontological ethical theories. According to act-consequentialist theories, "An action is right if and only if it promotes the best (or good enough) consequences," and according to deontological theories, "An action is right if and only if it conforms to the moral law." These principles are then filled out or made substantive by an account of best consequences (such as maximization of pleasure over pain or satisfying peoples' desires) and an account of the moral law (such as maxims that are universalizable or rules commanded by God), respectively. In a virtue-oriented ethical theory, what gives content to the principle of right action is an account of a virtuous agent or substantive accounts of the virtues. Thus, the virtues provide content to a virtue-oriented principle of right action in the same way that a value axiology gives content to a consequentialist principle of right action and an account of the moral law gives content to a deontological principle of right action.[2]

It is often said of virtue-oriented ethical theories that they are agent-centered or agent-focused in a way that modern ethical theories, such as utilitarianism and Kantianism, are not. This description is accurate so long as it is understood in the way indicated above: that the substantive content of a virtue-oriented principle of right action is provided by substantive accounts of virtues and vices, whereas the substantive content in a deontological principle is provided by a substantive account of the moral law and the substantive content of a utilitarian principle is provided by a substantive account of good and bad consequences.[3] However, this should not be taken to imply that within modern ethical theories an ethic of character is any less important than an ethic of action. Immanuel Kant was, and contemporary Kantians are, deeply concerned about character ethics, as are and have been many utilitarians.[4] Nor should it be taken to imply that in a virtue-oriented ethical theory, how one should act in concrete situations is any less important than the kind of person one ought to be.

A common objection to virtue-oriented principles of right action, particularly neo-Aristotelian ones such as Hursthouse's, is that they are circular. The criticism is that they define the virtuous person as the person who does the right thing, or define virtue as the disposition to do the right thing, but then define the right thing as what the virtuous person would do. This criticism is misplaced. It is possible to substantively characterize virtues, and thereby a virtuous person, without falling back on their being dispositions to do the right thing (although virtues are that as well). For example, the pluralistic teleological account of what makes a character trait a virtue has been defended and employed to generate substantive accounts of several virtues and vices without appealing to a conceptually or substantively prior principle of right action. Therefore, employing those virtues and vices to provide content to a virtue-oriented principle of right action will not be circular or question begging.

AGAINST QUALIFIED AGENT PRINCIPLES

As the standard for virtue-oriented principles of right action, Hursthouse's particular principle—"An action is right if and only if it is what a virtuous agent would do in the circumstances"—has received considerable critical attention from those friendly and hostile to virtue-oriented ethical theory, and several problems with it have been identified. Moreover, these problems apply to any qualified agent account of right action—i.e., any account that defines right action in terms of a virtuous agent's beliefs, desires, or actions.

The Underdetermined Problem

There is no such thing as "what the virtuous agent would do" in a particular situation. What any actual virtuous person would do in a given situation is contingent upon her particularity—e.g., abilities, commitments, positions, resources, and relationships. For this reason, two virtuous people, in the same situation and both acting from virtue, might do different things. If a child is being pulled out from shore by a riptide, one virtuous agent might go for help, since she cannot swim, while another might enter the water, since she is a trained lifeguard. Thus, virtue and circumstance frequently underdetermine what is right for an actual person, even an actual virtuous person, to do.

This problem for qualified agent principles persists even if one moves, as Hursthouse does, to an inclusive version of the principle—i.e., "An action is right if and only if it is what *some* virtuous agent would do in the circumstances." This is because the problem is not just that in many situations there is more than one action that some virtuous agent would perform, but also that which actions are right for a particular person depends, often crucially, on facts about that agent. It would be wrong for the trained lifeguard to waste time looking for help when she can make the rescue herself, even though it is what some virtuous agents would do.

The Rightness from Weakness Problem

There are actions that seem clearly right, or even obligatory, for a nonvirtuous person, that a virtuous person would not do. For example, it is appropriate for a nonvirtuous person to perform actions that would help her improve her character. But many of these actions—e.g., certain forms of self-monitoring or seeking certain types of counsel—are not things a virtuous person would do, since a virtuous person does not have the deficiencies those actions aim at remedying.

This reveals that the appropriateness of an action often depends not only on a person's particular knowledge, skills, and relationships but also on her actual character. This is an extension of the central point from the previous objection, and it implies that a "virtue-oriented theory of right action must take account of the fact that many actions are morally required of us only because we fail to possess the character traits or motives that we ought to possess."[5] Sometimes, because a person lacks virtue, it is right for her to do something that no virtuous agent would do.

The Wrongness from Weakness Problem

There are actions that seem clearly wrong for a nonvirtuous person, even though a virtuous person would perform them. For example, a person who lacks the fortitude, commitment, and reliability to effectively lead a community effort to oppose some undesirable land use ought not seek leadership of the effort, whereas a person who has both the skills and the strength of character might well do so. Similarly, a nonvirtuous person should avoid situations where her indulgences or emotions are likely to get the better of her, because she is intemperate, irascible, or envious, which a virtuous person need not avoid.

These problem cases for qualified agent principles arise in the not uncommon event that the appropriateness of an action depends in part upon the likelihood of success, and the likelihood of success depends in part upon some aspect of the agent's character. For example, the appropriateness of making a promise often depends on there being a high likelihood of its being kept, which in turn often depends upon whether the promiser is reliable and honest. In such cases, it will sometimes be wrong for those who lack the relevant virtues to do what the virtuous person would do—make the commitment, intervene, or assume responsibility. Like the previous problem, these cases reveal that the rightness of an action is sometimes contingent upon a person's actual character. When it is, the actions of a virtuous person can be an inappropriate guide for nonvirtuous people.

The Contextual Problem

Contextual factors can sometimes lead a virtuous person to do what seems clearly wrong, even when she is acting in character. Oedipus's actions are often taken to be a paradigmatic instance of this. Types of contextual factors that can lead virtuous agents astray include: incapacity, as when a virtuous agent is for no fault of her own sleep deprived; misdirection, as when an agent is for no fault of her own tricked; and ignorance, as when the agent is for no fault of her own unaware of ethically salient features of the situation.[6] When a virtuous person's actions under such conditions result in, for example, serious harm to an innocent person, the actions might be considered understandable or even reasonable, but not right.

This problem for qualified agent accounts arises because any actual virtuous person is physically, emotionally, and cognitively finite, and therefore subject to external pressures and fortune, in ways that can compromise the appropriateness of her actions. As a result, the performance of an action by a virtuous person acting in character is insufficient for its being right. It must also be performed under nondistorting conditions.

Some variation of these concerns is going be applicable to any qualified agent principle of right action. Because there is no such thing as what an abstract virtuous agent would do (or desire or believe) in some situation, any qualified agent principle must define right action in terms of what actual virtuous agents would do. But actual virtuous agents are virtuous humans. As humans they are cognitively, perspectivally, psychologically, and physically finite, and therefore susceptible to luck, ignorance, situational pressures, and missteps. Excellence in character does not preclude them from being limited in any of these ways.[7] Moreover, what a particular agent, virtuous or nonvirtuous, should do (or desire or believe) is in many situations a function of her character, as well as her particular knowledge, resources, positions, and abilities. Therefore, one person's actions (or desires or beliefs) are not always going to be an appropriate guide for others, even if (and sometimes because) she is virtuous.[8]

AGAINST IDEAL OBSERVER PRINCIPLES

The problems with qualified agent principles indicate that a virtue-oriented principle of right action must be sensitive to agent individuality without being susceptible to agent (including virtuous agent) fallibility. One approach to managing these complexities is to move to an ideal observer principle of right action, according to which an action is right if and only if it is what an ideal (i.e., unimpaired, fully informed, and perfectly virtuous) observer would advise (or judge or approve) one to do in the situation.[9] Alternatively, one might move to an idealized self principle, according to which an action is right if and only if it is what an idealized (unimpaired, fully informed, and perfectly virtuous) version of oneself would do (or judge, advise, or approve) in the situation.[10] The move to idealization eliminates the fallibility that the finitude of actual virtuous agents introduces. It also accommodates agent particularity, since the advisor (or approver, and so on) is knowledgeable regarding both a person's particularities and how those inform appropriate action for her. Therefore, properly formulated ideal observer principles pick out all and only right actions. From the constructed perspective of perfect contextual knowledge, perfect character, perfect understanding of the substantive content of the virtues (their bases and forms of responsiveness), and perfect practical reasoning, there is no space for an error (accidental or intentional) to occur. The idealized perspective, since it is designed in a way that eliminates all mistake-generating possibilities, is conceptually tied to right action.

Nevertheless, ideal observer principles do not explain right action. What an ideal observer endorses is right, but what makes it right is not that an ideal observer endorses it. For example, if a person were to encounter an injured child in pain and distress and she could help remedy that with little risk or cost to herself, then assisting the child would be the compassionate, helpful, and caring thing to do. Therefore, an ideal observer would recommend (or advise, and so on) her to assist in the ways appropriate to her (given her particular abilities, knowledge, strength, and so on) under the circumstances (i.e., the expertise of others nearby and the desires of the injured person). However, it is not the ideal observer's attitude that determines the rightness of giving assistance, it is the rightness of assisting that determines the observer's attitude. If a particular course of action is right, it is so because of the features of the situation and what constitutes appropriate responsiveness to those features, not because an idealized being would advise, allow, or endorse it from her perspective.

A similar point applies to qualified agent principles of right action. It is not a virtuous person's doing something that makes it right. A virtuous person does what is right because she possesses, constitutive of her virtue, the capacity to identify and deliberate properly upon the ethically salient features of the situation, and is well disposed conatively and affectively regarding them. A virtuous person sometimes gets things wrong because, as a finite human being, she misses (perhaps nonculpably) something relevant or is unable to reason or respond properly (perhaps for contextual reasons) regarding some relevant considerations. For these reasons, a virtuous person's actions do not always track right action. A fortiori, that a virtuous person does something is not right making. Thus, while it is conceptually true that an action is right if and only if an ideal observer would endorse it, and it is generally true that a virtuous person performs right actions, it is neither the ideal observer's endorsement nor the virtuous agent's performance that make an action right.

TARGET PRINCIPLES

In a virtue-oriented ethical theory, the primary evaluative concepts are the virtues. It is by specifying the substantive content of the virtues that moral considerability—the bases and forms of moral responsiveness appropriate to particular individuals or entities—is determined. It is thus through the virtues that the sorts of considerations that are reason giving with respect to actions are identified. Therefore, the virtues must be central in action guidance, and right action is best explicated in terms of them. Although ideal observer principles or sufficiently qualified actual agent principles can pick out all and only right actions, neither is explanatory of what makes an action right. If a principle is to track the rightness-making features, it must be formulated more directly in terms of the virtues than are ideal observer and qualified agent principles. Christine Swanton has argued for a "target-centered" virtue-oriented principle of right action that does this. According to Swanton, "An action is right if and only if it is overall virtuous."[11] Things are a bit more complicated than Swanton's principle suggests. Nevertheless, her general approach of incorporating the virtues into the definition of right action is the correct one.

Swanton distinguishes between an action from virtue and a virtuous act. An "action from virtue" is "an action that displays, expresses, or exhibits all (or a sufficient number of) the excellences comprising virtue... to a sufficient degree."[12] Whether an action is from virtue concerns only the state from which the agent acts. If she acts from the dispositions constitutive of the relevant virtues, then the action is from virtue. One need not look to its outcome, whether it is successful in accomplishing its aim, to determine if this is the case. Although actions from virtue will tend to be right actions, they can sometimes miss the mark, since a virtuous agent acting characteristically is nevertheless finite and subject to fortune. In contrast, an action is a "virtuous act" "if and only if it hits the target of [a virtue]," where "hitting the target of a virtue is a form (or forms) of success in the moral acknowledgement of or responsiveness to items in its field or fields, appropriate to the aim of the virtue in a given context."[13] Whether an act is virtuous is typically independent of the agent's motives or states from which she acts.[14] It is a matter of whether the considerations in the world to which the operative virtue is responsive are adequately addressed by the agent's action. With respect to compassion, it is a matter of whether the suffering is relieved. With respect to wonder, it is whether one is able to see the complexity of the natural world. With respect to tolerance, it is whether one is able to refrain from interfering with what one finds objectionable. A person might successfully hit the target of a virtue, despite not acting from the virtue or even possessing it. People often do the honest, compassionate, or just thing for the wrong reasons.

The target of a virtue also can be accomplished to a greater or lesser degree. For example, a person might alleviate some suffering, but not as much as she might have under the circumstances, and therefore only partly hit the target of compassion. Moreover, what counts as hitting the target (and to what degree it is hit) is often contextual. What constitutes, for example, successful beneficence, friendship, or fortitude can depend upon facts about the situation and the agent, beyond the considerations that are the basis of responsiveness.[15] Furthermore, the target of a virtue often involves desires and emotions, not just actions. For example, one might help, but grudgingly; one might tolerate, even while inappropriately disgusted; or one might persevere, even while irrationally fearful.[16]

The concept of "hitting the target of virtue" enables specifying right action directly in terms of the point of the virtues, rather than mediated by or filtered through an agent, actual or idealized. Therefore, target principles of right action capture well the way the virtues are reason giving with respect to actions.

THE AGENT-RELATIVE TARGET PRINCIPLE

Swanton endorses the principle that "an act is right if and only if it is overall virtuous, and that entails that it is the, or a, best action possible in the circumstances."[17] However, as the problems with qualified agent principles of right action revealed, a principle of right action must be sensitive to the abilities and limitations, including the character weaknesses, of an agent. Rightness must therefore be indexed to those particularities, which Swanton's principle does not do. On her view, "it may be the case on occasion that the *overall* virtuous act [and therefore right act] lies not merely outside the scope of an agent's wisdom, but also beyond her strength."[18] This is acceptable, she believes, because on her view (as on mine), blameworthiness and rightness can come apart. Therefore, an agent need not always be blameworthy for not being capable of doing the right thing. Swanton also points out that even if an action is right, "it is not necessarily obligatory."[19] This is the case, for example, with supererogatory actions and mere politeness. Therefore, putting rightness out of the reach of some agents does not necessarily violate the principle that "ought" implies "can." But the problem is deeper that these responses suppose. It is not just that some agents in some circumstances will be incapable of doing what is right (which may be problematic in itself), but that in many cases it would be wrong for an agent to even attempt the action that would be overall virtuous and therefore right if performed by a capable agent. Moreover, Swanton's account appears unable to distinguish between what is required and what is supererogatory in cases when they fall on a continuum of responsiveness to, for example, the widespread suffering caused by a natural disaster. If rightness is the best possible action, then there is no room in such cases for distinguishing right and obligatory from right and supererogatory.[20] These considerations favor moving to the following *agent-relative target principle* of right action:

> An action is right to the extent that it better hits the targets of the operative virtues taken together (i.e., it is more virtuous) than the other courses of action available to a particular agent under the circumstances; and an action is wrong to the extent that it misses the targets of the operative virtues taken together (i.e., it is less virtuous) than the other courses of action available to a particular agent under the circumstances.

This principle is not subtle. It simply packs in everything that is relevant to making an action appropriate for a particular agent: the facts about the agent, the facts about the situation, the virtues that are operative in the situation, and what hitting the target of those virtues involves.[21]

One implication of the principle that has already been emphasized is that an action that is right for one person can be wrong for another person. How a person can effectively hit the target of some virtue, or even what constitutes effectively hitting the target, is often dependent upon her abilities, positions, character, and resources.

A second implication of the principle is that it is possible for a person to act rightly and yet it be unfortunate that she could not do better, since the action is right for her only because of some lamentable weakness. For example, under some circumstances it might not be right for a person with low confidence and self-esteem to speak up in defense of a friend to those who are speaking ill of the friend behind the friend's back. The costs to her well-being might be high, and she might lack the ability to intervene effectively and only exacerbate the mockery. Her weaknesses might thereby make it better for her to avoid participation and inform her friend about the others' behavior. That course of action might, for her, hit the targets of friendship and prudence better than what would be preferable and what a confident, articulate person would be able to accomplish: effectively intervening without great distress to herself. Assessments of how well a person responds in some situation without accommodation for character weakness allow for interpersonal comparisons in a way that evaluating the rightness of people's actions does not. One person might do better in a particular situation than another, although they both act rightly.

A third implication of the principle is that a person can act rightly and yet not be praiseworthy. For example, the agent in the case described above might do the right thing in avoiding participation and informing her friend, but it might not be something of which she should be proud (either that she did the right thing or that it is the right thing for her), since it is regrettable that she could not have done better. Furthermore, she might be blameworthy if her inability to do better is to a significant extent her own fault. Of course, if her lack of confidence and self-respect is the result of poor treatment from others throughout her life and has persisted despite her efforts to address it, then that this is the best she can do would not be something for which she is blameworthy. As this case illustrates, assessments of culpability and assessment of rightness do not always track each other, since they have both different objects and different standards of evaluation.

These implications provide the basis for a response to a possible objection to the agent-relative target principle of right action: indexing rightness to agent particularity, including character particularity, seems to let people "off the hook" for just the wrong reason, their lack of virtue. This objection misunderstands the role that agent indexing plays. It does not function as an excuse for failing to act virtuously. It makes the principle sensitive to the fact that the particulars about an agent, even about her character, can influence the extent to and ways in which she is able to hit the target of the virtues. Moreover, it does not eliminate comparisons between people. Those who are supposedly "let off the hook" have worse character than those who are not, and sometimes their actions (even when right) are worse than the right actions of a virtuous person, and they can be culpable for that.

Another significant feature of the agent-relative target principle is that it defines rightness in terms of success, what actually hits the targets of the operative virtues, rather than what is reasonably expected to do so. One motivation for this is cases where contextual factors lead a virtuous person acting in character to do something that turns out horribly—e.g., Oedipus cases. What a person does in these cases might be reasonable and nonculpable, but hardly seems right, even though they have strong reasons to believe at the time of action that they are doing the right thing. Moreover, the negative assessment in such cases is more appropriately expressed in the evaluation of the act than in the evaluation of the agent, who by hypothesis is virtuous and not responsible for the contextual distortion. A second motivation is that when we deliberate about what we ought to do, we are trying to identify the action that is in fact the best, not the action that we can reasonably expect to be the best. Therefore, it seems appropriate that rightness track outcomes in the world, rather than our expectations about them.

One implication of defining rightness in terms of outcomes is that there is always some uncertainty at the time of action regarding what is the right thing to do. We never know, in the sense of having a belief that is not possibly false, that a particular action will hit well the targets of the operative virtues prior to seeing how things turn out. We are not equally epistemically handicapped in every case. In some situations we have strong reasons to believe a particular action will hit well the target of virtue, while in others there is substantial uncertainty. Moreover, it is incumbent upon us to dedicate appropriate resources to trying to identify which actions are right. Nevertheless, in every case it is possible that in the end we will have been mistaken. This is not a shortcoming of the agent-relative target principle of right action. It is an ineliminable feature of our situation. We ought to do what we believe is right based on the best available evidence, since it is all we have to go on. But it is always possible that the evidence, which due to our finitude is never entirely clear and complete, leads us in the wrong direction, even when we deliberate properly upon it.

A second, related implication of defining rightness in terms of outcomes is that factors that are unknowable, unpredictable, or uncontrollable at the time of action sometimes have a role in determining whether an action is right, since they can influence whether and to what extent an action hits the targets of the operative virtues. As with ineliminable uncertainty, this is not a shortcoming of the principle, but rather a feature of our situation that is a product of our finitude. We often make retrospective judgments that our actions, although they seemed right at the time, were wrong due to factors of which we were unaware (and could not have been aware) or over which we had no control. This does not imply that we acted unreasonably or are culpable. Nor does it imply that we should have acted differently given the evidence available, even though it would have been better if we had.

The reasons for favoring an actual outcome principle of right action over an expected outcome principle are not, however, so strong that reasonable people could not disagree about which is the better option. It is therefore worth noting that reformulating the agent-relative target principle of right action in terms of expectations about hitting the targets of the operative virtues would be a straightforward matter. Moreover, regardless of whether the principle is formulated in terms of actual outcomes or expected outcomes, it favors the same method of decision making. There is convergence between the two alternatives in ethical practice.[22]

DECISION MAKING

Like any principle of right action, the agent-relative target principle is general, and its usefulness in practice depends upon whether there is an effective method for identifying what it defines as right. A common criticism of virtue-oriented ethical theories is that they are insufficiently action guiding. Particularized to environmental ethics, the concern is that specifications of environmental virtues will provide an account of the dispositions people should have regarding the environment and perhaps derivatively indicate the general sorts of environmental behaviors they should engage in, but will not provide specific guidance in concrete situations or on concrete issues. To be viable, a virtue-oriented approach to environmental ethics must respond to this concern. The only way to do so is to provide an effective method of decision making that can be employed even by people who are not environmentally virtuous.

The bit of truth in the lack-of-action-guidance criticism is that many virtue-oriented ethical theories, including this one, do not provide a finite set of rules or principles that can be applied by anyone in any situation to yield a unique action-guiding prescription.[23] This is not to concede that they do not supply adequate action-guiding resources; it is merely to recognize that they do not provide guidance along that "scientific" model. The issue, then, is whether the alternative on offer is sufficient.

The virtue-oriented method of decision making, which reflects the agent-relative target principle of right action, includes virtue-rules (v-rules) that embody the substance of the virtues; the use of mentors, models, case studies, and collaborative discourse; and moral wisdom.

V-rules correspond to substantive specifications of particular virtues. For example, because a disposition to help alleviate the suffering of other people when there is little cost to oneself is partly constitutive of compassion, there is a v-rule: "help alleviate the suffering of other people when there is little cost to oneself." Because a disposition to avoid compromising the availability of basic environmental goods is among the virtues of sustainability, there is a v-rule: "do not compromise the availability of basic environmental goods." V-rules can be taught, learned, and applied in concrete situations by those who do not have the corresponding (i.e., virtuous) dispositions. They can also be derived through individual and collaborative reflection on what dispositions are constitutive of the virtues. Thus, V-rules are accessible by the same means (moral education and ethical reflection) and action guiding in the same way (by application to concrete situations) as laws within deontological theories and secondary principles within act-utilitarian theories. However, the greatest likeness to v-rules is found in rule-internalization forms of rule consequentialism, according to which an action is right if it is consistent with a code of rules, the general internalization of which promotes consequences as good as or better than any alternative code.[24] In fact, if the criteria for evaluating codes is their conduciveness to both human and nonhuman flourishing, and internalization is understood dispositionally, then the rules that make up the code will be similar in form, justification, function, and content to the v-rules of this virtue-oriented ethical theory.[25]

Deliberation in concrete situations involves identifying which virtues are operative (or which v-rules apply) and determining what actions they recommend. It also involves determining what to do in the event that different operative virtues (or v-rules) favor contrary courses of action. In cases where an agent has difficulty identifying the operative virtues (or applicable v-rules), is unable to determine which actions are favored by those that are operative, or there are conflicting v-rules, she can look to role models, advisors, case studies, and collaborators for assistance. Here the virtue-oriented approach deviates significantly from the scientific model of ethical reasoning. It denies that through proper application of rules and principles, every moral agent can determine, in any situation whatsoever, what is the right thing to do. There is no overarching priority principle or strict hierarchy of virtues that provides adjudication in each and every case. Moreover, in some cases, discerning which virtues are operative and how their targets are best hit by a particular agent under the circumstances requires moral wisdom or sensitivity regarding the application of virtues in particular contexts. This is not something that all moral agents possess to the same degree, since it is developed over time through attentive and reflective experience. It does not, however, follow that those who lack moral wisdom are without resources for guidance in difficult situations. They can look to those who are morally wise either as advisors, mentors, or models, and they can make use of precedents that provide information on how decisions in similar cases have worked out in the past. This is, in fact, something we often do. When we are unsure of how to act, we seek guidance from people we recognize as possessing more wisdom and experience in the relevant areas.

The difficulties involved in identifying which norms are applicable in a concrete situation and determining what they favor, both independently and all things considered, are not confined to virtue-oriented ethical theories. For example, deontological theories have notorious problems with the possibility of conflicting perfect (inviolable) duties. Act-utilitarian theories have notorious methodological problems applying the principle of utility (unknown and unforeseeable consequence problems, time-crunch problems, and value-assignment problems). Rule-consequentialist theories have notorious problems adjudicating between conflicting rules without falling back on act-consequentialism. Moreover, no ethical theory can eliminate the need for good situational judgment, regardless of how "mechanical" or "codifiable" its rules and principles. The best an approach to situational decision making can do is just what the virtue-oriented approach does: provide tools and resources that effectively assist people to make good judgments.

Objections have been raised against approaches to situational decision making similar to the virtue-oriented approach on the grounds that they require an unacceptable epistemology. One concern is that for moral wisdom to fulfill its role in such a decision-making procedure, the virtuous person (or the possessor of wisdom) must have some special access or faculty for discerning what is right. She somehow perceives rightness where others cannot. A second concern is that they exaggerate what moral wisdom enables. Due to human finitude and the complexity of many ethical situations, no single agent, regardless of how excellent her character or her wisdom, will be able to identify the correct course. However, the virtue-oriented approach does not rely upon an epistemology in which a virtuous person has privilege to facts, information, or properties of situations that are inaccessible to those who are not virtuous. It does not imply that wrong action is always, or even usually, the product of ignorance. Most people have some capacity to see, for example, what is just, honest, or loyal in most contexts. When people act wrongly, they often do so despite their knowledge. They either lack the dispositions to do what they recognize as right or situational factors are decisive in that instance. Nevertheless, it is true that a virtuous person or a person with moral wisdom often is attentive to different details, feels differently about them, takes them as having different normative force, conceptualizes them differently, and orients them within a different outlook than a nonvirtuous person. There is nothing remarkable about this. It is an implication of the fact that each person, no matter how virtuous or vicious, has limited and particular perspective. There is thus nothing objectionable about the claim that a virtuous person sees things in particular ways or that those who do not share her perspective cannot always grasp or make sense of it. Moreover, the virtue-oriented approach does not require that a virtuous person be able to perceive immediately the right course of action in all situations. A virtuous person is aware of her limitations and fallibility, and is realistic about the challenges involved in sorting out difficult matters. She seeks advice, assistance, and partners when appropriate, and possesses traits conducive to effective communication and collaboration— e.g., modesty, humility, attentiveness, patience, and honesty. Therefore, it is not the case that the virtue-oriented approach to situational decision making entails an unacceptably individualist epistemology.

According to the virtue-oriented approach, situational decision making proceeds and action guidance is accomplished through the application of the virtues or v-rules relevant to the situation, appropriately informed by moral wisdom and assisted by the counsel of mentors, the study of models, and collaborations with others. This is not the scientific model advocated by many Kantians and utilitarians, but it is a viable method for determining what one ought to do in a concrete situation. Moreover, it reflects quite well how ethical deliberations actually proceed. It is common for people to think about, for example, what would be the honest, compassionate, or loyal thing to do in a particular situation and explain their actions in virtue terms. As Wensveen's catalogue of environmental virtue and vice terms reveals, doing so is ubiquitous in environmental discourse. It is also common for us to seek advice, talk things through with others, and pattern our behavior on those we recognize as models of ethical excellence or insight. Both religious and secular ethical traditions exhibit these features. They provide exemplars, authorities, forums, and dialogical resources to assist in deliberations on difficult cases.

ENVIRONMENTAL DECISION MAKING

The virtue-oriented approach to environmental decision making proceeds in the way described above. When there are considerations that fall within the field of an environmental virtue, that virtue and its corresponding v-rule are operative. Moreover, environmental virtues are justified by the pluralistic teleological account and constitutive of human goodness in the same sense as personal and interpersonal virtues. Therefore, environmental concerns are not the default area of compromise. When an environmental virtue pulls in opposition to a personal or interpersonal virtue, there is no presumption that what the environmental virtue recommends is subordinate. Each case must be examined individually. On some occasions what an environmental virtue recommends will be properly subordinated, on others it will not. In most cases, a course of action that does not offend any virtue is preferable to one that does. This is significant, since there is nearly always an alternative to some environmentally insensitive behavior or policy that does not compromise the demands of other virtues.

The virtue-oriented account of right action and approach to decision making accommodate pluralism in the expression of environmental virtue. For example, any environmentally virtuous person will be opposed to unnecessary environmental degradation that compromises some peoples' access to environmental goods. But, depending upon a person's skills, abilities, positions, and resources, she might best hit the targets of care, compassion, justice, or other operative virtues by directly intervening, working to change the institutions or policies that enable or incentivize the degradation, or attempting to raise awareness about the degradation and the suffering it causes. The facts about a situation and the operative environmental virtues often underdetermine how a particular environmentally virtuous person is disposed to act in that situation, as well as what actions hit well the target of environmental virtue for a particular agent, environmentally virtuous or not.

What is distinctive about the virtue-oriented approach to environmental decision making is that the normative force of action-guiding prescriptions is drawn from the substance of the virtues. If a person ought not clear a stand of trees in her backyard in order to improve the view from her window, the reason is not that doing so would not produce the best consequences or that the maxim it embodies cannot consistently be willed to be universal law. The reason is that doing so misses the targets of care, compassion, ecological sensitivity, or other operative virtues. If an off-road vehicle driver treats a wilderness area as a playground to be run over and through, she fails to see the natural environment and the individuals that constitute it as part of her "community" and appreciate the ways wilderness areas are a shared public good. She may be having fun, enjoying herself, and taking her thrills, but she is uncaring, inconsiderate, and selfish, since her activity destroys habitat, disrupts migratory patterns, and degrades alternative forms of outdoor recreation. Her actions are wrong because they miss the target of virtues of communion with nature, virtues of respect for nature, land virtues, and virtues of stewardship, hitting instead the "targets" of their corresponding vices.[26]

These examples demonstrate the straightforward way the virtue-oriented approach to environmental decision making can be action guiding. They are simple cases, however, and decision making becomes more difficult when additional, nonenvironmental virtues become operative, particularly when they do not appear to favor the most environmentally virtuous course. In chapter 6 I treat in detail one such case: the use of genetically modified crops in agriculture.

CONCLUSION

An action is right to the extent that it better hits the targets of the operative virtues than the other courses of action available to a particular agent under the circumstances. This principle of right action supports a virtue-oriented method of decision making in which action guidance is accomplished through the application of the operative virtues or v-rules to a situation, appropriately informed by moral wisdom and assisted by the counsel of mentors, the study of models, and collaborations with others. This virtue-oriented approach provides action guidance in environmental contexts and on environmentally related issues.

5

The Virtue-Oriented Approach and Environmental Ethics

The theory of 'ideal utilitarianism'...seems to simplify unduly our relations to our fellows. It says, in effect, that the only morally significant relation in which my neighbours stand to me is that of being possible beneficiaries by my action. They do stand in that relation to me, and this relation is morally significant. But they may also stand to me in the relation of promisee to promiser, of creditor to debtor, of wife to husband, of child to parent, of friend to friend, of fellow countryman to fellow countryman, and the like; and each of these relations is the foundation of a prima facie duty, which is more or less encumbent upon me according to the circumstances of the case.

—W. D. Ross, The Right and the Good, 19

THE CASE FOR THE VIRTUE-ORIENTED APPROACH

The case in favor of the virtue-oriented approach as an environmental ethic has two parts. The first is the positive arguments for the central components of the approach: its theory of virtue, virtue-oriented principle of right action, and virtue-oriented method of decision making. These have been developed and defended in previous chapters. The second, which is the focus of this chapter, is the approach's capacity as an environmental ethic. The approach captures well the multifarious dimensions of our relationship with the environment and meets well the environmental ethics adequacy conditions (discussed below).

The approach's many pluralisms are key to its capacity as an environmental ethic. Therefore, I begin this chapter by revisiting the approach's

pluralistic aspects and locating it within the discourse among environmental ethicists regarding pluralism in environmental ethics. I then ex-
plicate three conditions for an adequate environmental ethic that emerge
from the environmental ethics literature, and argue that the virtue-oriented approach meets these conditions well and that objections to its
doing so are misplaced. Finally, I discuss whether the virtue-oriented approach is a form of environmental pragmatism, which is often associated
with pluralism in environmental ethics. This discussion helps to locate
the approach within the environmental philosophy terrain and clarify its
position on some prominent theoretical and methodological debates.

PLURALISMS

I have argued that the virtue-oriented approach's pluralisms enable it to
capture particularly well the range of environmental experiences, relationships, and entities that are ethically significant, without reducing, homog-
enizing, or otherwise distorting them. However, not everyone agrees that
pluralism in environmental ethics is to the good. Baird Callicott is critical of it on the grounds that embracing multiple theoretical approaches
to environmental ethics requires endorsing incompatible metaphysical
foundations. He believes that this undermines claims about the correct-
ness of any particular moral point of view, thereby rendering pluralistic
approaches to environmental ethics either incoherent or arbitrary.[1] The
variety of pluralism that is the target of Callicott's criticism is what Peter
Wenz has called "extreme pluralism": "The extreme pluralist adopts different ethical theories for different contexts, and/or for different general
subjects, of application."[2] Within environmental ethics, this means avail-
ing oneself of whatever theoretical approach, with its particular metaphysics of morals, conception of human nature, and moral psychology, is
best suited to an environmental issue or situation. Another type of pluralism is what Wenz has called "moderate pluralism," according to which
there are "a variety of *independent* principles, principles that cannot all be
reduced to or derived from a single master principle. Whereas extreme
pluralism involves a plurality of theories, moderate pluralism includes
only a plurality of principles (in a *single* theory)."[3]

A recounting of the virtue-oriented approach's pluralisms will be helpful for identifying where the approach falls among these types of plural-

isms, as well as for determining whether it is subject to Callicott's objections to extreme pluralism.

1. *Pluralism in what makes a character trait a virtue.* A character trait is a virtue to the extent that it is conducive to accomplishing certain ends. Among these is the agent's own flourishing (the constituents of which are plural), but they also include the flourishing of other human beings as well as the flourishing of nonhuman living organisms and the good of some environmental collectives.

2. *Pluralism in realizing virtue, including environmental virtue.* Sometimes a plurality of character traits regarding a particular field meet the criteria for virtue (roughly) equally well. Moreover, the demands of the world are sufficiently great and diverse that no moral agent can be disposed to meet all of them as well as possible. Two agents might both be virtuous even though their character traits are substantially different. Therefore, not all virtuous people are equally environmentally virtuous, and not all environmentally virtuous people have the same character traits.

3. *Pluralism in how environmental considerations are related to virtue.* Environmentally responsive virtues encompass within their field some environmental entities or interactions. Environmentally productive virtues promote or maintain environmental health and integrity, the flourishing of nonhuman living things, or other environmental goods or values. Environmentally justified virtues are justified at least in part by environmental considerations, such as the inherent worth of nonhuman entities, relationships that can be had with environmental entities, or resources the environment provides.

4. *Pluralism in varieties of environmental virtue.* Among the varieties of environmental virtue (inclusive of environmentally responsive virtues, environmentally productive virtues, and environmentally justified virtues) are virtues of sustainability, virtues of environmental activism, virtues of environmental stewardship, virtues of communion with nature, virtues of respect for nature, and land virtues.

5. *Pluralism in how environmental entities are morally considerable.* Different virtues are responsive to different objects, properties, or events (they differ in bases of responsiveness), and they are responsive in different ways (they differ in forms of responsiveness). Therefore, moral considerability is always relative to a particular virtue. Different environmental entities—living things, sentient animals, ecosystems, landscapes,

other environmental collectives—are morally considerable under different virtues. For example, aesthetic appreciation is appropriate to some
rock formations, but compassion is not; wonder is appropriate to the
functioning of barnacles, but loyalty and friendship are not. Moreover,
the target of some environmental virtues, such as compassion and care,
is productive, whereas the target of other environmental virtues, such as
gratitude, appreciation, and wonder, is expressive or experiential.

6. *Pluralism in right action on environmental issues and in environmental contexts.* An action is right to the extent that it hits the targets of the
operative virtues taken together better than the other courses of action
available to a particular agent under the circumstances. Which action is
right often depends upon an agent's particular skills, resources, positions, location, and character. Moreover, there may be several courses of
action available that would accomplish the target of the operative virtues
(roughly) equally well. Furthermore, there is no one way to appreciate or
express wonder toward nature, live modestly, simply, and temperately,
organize with others in support of ecological ends, or promote considerateness toward living things, for example. For these reasons, there is not
always a single right way for every agent to act in a particular environmental or environmentally related situation.

7. *Pluralism in resources for environmental decision making.* Sometimes
an environmentally virtuous person will see clearly and immediately
which environmental actions or policies are right. Sometimes it will be
obvious even to those who are not environmentally virtuous. However,
in more difficult cases, decision making might involve considerable deliberation about what virtues or v-rules are operative and what actions
or policies they favor. It might also require looking to role models or
case studies or seeking out experts, collaborators, or others who have
cultivated good judgment (wisdom) in the relevant areas. There is thus
a plurality of resources available to an agent to assist in environmental
decision making.

Although the virtue-oriented approach is pluralistic in each of these
ways, extreme pluralism, as defined by Wenz and criticized by Callicott, is not among them. The approach is one ethical theory all the way
through. The basic evaluative concepts, the account of right action, and
the approach and resources for decision making are consistent across
environmental contexts and issues. Therefore, it does not fall into the
theoretical arbitrariness or contrariness that concerns Callicott.

It is somewhat less clear whether the virtue-oriented approach is moderately pluralistic. Wenz identifies W. D. Ross's pluralism as paradigmatic of moderate pluralism. But Ross's pluralism is distinctively intuitionist. He endorses several *prima facie* duties that do not have a common basis or principle that underlies or justifies them.[4] In contrast, on the virtue-oriented approach, the virtues and their corresponding v-rules are each justified in the same way: by how conducive they are to promoting the ends. Nevertheless, the virtue-oriented approach admits a plurality of normative principles (virtues or v-rules), which are not reducible to a single principle and can conflict. Moreover, there is no overarching principle or strict order of priority that in all cases provides a clear resolution to any conflict so long as the principle is applied properly or the order of priority is adhered to faithfully. So, although the various virtues and v-rules have common justification, there is irreducible pluralism, uncodifiability, and an ineliminable need for good judgment to adjudicate in some cases where norms conflict. Thus, if moderate pluralism is defined as rejecting a strongly codifiable or hierarchical model of ethics according to which some finite set of rules or principles provides determinate action guidance across all contexts, then the virtue-oriented approach is moderately pluralistic.

ADEQUACY IN ENVIRONMENTAL ETHICS

There is general agreement among environmental ethicists that an adequate environmental ethic must provide a basis for advocating and promoting environmentally sustainable practices, policies, and lifestyles. This general adequacy condition does not presuppose any particular approach to environmental ethics. However, it is not merely a formal requirement. It involves a substantive commitment to sustainability (or the like). This commitment is rooted in analyses of how our considerable environmental challenges have arisen and what is required to address them. Moreover, it has been substantiated by the arguments in the preceding chapters concerning the relationships between environmental goods and human and nonhuman flourishing.

There is both a theoretical and a practical dimension to the general adequacy condition. To satisfy the condition, an environmental ethic must not be susceptible to pressures or preferences that could result in its endorsing environmentally unsustainable practices, policies, or lifestyles.[5] But it also must be efficacious in promoting solutions to real world environmental problems. It must help bring about, not merely justify, environmentally sustainable practices, policies, and lifestyles.[6] Therefore, an environmental ethic is adequate to the extent that it:

A. Provides a basis for reliable, sustained, and justified critique of environmentally unsustainable practices, policies, and lifestyles.
B. Provides action and policy guidance in concrete situations involving individual or communal interactions or relationships with the natural environment.
C. Provides arguments, reasons, or justifications that are efficacious in moving people to perform the actions or adopt the policies that are recommended.

Many environmental ethicists, including those who have done significant work on environmental virtue, believe that a virtue-oriented approach to environmental ethics cannot meet the adequacy conditions.[7] This estimation is based on several concerns regarding virtue-oriented ethics generally: it is not possible to provide objective specifications of virtues and vices; they cannot provide sufficient action guidance in concrete situations; and they are unacceptably agent centered or egoistic.[8] These general concerns give rise to the following specific objections to a virtue-oriented approach to environmental ethics:

1. It is not possible to provide objective specifications of environmental virtues and vices.
2. A virtue-oriented approach cannot provide sufficient guidance on concrete environmental problems and issues.
3. A virtue-oriented approach cannot justify constraints on human activities that affect the environment.
4. A virtue-oriented approach cannot critically evaluate obtaining cultural practices and policies regarding the environment.
5. A virtue-oriented approach cannot value environmental entities for their own sake.
6. A virtue-oriented approach is unacceptably anthropocentric.

Each of these objections concerns the normative resources of virtue-oriented ethics and the capacity of a virtue-oriented approach for meeting the first two adequacy conditions. Each of them is misplaced.

It Is Not Possible to Provide Objective Specifications of Environmental Virtues and Vices

This objection involves objectivity in two senses. The first sense is the scope of the norms of the ethic, or for whom they have normative force. All moral agents? Only those in particular cultures? Only those under certain conditions? The second sense is the basis of the normative force of the ethic, or what makes the norms appropriate to a person. Is it contingent upon a person's wants or desires? Existing cultural practices? Facts independent of obtaining attitudes or cultural norms? If the norms of an environmental ethic have force only for those cultures in which they are commonly accepted or only for people who have certain desires, then the ethic will not have the capacity to be critical of obtaining cultural attitudes and practices and therefore will not satisfy the first adequacy condition. To meet that condition, an environmental ethic must not merely organize and legitimize existing cultural and personal norms, and its normative force must not be contingent upon obtaining cultural practices or personal preferences or desires.

The central evaluative concepts of the virtue-oriented approach are the virtues. Therefore, the extent to which the ethic is objective in the senses described above depends upon the scope and basis of the normativity of the virtues. According to the pluralistic teleological account, a character trait is a virtue to the extent that it is conducive to a person in a world like ours realizing ends grounded in her own good, the good of other human beings, and the good of environmental entities with inherent worth. Neither the pluralistic teleological account nor the substantive specifications of the virtues that follow from it are simply reflections of cultural practice or personal preferences or desires.

But, perhaps character trait evaluation should be sensitive to cultural context. If one trait is more conducive than another to promoting the ends for individuals of one culture (in a particular environment) but less conducive than the other for individuals of a different culture (or in a different environment), why not relativize virtue to culture (or environment)? The reason given earlier for applying the pluralistic teleological account at the level of human moral agent was that when doing ethics, we are concerned with norms at that level of generality. It is justified by the ethical side of ethical naturalism. However, if that commitment should change, the account of what makes a character trait a virtue can be modified accordingly. The pluralistic teleological account can be pitched at various levels—e.g., human moral agent, culture, or culture-in-environment. Moreover, at whatever level it is pitched, the virtue-oriented approach would remain sufficiently objective because the proper commitment will define both the level of generality that an ethic must meet and the level at which the pluralistic teleological account is applied. Furthermore, there is a crucial sense in which the virtues would be objective even if relative to culture. They would depend upon the facts about which character traits in that culture actually are most conducive to realizing the ends. They would not be determined by the prevailing beliefs within the culture about which traits are most conducive to achieving the ends, what makes a character trait a virtue, or which traits are virtues. The account of what makes a character trait a virtue (i.e., teleological pluralism appropriately modified) would remain constant across cultures, and according to that account what makes a trait a virtue or vice is not reducible to obtaining cultural practices or individual attitudes. Finally, relativizing virtue to culture would not undermine the normative force of environmental virtues. It would still be the case that all people ought to cultivate and express environmental virtues, although the substantive dispositions that constitute them might differ from culture to culture or culture-in-environment to culture-in-environment. The normativity of the virtues would be grounded in their conduciveness to a person in her culture promoting the eudaimonistic and noneudaimonistic ends. So long as a person is a member of that culture, she ought to cultivate the virtues appropriate to it, environmental virtues included. The normative force of the environmental virtues would therefore remain independent of individual attitudes or prevailing cultural norms. Thus, modifying the pluralistic teleological account so that it is sensitive to cultural or environmental difference (or, for that matter, to different life stages) would not undermine the objectivity of environmental virtue or prevent the virtue-oriented approach from satisfying the adequacy conditions.

A Virtue-Oriented Approach Cannot Provide Sufficient Guidance on Concrete Environmental Problems and Issues

This objection is that, although specifications of environmental virtues provide descriptions of what sort of dispositions a person should have regarding the natural environment and indicate the general sorts of environmental behaviors a person should engage in, they do not provide specific action guidance in particular situations or a decision-making mechanism for people who are not already environmentally virtuous to determine what actions they should perform and what policies they should support.

As has already been discussed, the virtue-oriented approach does not provide a finite set of rules or principles that can be applied formulaically by anyone in any situation to yield a unique action-guiding prescription. The approach is pluralistic and uncodifiable. Nevertheless, it does provide a principle of right action and is replete with action-guiding resources, such as v-rules, role models, and collaborative discourse, that can help a person identify which courses of action hit well the targets of the operative virtues in a particular situation. That the virtue-oriented approach has the normative resources to provide action guidance in environmental and environmentally related contexts is demonstrated further in the next chapter, when the approach is applied to the issue of genetically modified crops in agriculture.

A Virtue-Oriented Approach Cannot Justify Constraints on Human Activities That Affect the Environment

This objection is related to the previous one. It gains traction from the idea that, although virtues (and vices) might indicate general sorts of behaviors we should engage in (or avoid), they do not define strict obligations (or prohibitions) in concrete situations. However, environmental virtues have normative force for all human moral agents, even if their substantive content is relativized to culture or culture-in-environment. Moreover, it is wrong to fail to hit the targets of the operative environmental virtues in a particular situation, absent overriding justification. So, any action that fails to hit the target of environmental virtue is, all other things being equal, impermissible. If eating certain types of meat produced in certain ways is contrary to virtue in a particular context, then there is a constraint against eating those types of meat produced in those ways in that context. There will be occasions when it is difficult to make relative judgments about the extent to which available courses of action hit the targets of the operative virtues. But this limited epistemological challenge does not undermine the capacity of the approach to provide constraints and prohibitions. It merely reflects the fact that it can sometimes be difficult to identify them.

A Virtue-Oriented Approach Cannot Critically Evaluate Obtaining Cultural Practices and Policies Regarding the Environment

This objection is derivative upon the previous ones. If it were not possible to provide objective specifications of environmental virtues and vices or generate action guidance on the basis of them, then virtue-oriented environmental ethics would seem capable of little more than clarifying, organizing, and legitimizing existing cultural attitudes and practices regarding the environment. This would be problematic because to meet the adequacy conditions, an environmental ethic must provide reasons for thinking that environmental degradative and exploitative practices and policies are wrong, even for societies or individuals that lack environmental concern. However, as discussed above, the virtue-oriented approach does provide adequately objective specifications of environmental virtues and vices. The character traits constitutive of environmental virtue are not determined by cultural practices or people's attitudes, and environmental virtue is normative for all human moral agents. Moreover, the approach provides action guidance in concrete situations and grounds constraints on the treatment of the environment. It thereby has the normative resources to critically evaluate obtaining cultural attitudes, policies, practices, and lifestyles.

A Virtue-Oriented Approach Cannot Value Environmental Entities for Their Own Sake

Holmes Rolston III has formulated this concern as follows: "Environmental virtues, as achieved by humans, will initially involve concern for human quality of life. But our deeper ethical achievement needs to focus on values as intrinsic achievements in wild nature. These virtues within us need to attend to values without us.... The other cannot be seen simply as a source of personal transformation. We must make the model at least an ellipse with two foci: human virtue and natural value."[9]

Rolston's concern is based on a misconception of the sense in which virtues are human excellences. They are not excellent in themselves, abstracted from the rest of the world. They are excellences in relating to the world. The facts about us (the sort of beings we are) and our world (the sort of demands there are for beings like us) are what make particular character traits virtues or vices. The bases of the virtues, therefore, include entities with inherent worth and values "without us." Moreover, they justify responsiveness to all sorts of environmental entities, including landscapes, ecosystems, living things, and sentient beings. Thus, there is no danger of environmental virtue losing touch with values or worth in the natural world.

Part of what makes this objection seductive is the tendency to identify virtue-oriented ethics with a claim about the source of value. Either the virtues are the basis of value in the world or value in the world is the basis of the virtues. Any ethic that accepts the former is a virtue-oriented ethic. However, things are more complex than this. Environmental virtues are intrinsically valuable, in the sense of being constitutive of human excellence, because they dispose their possessor to meet well the demands of the world. The dispositions constitutive of environmental virtue are not intrinsically valuable absent those demands. Moreover, the relationship between virtue and values in nature is mutually informative. The bare fact that nature has inherent worth or intrinsic value does not imply anything in particular about how an agent ought to respond to that value. Therefore, it does not make any particular normative claims or demands. The facts about us and our way of going about the world "translate" natural values and worth into practical norms for us.[10]

This last point is telling regarding a question that is sometimes considered crucial to environmental ethics: Would there be value in the world absent any valuers? While this may be a compelling metaphysical question, it has little if anything to do with ethics, since ethics presupposes the existence of moral agents. The question is not, What values would be in the world absent moral agents? but rather What things in the world ought to be valued by human moral agents? Looking from a virtue-oriented perspective at the "last man" cases that embody this issue—whether the last man on earth does wrong by destroying or planning the destruction of natural landscapes, living things, or other environmental entities just before he dies[11]—the answer is straightforward. What the last man does is wrong because the destruction is ecologically insensitive, cruel, wanton, disaffected, and indifferent to the worth of living things and the goods that the natural environment has provided him over his life. Establishing the vices that inform this assessment does not require appealing to any values absent agents.

A Virtue-Oriented Approach Is Unacceptably Anthropocentric

There are at least four ways in which the virtue-oriented approach is anthropocentric. First, it is concerned with how we ought to live. Because the aim of ethics is to identify what sort of person we ought to be and how we ought to behave, every environmental ethic is inescapably anthropocentric in this respect.

Second, the approach is an attempt by us to figure out how we ought to live. This is another type of inescapable anthropocentrism. Even when people advocate doing ethics by "listening to god" or "listening to nature," they are making substantive claims about how we ought to go about answering ethical questions. At a minimum, we decide whether to try to figure things out on our own or defer to some other "authority." So even if "listening to god" or "listening to nature" represents a legitimate method for determining how we ought to live, there is no avoiding this variety of anthropocentrism.[12]

Third, the approach proceeds from our human perspectives. This too is a type of anthropocentrism that cannot be separated from ethics. Since ethical questions must be answered by us and we are finite and limited, ethical inquiry is constrained to the perspectives possible for us. This is not to claim that all perspectives are equally insightful or that we cannot obtain greater or lesser degrees of clarity or impartiality, it is merely to note that whatever clarity or impartiality we can achieve is what we are capable of as human moral agents given our cognitive, physical, and affective limitations. The virtue-oriented approach, like all ethics, is anthropocentric in this respect.

Fourth, the norms the approach advocates are sensitive to the facts about us and our world. If we were not the way we are—possessing certain cognitive and psychological predispositions and tendencies, dependent upon the natural environment for basic goods, capable of significantly degrading the environment and depleting our resources, unable to survive as newborns on our own, social, fallible, vulnerable,[13] and so on—the substantive content of virtues, including environmental virtues, would be much different. This type of anthropocentrism, unlike the types discussed above, is not inherent to ethics. It arises from a commitment to ethical naturalism and its corollary: questions about ethics are questions about how we should live as the particular kind of beings that we are, given the particular world we are in. Therefore, this type of anthropocentrism is acceptable to the extent that the naturalistic premise and its corollary are acceptable.

However, there are also a number of respects in which the virtue-oriented approach is not anthropocentric. It is not the case that only humans are morally considerable; that only humans have inherent worth; that the value or worth of all environmental entities is derived from the worth of humans; that the only demands of the world are agent or human flourishing; that humans are afforded a special, privileged place within nature (or outside of nature); or that special moral standing is attributed merely for membership in the species *Homo sapiens*. In denying each of these, the approach avoids what most environmental ethicists rightly find objectionable about some forms of anthropocentrism: unjustified bias toward humans to the detriment of nonhumans.

Because each of these objections to the virtue-oriented approach is misplaced, and on the basis of the positive arguments for its central components, the normative adequacy of the approach is established. The virtue-oriented approach meets well the first two environmental ethics adequacy conditions.

What, then, of the third adequacy condition: that an adequate environmental ethic must provide arguments, reasons, or justifications that are efficacious in moving people to adopt or implement the recommended practices or policies? Is the virtue-oriented approach well positioned to meet this condition, in comparison with other approaches to environmental ethics?

People's conceptualizations of environmental issues are neither uniform nor static. Environmental issues can be framed as human health issues, wilderness issues, quality of life issues, future generations issues, resource issues, or animal welfare issues, for example. An environmental ethic is likely to be practically efficacious to the extent that it is able to engage the multifaceted and dynamic discourses and motivations that these many frames generate. Wensveen's study of environmental virtue language, which found it to be integral, diverse, dialectic, dynamic, and visionary, suggests that a virtue-oriented approach to environmental ethics can be well positioned in this respect. The many pluralisms of the virtue-oriented approach reinforce this. The more pluralistic an ethic, particularly with respect to norm justification and moral considerability, the more possible points of resonance with public discourse and personal motivations. So, in comparison with less pluralistic approaches to environmental ethics, the virtue-oriented approach is well resourced for satisfying the third adequacy condition.

However, it is important to be realistic about what this means. A majority of Americans report that they worry either a fair or a great deal about the quality of the environment.[14] Therefore, one might reasonably expect that Americans would be living, or at least making an effort to live, environmentally considerate lives. But, while we describe ourselves as concerned about the environment, it is not expressed in our lifestyles. For example, we continue to purchase vehicles with low fuel efficiency, take our recreation in environmentally destructive forms, and sprawl out from population centers, paving and leveling as we go. We are even aware of the discrepancy between our environmental attitudes and behavior. Nearly half of Americans describe themselves as sympathetic but inactive regarding the environmental movement.[15]

This should give environmental ethicists pause. The practical efficacy condition claims that an adequate environmental ethic must encourage policies, practices, and lifestyles that are environmentally sustainable and nondegradative. But the dissociative state of Americans' environmental concern and behavior raises questions about how efficacious environmental ethics can be. People's attitudes are already pro-environmental, yet they are not moved to adopt a more sustainable lifestyle. Are additional attitudinal or evaluative adjustments along the dimensions addressed by environmental ethics likely to fare any better? This is an empirical question. Answering it requires determining what attitudinal changes particular environmental ethics attempt to elicit, whether the ethics' arguments change peoples' attitudes in the intended ways, and whether those changes in attitude translate into changes in individual behavior. I do not know of any study that attempts to answer these questions in a systematic way for any environmental ethic. But the data discussed above suggest two points that are relevant here. First, the practical efficacy condition must be interpreted reasonably. No theory of environmental ethics is going to have an overwhelming effect on people's environmentally related behavior. Second, it appears that what is needed, at least as much as generating awareness of environmental issues, is raising the salience of the issues and removing behavioral barriers by making pro-environmental behavior easier and less costly (or making environmentally degradative behavior harder and more costly). I do not know of any study of how effective different approaches to environmental ethics are in these regards (again, empirical questions). However, one plausible way to raise the salience of environmental issues is to emphasize how they are implicated in the quality of our own lives, as well as in the many things we care about. The pluralisms of the virtue-oriented approach make this explicit.

Therefore, the virtue-oriented approach appears to be well positioned to satisfy the practical efficacy condition (reasonably interpreted), in comparison with other approaches to environmental ethics. Since the virtue-oriented approach also meets well the normative adequacy conditions, it is an adequate environmental ethic. It is possible that several approaches to environmental ethics meet well the adequacy conditions. Thus, satisfying the conditions may not establish any one environmental ethic as superior, or any one ethical theory as preferable, to all the alternatives. However, the case for the virtue-oriented approach as an environmental ethic does not rest entirely on its meeting well the adequacy conditions. It also rests on how well the approach captures the complex ethical dimensions of our relationships and interactions with the natural environment, as well as the positive arguments for its theory of virtue, principle of right action, and method of decision making.

IS THE VIRTUE-ORIENTED APPROACH PRAGMATIC?

The case in favor of the virtue-oriented approach as an environmental ethic draws heavily on its pluralistic dimensions. An approach to environmental ethics often associated with pluralism, as well as with an emphasis on practical efficacy, is environmental pragmatism. In this section, I discuss the ways the virtue-oriented approach is pragmatic in order to further clarify its position on several prominent theoretical and methodological issues in environmental ethics. Environmental pragmatism, as I understand it, is a family of "theories" that emphasize certain normative, perspectival, methodological, and metaethical themes. Most environmental ethics that are self-described as pragmatic endorse some combination of a significant number of the following:[16]

Normative Themes

1. There is at least moderate pluralism.
2. There is uncodifiability—i.e., "No list of virtues, no list of rights and duties, no table of laws, no account of the good should be expected to serve in every possible situation that we confront."[17]

3. There is an area of practical "convergence" among contrary theoretical approaches to environmental ethics. Rather than focusing on mere theoretical differences between views, we should embrace justifications for the converged-upon positions that can effectively engage public and political discourse and individual motivations.

Perspectival Themes

4. Environmental issues are social and ethical issues that only human beings can resolve. Although we can attempt to represent the interests of nonhumans in environmental decision making, "the *human* organism is inevitably the one that discusses value. This is so because human experience, the human perspective on value, is the only thing we *know* as humans."[18]

5. Environmental ethics is always done from the middle of things. We must attempt to make our way the best we can on the basis of the information about ourselves and our world to which we have access through our present and past experiences, both personal and societal.

6. Each of us has only a finite, partial perspective of the world. This is an inescapable feature of being human, and we must not pretend to be able to transcend to an "objective" or "impartial" point of view free from individual contingencies, idiosyncrasies, or biases.

Methodological Themes

7. We are inextricably located in personal, social, and historical contexts. If change is to occur, it must proceed from this position through critical, creative, and communal reflection and practice. This is our best, if not our only, option.

8. The traditional distinction between reasoning about means and reasoning about ends ought to be given up. "The notion of fixed ends [should be] replaced by a picture of values dynamically interdepending with other values and with beliefs, choices, and exemplars: pragmatism offers, metaphorically at least, a kind of 'ecology' of values."[19]

9. Environmental issues are best addressed through public and democratic decision making. The appropriateness of the decision-making process legitimates or justifies the outcome. "While a pragmatist might endorse a policy framed in the language of rights or utility, the philo-

sophical justification for this endorsement will be procedural, and hence not an endorsement of rights or utility theory."[20]

Metaethical Themes

10. Environmental ethics ought to be practice oriented. Adequately addressing our environmental problems should be prioritized over obtaining "certainty" or "truth," and over settling disputes regarding abstract philosophical claims. We ought not get bogged down or distracted by perhaps irresolvable and often divisive metaphysical machinations and their epistemological counterparts—e.g., regarding the ontological status of ecosystems or the extent to which different environmental entities express "being."

11. Environmental ethics must avoid metaethical dogmatism. We ought not believe from the outset that only one sort of environmental ethic, such as nonanthropocentric, holistic, or intrinsic value-based environmental ethics, can be adequate.

12. There is no strong human-nature dichotomy. Humans are biological and environmentally embedded beings. We do not stand outside of nature. We are both permeated by and constitutive of it.

13. There is no need for a foundational approach to environmental ethics. Foundationalist theories tend to be static and removed from experience and practice. They are often insensitive to the political and social facts that are part of most environmental issues and therefore unable to adequately engage public environmental discourse. They also tend to be steeped in problematic metaphysical and epistemological commitments.

14. The traditional distinction between instrumental value and intrinsic value ought to be given up. If appeals are made to "intrinsic value," they must be to a conception that is not metaphysical, universal, and foundational. Instead, it must be "contextualized," emerging though our attempts to respond to situational demands, and "justified in terms of [its] ability to contribute to the resolution of specific environmental problems."[21]

Many of these themes are taken to reinforce or justify others, though none of them represents an environmental pragmatism doctrine or manifesto. Perhaps it is best, then, to think of an environmental ethic as more or less pragmatic according to how many of these commitments or positions it endorses (or, at least, with which it is consistent) and how central or peripheral they are.

On this standard, the virtue-oriented approach is considerably pragmatic. It embraces moderate pluralism, uncodifiability, the denial of a human-nature dichotomy, and that ethics must proceed from "the middle of things" by means of individual and communal reflection and practice. It also embraces each of the perspectival themes, although it is necessary to put a virtue-oriented gloss on what sorts of "objectivity" and "impartiality" are and are not attainable, given our finitude. Furthermore, it rejects metaethical dogmatism and supports a practice-oriented commitment, although not with the attendant de-emphasis on truth.

However, there are also considerable areas of divergence between the virtue-oriented approach and the positions described above, which preclude the approach's being considered a pragmatic environmental ethic. First, the approach is foundational. It is rooted in particular conceptions, formal and substantive, of what constitutes human flourishing, human goodness, and the demands of the world, which are developed from our best science, some metaethical commitments, and our lived experience.

Second, the approach involves a conception of inherent worth that supports a distinction between reasoning about means and reasoning about ends, as well as between instrumental and noninstrumental value. I have argued that living organisms and some environmental collectives have a good of their own that we need to be responsive to and that justifies virtues of respect for nature. This is a fairly traditional conception of noninstrumental value, and it is certainly not a conception of value that is only "justified in terms of [its] ability to contribute to the resolution of specific environmental problems." It is a type of value that helps define and identify environmental problems and constrains what counts as acceptable resolutions to them.

Third, the approach does not begin with, or have any special commitment to supporting or preserving, an area of practical "convergence" among environmentalists or theories of environmental ethics. This is not to deny that there is such an area. It is merely to note that whether there is one is immaterial to the development of the approach and the evaluative resources that it provides. In this way, the approach's direction of development is contrary to that described above—practical convergence to theory.

Finally, the approach rejects procedural pragmatism, according to which the appropriateness of the decision-making process is the rightness-making or justifying feature of the policy or practice outcome.[22] Whether an environmental policy or practice is justified depends upon the extent to which it involves appropriate responsiveness to the features of the situation, as understood through the virtues, and hits well the targets of those virtues taken together. Therefore, the approach allows that mistakes can be made even when appropriate decision-making procedures are followed. This is not to eschew public discourse, democratic process, or collaborative decision making. As has been discussed, a virtuous person knows that she is not an expert on all matters, has limited resources, and does not occupy all perspectives. An environmentally virtuous person recognizes that in complex environmental scenarios, where ethics, science, public policy, social movements, media, culture, and ecology converge, it may take considerable cooperative effort just to determine what the issue is and what is at stake, let alone identify and effectively promote an acceptable resolution. Among the environmental virtues are virtues of environmental activism and virtues of environmental stewardship, which include social virtues, dialogical virtues, and virtues of cooperation. Nevertheless, it is not the social discourse or the procedure that justifies one course of action, practice, or policy over another. It is the effectiveness of collaboration and cooperation in identifying the right course, as well as respect for the autonomy of other stakeholders, that legitimates the method.

Thus, the virtue-oriented approach largely shares the pragmatic conception of the human ethical situation: ethics begins with the problem of what to do in our concrete situations, we are already inextricably in the middle of things, we cannot get outside our own finite perspective, and we have only the information about ourselves and our world to go on. Where the approaches diverge is on what can be accomplished from this position. Pragmatic views are skeptical about the prospects of establishing a "universal," "objective," or "true" metaphysic, foundation for ethics, or account of agent-independent value that would support a distinction between instrumental and inherent value, support a distinction between means and end reasoning, or provide for discriminating against some wants and desires in decision making. In contrast, according to the virtue-oriented approach, agent-independent values and foundations are established from this position. Because of this, identifying proper environmental practice and policy is not reducible to appropriately public deliberations or democratic decision making. Sometimes these procedures will be dominated by uninformed, short-sighted, distorted, biased, or base preferences. Dogmatism in value theory, metaethical commitments, or other components of ethical thought should be avoided. The available information might change or errors in reasoning might be revealed. However, openness to reconsidering and testing ethical theories and norms in light of new evidence or challenges is not the same as regarding them as one nonfoundational, nonconstraining perspective among others in a public decision-making process.

CONCLUSION

The virtue-oriented approach satisfies well all three adequacy conditions. Each of the objections to the approach meeting the normative adequacy conditions is misplaced, and it appears to be as well resourced for satisfying the practical efficacy condition as can be reasonably expected of any environmental ethic. Taken together, the positive arguments for the approach's theory of virtue, virtue-oriented account of right action, and method of decision making, its meeting well the adequacy conditions, and its capacity to accommodate the many ethically significant dimensions of the human relationship with nature recommend it as an environmental ethic. Although it has much in common with pragmatic approaches to environmental ethics, the virtue-oriented approach involves several normative, methodological, and metaethical positions that preclude its being a member of the environmental pragmatism family.

6

A Virtue-Oriented Assessment of Genetically Modified Crops

One possibility is just to tag along with the fanaticists in government and industry who would have us believe that we can pursue our ideals of affluence, comfort, mobility, and leisure indefinitely. This curious faith is predicated on the notion that we will soon develop unlimited new sources of energy.... This is fantastical because the basic cause of the energy crisis is not scarcity; it is moral ignorance and weakness of character. We do not know *how* to use energy, or what to use it *for*. And we cannot restrain ourselves.... If we had an unlimited supply of solar or wind power, we would use that destructively, too, for the same reasons.

—*Wendell Berry*, The Unsettling of America:
Culture and Agriculture, *13*

The increase in man's power over his environment has not been accompanied by a concomitant improvement in his ability to make rational use of that power.

—*Daniel Kahneman, "Human Engineering Decisions," 190*

GENETICALLY MODIFIED CROPS

Ninety-nine percent of the genetically modified (GM) crops currently in the field are corn, cotton, soybeans, and canola that have been engineered for herbicide tolerance, insect resistance, or both. The most common herbicide-tolerant GM crop is soybeans engineered to be resistant to Monsanto's Roundup herbicide. The most common insect-resistant crops are corn and cotton engineered with genes from the bacterium *ba-cillus thuringiensis* so that they produce *B.t.* spores, a common insecticide used against cotton bollworm and European corn borer.[1] In 2006, GM crops constituted 61 percent of the corn acreage, 89 percent of the soybean acreage, and 83 percent of the cotton acreage planted in the United States.[2] Worldwide in 2005, 8.5 million farmers cultivated GM crops on 222 million acres for an estimated market value of $5.25 billion.[3]

GM organisms are created by the intentional transfer of genetic material between organisms using recombinant DNA techniques.[4] There is considerable disagreement regarding whether this method of genetic modification is just a more sophisticated form of the kind of agricultural innovation that humans have been practicing by means of selective breeding and hybridization since the beginning of agriculture.[5] However, the issue of whether the technology is new in degree or new in kind has been overemphasized in the context of ethical assessment.[6] Changes in degree can be ethically significant—discipline can become abuse, for example—and changes in kind can be ethically insignificant—replacing one's knitting hobby with online gaming, for example. Therefore, the acceptability of GM crops must be determined by considering the technology itself, process and product, and its social and environmental implications directly, not by reflecting on how or to what degree it is unlike what came before it.

In this chapter I apply the virtue-oriented approach to the issue of GM crops. I argue that the approach justifies a general presumption against the use of these technologies as the primary strategy for meeting agricultural challenges. However, under some circumstances particular GM crops ought to be supported as part of an integrated approach that also addresses the social, economic, political, and ecological dimensions of those challenges. Therefore, the virtue-oriented approach favors a position of selective endorsement regarding GM crops.

ENVIRONMENTAL GOODS

According to the virtue-oriented approach, assessment of a particular agricultural biotechnology involves determining whether promoting, developing, supporting, or employing the technology hits well the targets of the relevant virtues, in comparison with the available alternatives.

The virtues operative in the case of GM crops are environmental, since GM crops involve living organisms and environmental exposure, as well as interpersonal, since GM crops are intended for human use and consumption and have social ramifications. Among the operative environmental virtues are dispositions to maintain environmental goods necessary or favorable for the cultivation of moral agency and human flourishing. Are agricultural technologies produced by manipulating the genetic sequences of plants by means of recombinant DNA techniques likely to imperil these goods (e.g., food, water, and recreation), and thereby miss the target of some virtues of sustainability or virtues of environmental stewardship?

On first appearances, it seems not. These technologies are designed to produce agricultural goods, and their advocates tout them as productively superior to nonengineered alternatives. They are purported to produce a product that is more nutritious or flavorful, yields greater quantities, is less expensive or labor intensive, or can be produced under otherwise forbidding conditions.[7] Opponents of GM crops often deny these claims, arguing that the technologies actually provide an inferior product, less agricultural security, or less product in the long run.[8] But no one denies that they produce agricultural goods. If they did not, they would not be as common as they already are.

However, there is the potential for unintended consequences with the adoption of any innovation. Opponents of GM crops have argued that they are likely to affect natural ecosystems or the conditions that support agriculture in ways that will ultimately undermine the production of environmental goods. There are concerns that unintended gene flow between GM crops and their natural relatives will result in either superweeds that will require increasing volumes of more and more concentrated herbicides to control or organisms that will aggressively expand beyond their current ecological niche and compromise ecosystem stability and biodiversity.[9] There are concerns that GM crops will themselves escape into the environment and outcompete, interbreed with, or contaminate native species, which might compromise ecosystem stability, biodiversity, or some food supplies.[10] There are concerns that pests' resistant to the insecticides produced by GM crops will increase, rendering insecticides ineffective and pest problems worse than before the modified crops were introduced, leading to more frequent and intensive applications of chemical pesticides.[11] There are even concerns that the crops will decrease soil nutrient quality, thereby requiring intensive use of chemical fertilizers and leading ultimately to a decrease in production and the destruction of wild habitat to replace exhausted agricultural lands.[12]

These are appropriate concerns within the virtue-oriented framework. If a particular technology is likely to cause ecosystem disruption or undermine the production of goods necessary for the cultivation of moral agency, virtue, or human flourishing, then that technology misses the target of virtues of sustainability and stewardship. However, to recognize the legitimacy of these concerns is not to concede that they render all GM crops unacceptable. Rather, what it implies is that each GM crop must be evaluated against an external goods criterion (or v-rule): a particular technology should only be supported if there are reasons to believe that it will not disrupt the integrity of natural and agricultural ecosystems we depend upon for environmental goods or that the prospects for continued production of those goods without adoption of the technology are worse than they would be if it were adopted. Moreover, the effects of a particular technology must be examined synergistically. What is crucial is not what ecological effects it has in isolation, but what cumulative effects it has given any other technologies in use, as well as any ecosystem stresses—such as biodiversity loss, recreational use, or climate change.

The GM corn, cotton, soybeans, and canola that make up the vast majority of GM crops currently in the field are an extension of the chemically intensive and monocultural approach to agriculture that has become increasingly dominant over the last fifty years. This approach has taken a significant toll on the ecosystems that support the production of environmental goods. Among its effects are elimination of nonpest species (plant, animal, and insect), soil erosion, desertification, depletion of soil nutrients, decreased nutritional value in agricultural products, topsoil loss, contamination of aquifers and waterways, and emergence of resistant species of pests. It has also had detrimental effects on food security in many southern nations. For these reasons, close scrutiny of these new technologies is justified. In fact, many of the environmental goods objections to GM crops are based on the expectation that they will further promote chemical and monocultural agriculture and the deleterious effects associated with it.[13] The others concern the potentially detrimental effects the unintended dispersal of GM crops, or their modified genes, will have on supporting ecosystems.[14] When assessed according to the external goods criterion, then, the acceptability of a particular GM crop is largely determined by whether it is likely to encourage increased monocultural and chemical agriculture, as well as whether it or its genes are likely to disperse beyond their intended fields and be ecologically problematic.

Whether a particular GM crop promotes chemical and monocultural agriculture or disperses into and disrupts nonagricultural ecosystems are empirical questions. At present, the data on these issues for most GM crops are limited. I know of no study of whether GM soybeans, cotton, corn, or canola promote monoculture. Furthermore, only a few field studies for only a few GM crops have been completed on seed or gene dispersal and effects on wildlife.[15] A few more have been done on the effects of GM crops on pesticide and herbicide use.[16] Nevertheless, it is possible to make informed projections about particular GM technologies on the basis of what research has been done, the facts about the technologies (e.g., their intended use, who controls them, and how they are modified), and historical precedents in agriculture and technology more broadly.

One reasonable expectation regarding the environmental effects of GM crops that has been confirmed by existing research is that they vary from crop to crop. Not all GM crops affect pesticide and herbicide use in the same way. They have different dispersal qualities, exhibit different fecundity in the wild, and affect wildlife differently. Moreover, what risks a particular crop poses vary depending upon the methods by which it is cultivated and the ecosystems in which it is located. The upshot is that the environmental effects of each GM crop must be considered individually. The question is not whether GM crops pass the external goods criterion established on the basis of the virtues of sustainability and environmental stewardship, but whether this or that GM crop does so when cultivated in a particular way, under particular conditions, and in proximity to particular ecosystems. Are there any crops that can be reasonably expected to do so?

There is at least one: golden rice. Golden rice was engineered by scientists at the Swiss Federal Institute of Technology by inserting two daffodil genes and one bacterium gene into the rice genome. The modification enables the production of beta-carotene, the precursor to vitamin A, which is not otherwise present (or present in only trace amounts) in traditional rice varieties. Scientists plan to crossbreed the engineered rice with local varieties favored by farmers in developing countries. Efforts to do so by the International Rice Research Institute are already under way in the Philippines. The result will be varieties of rice, made freely available to poor farmers in developing countries, that are well adapted to local environments and will provide a reliable source of vitamin A. This is significant because between 140 and 250 million children, many of whom live in developing countries where rice is a staple food, suffer from vitamin A deficiency, which in severe cases causes symptoms ranging from vision impairment to increased susceptibility to diarrhea and measles.[17] The United Nations Children's Fund (UNICEF) reports that between 250,000 and 500,000 severely vitamin A-deficient children go blind each year,[18] and estimates that vitamin A deficiency is a significant contributing cause to a million childhood deaths each year.[19] UNICEF also reports that many of the childbirth-related complications that cause the deaths of nearly 600,000 women each year could be significantly reduced by remedying vitamin A deficiency among pregnant women.[20]

By incorporating the technology into locally favored seed varieties, rather than in a single product that would be patented and controlled by transnational corporations such as Monsanto or Pioneer, golden rice is being distributed in a way that will not displace local seed varieties, although they will be genetically altered versions. It is also significant that golden rice is not being promoted as a panacea for vitamin A deficiency. Researchers project that it will provide only 15 to 20 percent of the recommended daily intake of vitamin A.[21] Therefore, it is intended as a complement to traditional sources of vitamin A, not as an alternative to crop diversity approaches for addressing the problem.[22] As a result, golden rice should not encourage chemically intensive and monocultural agriculture.

Moreover, because the transplanted genes increase beta-carotene production rather than hardiness, aggressiveness, fertility, or toxicity, it is difficult to construct a reasonable scenario in which the transplanted genes would be detrimental to biodiversity even were they to spread through gene flow, interbreeding with wild plants, or unintended dispersal of the seed. The genetic modification does not confer any obvious fitness advantage under plausible environmental conditions. There is the possibility that such characteristics will be accidental to the genetic modifications of golden rice. But that can be determined from controlled field tests, which should go forward, given the promise of the technology and the considerable reasons to think that it will not damage the capacity of natural and agricultural ecosystems to produce environmental goods. The results of those tests would provide additional evidence as to whether golden rice satisfies the external goods criterion.[23]

Most of the considerations that collectively suggest that golden rice is likely to meet the external goods criterion do not apply to the preponderance of GM crops currently in use. The GM soybeans, corn, cotton, and canola that make up most of the GM plants cultivated in the world are designed to help large monocultural and chemically intensive farming operations improve their yield, and thereby turn a profit for the transnational corporations that manufacture and sell them. Indeed, they appear to be inextricable from the intensive monocultural and chemical approach to agriculture that has greatly contributed to our agricultural and environmental problems. Therefore, their use can be reasonably expected to promote or perpetuate it. This is so even if in some cases they lead to reductions in per acre pesticide or herbicide use.[24]

Concerns about the unintended ecological consequences of GM crops ought to be taken seriously and can render particular technologies unacceptable, but they do not justify global opposition to them. Each technology and the conditions of its adoption must be assessed individually. The details are crucial to whether a particular technology cultivated in a particular social, economic, and ecological context meets the external goods criterion.

RESPECT

GM crops that satisfy the external goods criterion might still be objectionable if employing them misses the target of other virtues. Some critics of GM crops have argued that they are disrespectful of nature or living organisms. Therefore, it is necessary to inquire whether promoting or cultivating GM crops is inconsiderate of individual organisms or collectives with inherent worth, or otherwise misses the target of an operative virtue of respect for nature, such as care, compassion, or ecological sensitivity.

In assessing this, we need only consider those GM crops that meet the external goods criterion. This criterion is, in part, concerned with the effects a technology has on wild ecosystems and individuals. So if some technology meets the criterion, its likely effects on those entities

are comparable to those of acceptable non-GM crops. Therefore, cultivating GM crops that meet the external good criterion will not be any
more inconsiderate, callous, uncaring, ecologically insensitive, or otherwise disrespectful to wild individuals (and collectives) than cultivating
non-GM crops. The same point applies to whether GM crops disrespect
agricultural ecosystems. If a GM crop meets the external goods criterion, then its effects on the ecosystems that support the agriculture are
comparable to those of non-GM crops.

Perhaps, then, it is GM plants themselves that are disrespected. However, it is difficult to maintain that GM plants are disrespected without
being led to a similar conclusion regarding non-GM crops. If genetic
modification by recombinant DNA techniques is disrespectful to the
modified plants, it must be so in virtue of what it involves doing to them.
But the candidates—e.g., it combines species, is anthropogenic, or alters
species from how they appear in nature—are each something found in
conventional agriculture, both modern and traditional. Nor is there necessarily a greater degree of genetic recombination in genetic engineering
(golden rice contains only three inserted genes) than in hybridization. As
discussed earlier, likeness to what came before is not itself an adequate
measure of ethical acceptability. But in this case, there is also the fact that
GM plants are not any better or worse off than non-GM plants. Indeed,
a particular GM plant would not exist at all if it were not genetically engineered, so it could not be worse off (or better off) than it would have
been were it not genetically engineered. Therefore, even given that agricultural plants have a good of their own, genetically engineering them is
not disrespectful to them in any unique way or to any unique degree, in
comparison with traditional and widely accepted forms of plant modification in agriculture.

One response to these arguments might be to claim that all crop
agriculture is disrespectful. However, virtues of respect for nature are
shaped by the inherent worth of living things as well as our form of
life. Any conception of respect for nature that violates the appropriation criterion is, in fact, a misconception. Therefore, agriculture *per se*
cannot be disrespectful. Moreover, those who oppose GM crops would
not welcome the conclusion that all crop agriculture is disrespectful.
They might, however, argue that all industrial agriculture is disrespectful, although more traditional or sustainable forms are not. But even if
this is true, it does not imply that the use of GM crops in nonindustrial

agriculture is disrespectful. Nor does it imply that there is greater or special disrespect, beyond whatever disrespect is inherent to industrial agriculture, when GM crops are used. The implication of this for golden rice, which is not embedded in industrial agriculture, is that it is no more disrespectful to support, develop, or cultivate it than to support, develop, or cultivate non-GM rice.

HUBRIS

Some critics of GM crops and other agricultural biotechnologies have argued that they do not fit with the image of ourselves and our place in the world that we ought to embrace. In particular, they often claim that to engage in or support these technologies is to express hubris rather than humility.[25]

Bill McKibben defends humility as an environmental virtue in his influential book *The End of Nature*. McKibben argues that humans "have ended the thing that has, at least in modern times, defined nature for us—its separation from human society."[26] Anthropogenic global warming, ozone depletion, and other climatic alterations "have killed off nature—that world entirely independent of us which was here before we arrived and which encircled and supported our human society."[27] Thus, the idea of nature as an independent force is no longer tenable. Human society is now surrounded by an artifactual "nature" that is both new and unpredictable. McKibben is not prepared to say that it is a worse nature, but he doubts that it will provide the relatively safe and stable context for human society that we have heretofore enjoyed.[28] So, while the new "nature" may not be in any objective sense worse than the old, the end of nature does have a legacy. First, we need to work out our relationship with this new nature. Second, we must face the environmental threats to human and nonhuman well-being that our ending nature has produced. Among these are the prospect of rising ocean levels, a significant decrease in the amount of accessible and usable fresh water, disruptions and inconsistencies in food production, increased outbreaks of diseases, and increased prevalence of extreme weather. Given this legacy, it is incumbent upon us to inquire into the proper attitude we should have toward this new nature and the challenges that it presents, since how we engage it will depend upon what attitudes we take. McKibben considers two general dispositions we might have regarding this new nature and situation: a disposition to further control nature and a disposition to accommodate ourselves to nature.

> So we need to "adapt" in some other fashion as well. The question is: How? We could, perhaps, figure out some way to drastically trim our ways of life and our numbers. But our impulse will be to adapt not ourselves but the earth. We will, I think, try to figure out a new way to continue our domination, and hence our accustomed life-styles, our hopes for our children. This defiance is our reflex.[29]
>
> The inertia of affluence, the push of poverty, the soaring population— these and other reasons listed earlier make me pessimistic about the chances that we will dramatically alter our ways of thinking and living, that we will turn humble in the face of our troubles.[30]

McKibben is not alone in advocating for a disposition of humility rather than domination regarding our relationships with the natural environment. When discussing environmental restoration, Eric Katz admonishes that "the human presumption that we are capable of [the] technological fix demonstrates (once again) the arrogance with which humanity surveys the natural world. Whatever the problem may be, there will be a technological, mechanical, or scientific solution."[31] Val Plumwood concurs:

> According to the naturalistic version of the dominant narrative, the blame for our [environmental] plight should be allocated in the usual place, to the symbolically-female, nature side of the hyperseparated and warring pair, reason versus nature.... And it is reason intensified that will be our hero and saviour, in the form of more science, new technology, a still more unconstrained market, rational restraints on numbers and consumption, or all of these together.... Reason in the form of scientific or technical fix also plays the hero in some alternative rationalistic and techno-optimistic scenarios. Science will save us, provided we do not lose our nerve or our faith in techno-reason and our will to continue along our current path, however precarious it may seem.[32]

Among environmentalists, Rachel Carson was an eloquent and persistent critic of human hubris regarding the natural environment.

The "control of nature" is a phrase conceived in arrogance, born of the Neanderthal age of biology and philosophy, when it was supposed that nature exists for the convenience of man.... [The] extraordinary capacities of life have been ignored by the practitioners of chemical control who have brought to their task...no humility before the vast forces with which they tamper.[33]

Carolyn Raffensperger expresses these same sentiments regarding agricultural biotechnology.

Humility would stand us in good stead, because we do not know all the consequences of engineering species. There are, of course, apparent benefits of biotechnology, and apparent beneficiaries. But we do not know enough even to understand whether those benefits are true or false, or whether they will lead to greater problems....

The restraint we must practice is restraint from the hubris that has gotten us into such technological messes time after time. Respect, humility, restraint, even humor—that we have to learn all these lessons time and again—are as important as scientific knowledge and investigation and our boundless technological creativity. We cannot afford to leave values such as these at the door when talking about biotechnology.[34]

Carson, Raffensperger, Katz, Plumwood, and McKibben each favor a disposition of humility over one of control and domination. They believe that we are better off with nontechnological, nonmanipulative responses to our environmental and agricultural challenges. But why? What reasons can they provide that will show them to be other than mere Luddites?

In defense of their position, they each offer reflections on our present ecological situation and the history that has led to it. We are, they claim, facing serious agricultural and environmental difficulties, such as chemical contamination of the air and water, topsoil loss, desertification, salinization, soil contamination, diseases and pests that can destroy entire crops, and biodiversity loss. This is something that advocates of agricultural biotechnology and GM crops will surely concede, since the promise of these technologies is that they will make a significant contribution to addressing our imminent agricultural and environmental challenges.[35] But how did we come to be in this situation, faced with these considerable difficulties? The answer to this question is of course complex, and most environmental thinkers would agree that an adequate answer must incorporate a variety of social, political, economic, ecological, and technological factors. But Carson, Katz, McKibben, Plumwood, and Raffensperger make a compelling case that it must also consider the attitudes toward natural and agricultural environments that have enabled the development and adoption of the agricultural practices and environmental policies that have been the efficient causes of these problems, and have thereby been detrimental to both human and nonhuman flourishing. The modern Western attitude toward the environment has been characterized by a disposition to control and dominate it, and this is "a key part of the problem, leading us to reproduce continually the same elements of failure—including the arrogance and ecological blindness of the dominant culture—even while we seek desperately for solutions within it."[36] This disposition is expressed in such practices as damming rivers, filling wetlands, cultivating water-intensive crops in arid locations, clearing forests, monocultural and chemical agriculture, species introduction, and species eradication. Humility in our environmental and agricultural practices is justified because it is more conducive to promoting and preserving goods necessary for and conducive to human and environmental flourishing than a disposition to promote them through domination and control.

One response to this claim might be to argue that it is domination and manipulation of our environment that has enabled humans to expand our range and population, as well as increase the length and comfort of our lives. Admittedly, the response continues, our pursuit and implementation of technology has generated some very serious environmental and agricultural problems, but these are relatively recent, and once we focus our technological ingenuity upon them, we will surely be able to handle them. After all, it is our technology that enabled us to get to where we are now in terms of longevity, health, and comfort. However, this response relies on an inaccurate framing of the historical case against technological domination and manipulation, as well as a misunderstanding of what humility with respect to technology and the environment involves. The sort of technological power at issue is the kind realized with the industrial revolution. Given that starting point, our ecological and agricultural challenges have arisen with remarkable rapidity and on a global scale. In just a few hundred years our technology has enabled us to significantly and detrimentally reduce the availability of fresh water in many places around the world, as well as significantly alter the earth's climate, for example. Moreover, the argument is not against the use of technology as part of an attempt to resolve our current ecological and agricultural challenges. Rather, it is against relying on technology as a "quick fix" or as "the solution" to those challenges. The claim is that it is hubris to rely narrowly on technology to address them, not that it is hubris to make use of technology as part of a comprehensive approach that also addresses their social, cultural, economic, political, lifestyle, and character dimensions.

Given a proper framing of the historical record, a comprehensive accounting of the causes of our environmental and agricultural challenges and what is required to address them, and a proper understanding of what humility regarding technology and the environment involves, it does appear to be hubris for us to rely primarily on further manipulation and domination, in the form of technological solutions, for addressing our agricultural and environmental challenges.

IMPLICATIONS

The propensity to rely on GM crops as the technological fix to our agricultural challenges is an expression of the disposition to attempt to meet our material needs primarily by domination and manipulation. Of course, most scientists, political leaders, and industry representatives who promote GM crops in this way do not think of themselves as engaged in or promoting a practice of domination. Nevertheless, that is exactly what they are attempting to do. When faced with the considerable problems discussed above, they are disposed to turn to technological solutions that rely on our "ability" to control our natural and agricultural environments by manipulating the DNA of some of the individual organisms that constitute them. Thus, while their motives may not be base, their actions express a disposition toward dominating and controlling nature, and they fail to hit the target of humility.

The foregoing is not, however, a criticism of GM crops themselves or even of the use of GM crops, or technology more generally, in addressing environmental and agricultural problems. Rather, it is a criticism of a certain type of approach to these problems, one that privileges domination and control over other possibilities, on the grounds that it fails to hit the target of a relevant virtue, humility. It justifies opposition to GM crops when they are proffered as "magic bullets" or focused technological solution. Pesticides in agriculture is a paradigmatic example of the magic bullet strategy. The target through which the solution is pursued—killing the pests—is narrow when considered in light of the social, economic, cultural, ecological, and evolutionary contexts in which agricultural pests arise and operate.[37] Pesticides also focus on treating the effect rather than the systemic causes of the problem, since they aim at killing the pests rather than addressing the origins of pest infestations and how our practices and polices contribute to them. Magic bullet strategies in agriculture are, because of their narrowness, highly susceptible to unanticipated and undesirable ecological, agricultural, and social consequences. Moreover, they depend for their success upon our ability to dominate and control the environment, as well as on our capacity to find a new technological fix for whatever undesirable side effects the latest magic bullet might have.[38] Thus, it is when GM crops are pursued and promoted as "the answer" to our agricultural challenges that the hubris charge is appropriate. Corn, cotton, and soybeans engineered for insect or herbicide resistance, the three big GM crops, are clear cases of magic bullets. They are part of the general chemical pesticide and herbicide strategy, and as such do not address the larger social, economic, ecological, and evolutionary contexts that give rise to the need for a "GM solution" in the first place.[39]

Instead of relying on the development and dissemination of GM crops to solve our agricultural problems, we should work toward modifying our lifestyles, including our diets, and our agricultural practices so that they are more attuned to the limits and distribution of our agricultural and environmental resources. We should also work to address the social, economic, and institutional factors that contribute to our environmental and agricultural challenges—e.g., agricultural subsidies, regulatory capacity and infrastructure, market and distribution mechanisms, international trade practices and agreements, access to technology and resources, intellectual property protections, and political instability and insecurity. This is not to claim that GM crops or other agricultural technologies cannot be included in such a comprehensive approach. There is nothing about GM crops that precludes them from being part of, for example, crop diversity or integrated pest management techniques in agriculture or reforms in resource allocations and distribution systems. Nor is there anything about them that requires that they be controlled by large transnational seed corporations and unregulated (or inadequately regulated) by national governments.[40] Again, the arguments above show that it is hubris to rely narrowly on technological fixes for agricultural challenges when the problems they aim to address are social, political, economic, and lifestyle problems as well. They are not arguments against the use of technology in agriculture.

The upshot of these considerations for the promotion and advancement of GM crops is that, although there is a presumption against their use as the primary means for addressing agricultural challenges, some GM crops are acceptable under certain circumstances, particularly if there are compelling virtue-oriented considerations that favor their use and they are part of an integrated approach for addressing a significant agricultural challenge. Of course, also relevant is whether there are additional virtue-oriented considerations against their use. For example, the promotion of a technology might be contrary to justice if those who would benefit from its development are not the ones who would bear the associated burdens.[41] This is the case, for example, when Midwestern family farmers' tax dollars are used to support research at public institutions to develop GM crops that benefit large corporate farms to the detriment of the farmers who were compelled by taxation to support the research.[42] This is also thought by some to be the case with "biopiracy"—i.e., when a government grants patent rights to an individual or corporation for the modification of a species that has traditionally been used or cultivated by an indigenous community.[43]

The GM soybeans, corn, and cotton promoted by transnational agricultural corporations fail to meet these conditions, just as they earlier failed to meet the external goods criterion. These technologies do not do significant work to alleviate the suffering of the impoverished, eliminate global inequalities, or reduce the negative ecological effects of modern agriculture. There are no social or ecological problems that these particular GM crops are likely to resolve that integrated approaches could not address more effectively or without the attendant promotion and perpetuation of monocultural chemical agriculture. Thus, in regard to these particular technologies, the presumption against the use of GM crops as the primary means of solving agricultural problems is not overcome. Once again, they ought not be supported.

This is not the case with golden rice, however. Golden rice appears capable of making a significant contributing to alleviating the suffering of some of the world's economically worst-off. It has, in fact, been designed specifically for this purpose. It will be freely distributed to the neediest, and is intended as a supplement to rather than a replacement for traditional sources of vitamin A. It will not promote monocultural chemical agriculture, nor will it diminish biodiversity, since it is being engineered into locally favored seed varieties. Moreover, there is no better alternative currently available, since the cost and infrastructure limitations on a vitamin distribution solution are substantial, and such a solution would only treat rather than resolve the problem. So, for golden rice, there is a compelling virtue-oriented reason, rooted in compassion for the suffering of others, that favors use of the technology as part of an integrated approach to addressing the problem of vitamin A deficiency. Since golden rice was also found to be acceptable according to the external goods criterion and not contrary to respect, the virtue-oriented assessment of golden rice is that it ought to be supported and field tests of the technology should be permitted to go forward.[44]

THE FUTURE

Virtue-oriented concerns regarding GM crops are not always without merit. There are considerable historical reasons to be wary of the disposition to trust and defer to technological fixes for agricultural problems, and some GM crops do pose considerable risks to environmental goods. However, this does not justify opposition to all GM crops. Instead, it justifies a measured pursuit of them in combination with lifestyle, social, and cultural changes, in an effort to meet our immediate and long-term agricultural needs. Each technology must be evaluated on its own merits, since one might be cruel while another is compassionate, unjust while another is just, or ecologically risky while another is safe. Thus, the virtue-oriented approach favors a position of selective endorsement of GM crops.[45]

There are a few reasons to be optimistic that the social and political "discourse" regarding GM crops is moving from the rhetoric that has characterized it thus far to a more productive discussion capable of discriminating assessment. First, the amount of credible scientific research on the ecological and human health effects of GM crops is slowly but steadily increasing. Research by the United Kingdom's Department of Environment, Food, and Rural Affairs (DEFRA) on the effects of GM crops on farmland wildlife is an example of this. Reliable data on the empirical claims that are central to the arguments regarding GM crops reduce the capacity for each side to rely on "our scientists" while attacking "their scientists," which has forestalled progressive dialogue.

Second, there is growing recognition among some major actors, including some who are central to defining the discourse and some who are responsible for regulating the technologies, that both a global opposition position and a global endorsement position are untenable. The move toward individual evaluation of particular technologies by these entities discourages rhetoric by requiring participants to address the substantive ecological, distributive justice, and human health issues raised by the technology under assessment. A report on agricultural biotechnology by the Food and Agriculture Organization (FAO) of the United Nations, *The State of Food and Agriculture 2003–2004, Agricultural Biotechnology: Meeting the Needs of the Poor?*, has emphasized the need for case-by-case assessment of GM crops, and DEFRA and the New Zealand Ministry for the Environment, for example, have committed to doing so.[46]

Third, in *The State of Food and Agriculture 2003–2004*, the FAO recognizes that, while it would be risky and hubris to expect GM crops to work as a magic bullet for all of our agricultural challenges and problems, these crops can be a valuable part of an integrated approach for addressing them. As discussed above, GM crops need not always preclude traditional farming techniques, nontechnological innovations, or revisions of social and cultural practices and institutions as part of a comprehensive approach to improving agricultural production and distribution.

Thus, there is a growing recognition of a middle way between pushing forward full tilt with the development of GM crops and not developing them at all: a discriminating pursuit of the technology as part of an inclusive strategy for addressing significant agricultural challenges. This is just what the virtue-oriented approach advocates.[47]

CONCLUSION

This discussion of GM crops should put to rest any lingering concerns about the capacity of the virtue-oriented approach to provide guidance on concrete issues or in concrete situations. By reflecting on which virtues are operative in the case of GM crops and what would constitute hitting the target of those virtues, guidelines for assessing which GM crops ought to be promoted and pursued and which ought to be resisted have been developed. There will, of course, be some difficult cases, and while the approach provides resources for working through them, it does not eliminate the need for good judgment and discernment. But, as has been discussed several times, this is not a shortcoming of the approach. It is an ineliminable feature of ethical decision making.

Conclusion

A Virtue-Oriented Alternative

"Neither the modified dominant position nor its Western variants, obtained by combining it with the lesser traditions, is adequate as an environmental ethic.... A new ethic *is* wanted."
—Richard Routley, "Is There a Need for a New, an Environmental, Ethic?" 48

WORK DONE

The central project of this book has been primarily a positive one. I have focused on what a virtue-oriented approach to environmental ethics can provide, rather than on what other approaches to environmental ethics cannot. In particular, I have:

1. Defended a pluralistic, teleological, and naturalistic account of what makes a character trait a virtue (chapter 1).
2. Demonstrated that this account of what makes a character trait a virtue can be employed to specify the dispositions constitutive of environmental virtues and vices (chapters 2 and 3).
3. Defended a virtue-oriented, agent-relative target principle of right action and a corresponding virtue-oriented method of decision making (chapter 4).
4. Shown that this virtue-oriented ethic accommodates well the many ethically significant dimensions of our relationships with the natural environment (chapters 2, 3, and 5).

5. Shown that this virtue-oriented ethic meets well the environmental ethics adequacy conditions (chapter 5).

6. Demonstrated that this virtue-oriented ethic can be employed to provide action and policy guidance on concrete environmental issues (chapters 4 and 6).

However, the virtue-oriented approach is not properly an environmental ethic, if by "environmental ethic" is meant an ethic peculiarly concerned with or oriented around environmental issues. The approach does not suppose that interactions and relationships with the environment constitute a discrete ethical sphere, or that environmental problems and issues require a distinctive form of practical reasoning, moral epistemology, method of ethics, set of evaluative resources, or metaethical framework. It does not involve rejecting the perennial questions, methods, and categories of Western philosophical ethics, or infusing it with aspects of non-Western traditions. It is, rather, a type of ethic familiar to the Western tradition that has been updated on the basis of contemporary work in moral philosophy, current scientific and ecological understanding, and current social and technological realities. The result is a new, environmentally informed, justified, and responsive ethic, which is sensitive to values independent of us in nature and the range of environmental goods in our lives.

The account of what makes a character trait a virtue, the virtue-oriented principle of right action, and the virtue-oriented method of decision making that constitute the virtue-oriented approach are therefore as much "personal" and "interpersonal" as they are "environmental." Moreover, that this approach constitutes an appealing environmental ethic recommends it not only as an environmental ethic but also as an ethical theory more generally. Ethical theories must be evaluated according to their capacity to capture well, and provide guidance on, personal, interpersonal, and environmental relationships, actions, and practices. Too often moral philosophers have marginalized the environmental aspects of the human situation in their assessments of competing ethical theories. If virtue-oriented ethical theory in general, and the virtue-oriented approach defended here in particular, is better resourced for environmental ethics than is, for example, contractarianism or utilitarianism, then, other things being equal, it is a superior ethical theory.

WORK AHEAD

The issues relevant to developing and defending a virtue-oriented approach to environmental ethics are distributed widely over the philosophical ethics and environmental ethics terrain. My treatment of them has been of necessity selective and programmatic. I have made several assumptions—for example, concerning ethical naturalism and interpersonal benevolence—and have not provided as much depth as I might have on some topics—for example, concerning aesthetic values in nature, what a character trait is, and stewardship as it relates to future generations. These and many other issues afforded only brief or passing consideration are significant, and their not being treated in greater depth is not a comment on their relative philosophical or ethical importance. Rather, it is the result of attempting to keep the project focused and emphasizing what is distinctive, novel, and promising about the virtue-oriented approach. There is thus quite a lot of work left to do on the issues associated with virtue-oriented environmental ethics. There is also much more to do with respect to specifying the particular dispositions constitutive of environmental virtues and vices. This is crucial, since environmental virtues and vices are the normative heart of the ethic and as yet are only partly and, in some cases, superficially specified in the environmental ethics literature. It is one thing to claim that we ought to be humble, sensitive, open, compassionate, frugal, appreciative, and tolerant. It is quite another thing to detail the dispositions constitutive of those traits. For all these reasons, this book is not intended as the final word on virtue-oriented approaches to environmental ethics, environmental virtue and vice, or the relationship between character and environment.

This is all the more the case since I have not shown that the virtue-oriented approach is preferable to all its alternatives. I have argued that it is superior to standard monistic approaches and that it incorporates what is insightful about environmental pragmatism, while avoiding some of pragmatism's problematic features. I have also emphasized the pluralistic aspects of the approach, which capture particularly well the many dimensions of our relationship with the natural environment, an appreciation of which is necessary for understanding and responding adequately to complex, diverse, and dynamic environmental challenges. However, I have not provided detailed comparative assessments with the more sophisticated versions of the familiar approaches or other pluralistic approaches to environmental ethics.

The aim of this book, in addition to identifying the ethically significant aspects of the relationship between human character and the natural environment, has been to make such comparisons necessary. There is a virtue-oriented alternative with considerable appeal and potential that ought to be considered alongside those other approaches. Upon final assessment, the virtue-oriented approach may even be found preferable to them.

NOTES

Introduction: A Virtue-Oriented Alternative?

1. Leopold, *A Sand County Almanac*, viii. John Muir concurs, "No dogma taught by the present civilization seems to form so insuperable an obstacle in the way of a right understanding of the relations which culture sustains to wildness as that which regards the world as made especially for the uses of man" ("Wild Wool" 364).
2. Carson, *The Sense of Wonder*, 88.
3. Muir, *The Yosemite*, 256.
4. Van Wensveen, *Dirty Virtues: The Emergence of Ecological Virtue Ethics*, 5.
5. Van Wensveen, *Dirty Virtues: The Emergence of Ecological Virtue Ethics*, 18. It is because of the ubiquitousness and multifariousness of our relationship with the natural environment that environmental virtues and vices are legion and their fields pervade our lives.

1. What Makes a Character Trait a Virtue?

1. Cafaro, "Thoreau, Leopold, and Carson: Toward an Environmental Virtue Ethics," 13, 14, 15, 16. See also Cafaro, "The Naturalist's Virtues" and *Thoreau's Living Ethics: Walden and the Pursuit of Virtue*.
2. Frasz, "What Is Environmental Virtue Ethics That We Should Be Mindful of It," 11.
3. They are those that make for a person willing to "devote a substantial percentage of one's thoughts and efforts to maintaining or enhancing the condition of some thing(s) or person(s), not primarily for the steward's own sake" (Welchman, "The Virtues of Stewardship," 415).
4. Aristotle, *Nicomachean Ethics*, Book 2, chs. 4–6.
5. Aristotle, *Nicomachean Ethics*, 1116a5–9.

6   Many of the major ancient Western philosophical schools (e.g., Platonic, Aristotelian, and Stoic) advocated some version of this eudaimonistic theory of virtue, although they often differed in their views on the strength of the relationship between virtue and flourishing. Some believed that the virtues are sufficient for flourishing; some believed that they are necessary for flourishing; and some believed that they are merely most conducive to flourishing. Among the prominent contemporary advocates of eudaimonism are Rosalind Hursthouse (*On Virtue Ethics*), Lawrence Becker (*A New Stoicism*), Julia Annas (*The Morality of Happiness*), Martha Nussbaum (*The Fragility of Goodness* and *The Therapy of Desire*), and Philippa Foot (*Natural Goodness*). For example, according to Hursthouse, "A virtue is a character trait a human being needs for eudaimonia, to flourish or live well" (*On Virtue Ethics* 167).

7. Hursthouse, *On Virtue Ethics*, 226. See also 195–97, 205–6. Here is Foot's formulation of the view: "My belief is that for all the differences that there are, as we shall see, between the evaluation of plants and animals and their parts and characteristics on the one hand, and the moral evaluations of humans on the other, we shall find that these evaluations share a basic logical structure and status. I want to suggest that moral defect is a form of natural defect not as different as is generally supposed from defect in sub-rational living things" (*Natural Goodness* 27). See also Foot, *Natural Goodness*, 26–27, 51.

8. Foot, *Natural Goodness*, 26–27. See also Hursthouse, *On Virtue Ethics*, 195–97, 205–6, and Foot, *Natural Goodness*, 2–4, 51.

9. Hursthouse, *On Virtue Ethics*, 202.

10. "Thus, evaluation of an individual living thing in its own right, with no reference to our interests or desires, is possible where there is intersection of two types of propositions: On the one hand, Aristotelian categoricals (life-form descriptions relating to the species), and on the other, propositions about particular individuals that are the subject of evaluation" (Foot, *Natural Goodness*, 33).

11. Hursthouse, *On Virtue Ethics*, 204.

12. Hursthouse, *On Virtue Ethics*, 206–207.

13. For each theory of virtue formulated in this chapter—each account of what makes a person ethically good or what makes a character trait a virtue—there is a corresponding account of what makes a character trait a vice: a character trait is a vice to the extent that is detrimental to realizing the specified ends.

14. Hursthouse, *On Virtue Ethics*, 219–20; Foot, *Natural Goodness*, 43.

15. "[Scientists] have documented the inordinate diversity of individuals and societies in areas as different as sexual preferences and political systems.

In light of this scientific progress, I want to highlight human *natures*: the diverse and evolving behaviors, beliefs, and attitudes of *Homo sapiens* and the evolved physical structures that govern, support, and participate in our unique mental functioning. Even though our bodies and behaviors share many common attributes, it's far more fruitful to consider not one human nature but many. The universals that bind together at any point in our evolution are covered in the word *human*. The word *natures* emphasizes the differences that give us our individuality, our cultural variety, and our potential for future genetic and—especially—cultural evolution" (Ehrlich, *Human Natures: Genes, Cultures, and the Human Prospect*, ix–x).

16. Richerson and Boyd, *Not by Genes Alone.*

17. "For it can be said that while animals go for the good (thing) *that they see*, human beings go for *what they see as good.* . . . Human beings not only have the power to reason about all sorts of things in a speculative way, but also the power to *see grounds* for acting in one way rather than another" (Foot, *Natural Goodness*, 56).

18. "Our way of going on is just one, which remains the same across all areas of our life. Our characteristic way of going on, which distinguishes us from all the other species of animals, is a rational way. A 'rational way' is any way that we can rightly see as good, as something we have reason to do. Correspondingly, our characteristic enjoyments are any enjoyments we can rightly see as good, as something we in fact enjoy and that reason can rightly endorse" (Hursthouse, *On Virtue Ethics*, 222).

19. Hursthouse, *On Virtue Ethics*, 223. Another reason Hursthouse believes that ethics is not "just a branch of biology or ethology" is that ethical reflection cannot proceed independent from or outside of one's "acquired ethical outlook" (165–66) and therefore should have "no pretensions to establishing conclusions from scientific foundations accessible from a neutral point of view" (224).

20. Hursthouse, *On Virtue Ethics*, 221–26.

21. Copp and Sobel, "Morality and Virtue: An Assessment of Some Recent Work in Virtue Ethics," 534–36.

22. Should these commitments require revision, so too will the account of what makes a trait a virtue. For example, if it turns out that we ought really to be concerned with norms at the cultural level, then the account can and must be modified so that a character trait is a virtue to the extent that it is conducive to its possessor flourishing *as a member of culture X* or *within the context of culture X*. In that event, what makes a character trait a virtue would be constant across cultures, while the substantive dispositions constitutive of virtues may differ between cultures.

23. Aristotle, *Nicomachean Ethics*, 1106b17–24; Hursthouse, *On Virtue Ethics*, 206–208.

24. "Hence whoever stands firm against the right things and fears the right things, for the right end, in the right way, at the right time, and is correspondingly confident, is the brave person; for the brave person's actions and feelings accord with what something is worth, and follow what reason prescribes" (Aristotle, *Nicomachean Ethics*, 1115b17–19). Skills or abilities (e.g., to effectively organize and motivate others, clearly evaluate one's capacity to handle threats, or commit fully to pursuit of one's goals) are not virtues (e.g., leadership, courage, or fortitude) if they are used in support of unacceptable means or to achieve unacceptable ends. "*Talents* of mind" and "qualities of *temperament*" can, as Kant claims, "be extremely evil and harmful if the will which is to make use of these gifts of nature, and whose distinctive constitution is therefore called *character*, is not good" (*Groundwork of the Metaphysics of Morals* 7).

25. Much of the competition for resources (e.g., water, nutrients, and pollinators) is between individuals of the same species. An individual is not a good specimen if it merely "makes way" for other (genetically distant) members of its species. Rather, it is a good specimen to the extent that its parts, operations, actions, and so on are well suited to the continuance of the species with its own genetic material. Thus, an individual has the end of the species going on in the form of its offspring or sufficiently close genetic relatives. This does not imply that all the ends collapse into the promulgation of genes. While promulgation of genes will often be central to explaining why individuals of a species are the way they are, it is how living things actually make their way in the world that is of primary evaluative importance. Evolution has thrown up living things that are, from the perspective of the individual, more than mere genetic vessels (though they are that as well). In what follows, the "continuance of the species" end is meant in the way just described—as sensitive to the fact that the genes with which an individual's species continues is relevant.

26. Hursthouse, *On Virtue Ethics*, 208–11. See also Driver, *Uneasy Virtue*, 74, 104–105.

27. Hursthouse, *On Virtue Ethics*, 218.

28. It is possible that autonomy and knowledge are accounted for as part of our characteristic, rational way of realizing the ends. If so, the following discussion of them simply makes explicit what already is included implicitly in Hursthouse's account.

29. Nielsen, *Ethics Without God*, ch. 8; Metz, "Recent Work on the Meaning of Life."

30. The distinction here is one of degree. Groups and individuals of some nonhuman species use tools, farm, learn from each other, cooperate, deceive, alter their environment, and so on. But no nonhuman species that we know of innovates or accumulates social practices and technologies (i.e., culture) on anything approaching the scale, complexity, or pace as do humans.

31. The conception of "capability" intended here is the one developed by Nussbaum (*Women and Human Development: The Capabilities Approach*).

32. For example, if health or subjective well-being are not adequately accounted for by the stated ends—i.e., are not merely instrumental or reducible to them—then perhaps they should be included as distinct ends.

33. Roco and Bainbridge, *Converging Technologies for Improving Human Performance: Nanotechnology, Biotechnology, Information Technology and Computer Science (NBIC)*. The United States Department of Defense's Defense Advanced Research Projects Agency (DARPA) also has human enhancement research programs (DARPA, "Darpa Programs").

34. Roco and Montemagno, "Preface," vii.

35. Roco, "Science and Technology Integration for Increased Human Potential and Societal Outcomes," 3.

36. Roco and Bainbridge, "Overview," 17.

37. By "strictly naturalistic" I mean independent of technological modification. However, in another (inclusive) sense, technologies are naturalistic and biological: they are adaptations made possible by, and longitudinal expressions of, human biology in particular environments (Pinker, *The Blank Slate: The Modern Denial of Human Nature*; Richerson and Boyd, *Not by Genes Alone*).

38. Roco puts the timeline for "Converging technology products for improving human physical and mental performance (brain connectivity, sensory abilities, etc.)" at one generation and "evolution transcending human cell, body, and brain" at (a cautious) n generations ("Science and Technology Integration for Increased Human Potential and Societal Outcomes" 6). Ray Kurzweil, a well-known technologist and futurist, projects 2045 as the year when the merging of human and machine intelligence will bring about "a profound and disruptive transformation in human capabilities" (*The Singularity Is Near: When Humans Transcend Biology* 136). Even Bill Gates has said that he expects a future, still some generations off, that includes direct brain-machine interfaces (Sullivan, "Gates Says Technology Will One Day Allow Computer Implants—But Hardwiring's Not for Him"). But while the timeline is vague and contested, the language is telling. Those who are promoting technologies of this sort speak of human-technology coevolution, posthuman evolution, human-cyborg evolution,

and transhuman evolution. They advocate extending human and social development beyond the "constraints" of our biology.

39. Sandler, "Nanotechnology and Human Flourishing: Toward a Framework for Assessing Human Enhancements."

40. This is not to claim that eudaimonistic virtue theories are egoistic. There may be eudaimonistic reasons for cultivating genuine concern for the welfare of others for their own sake and for being motivated to act on that basis (Annas, *The Morality of Happiness*, 58–260). The claim here is that there may be noneudaimonistic reasons for cultivating such concern and motivation as well.

41. Swanton, *Virtue Ethics: A Pluralistic View*, 2.

42. Hume, *An Enquiry Concerning the Principles of Morals*.

43. Slote, *Morals from Motives*.

44. Swanton, *Virtue Ethics: A Pluralistic View*, 93.

45. Hursthouse has argued that Hume's theory of virtue is actually quite close to this ("Virtue Ethics and Human Nature").

46. For a contrary view, see McDowell, "The Role of Eudaimonia in Aristotle's Ethics." For discussion of this issue, see Swanton, *Virtue Ethics: A Pluralistic View*, ch. 4, Hursthouse, *On Virtue Ethics*, ch. 8, and Foot, *Natural Goodness*, ch. 6.

47. This example is used also by Hursthouse, *On Virtue Ethics*, 227–28, "Virtue Ethics vs Rule-Consequentialism: A Reply to Brad Hooker," 46–50, and "Applying Virtue Ethics to Our Treatment of the Other Animals," 141–43.

48. Driver, *Uneasy Virtue*, 82. The pluralistic teleological account also has significant similarities with Ben Bradley's formulation of virtue consequentialism ("Virtue Consequentialism"). It is both contrastivist—i.e., character traits are virtues to the extent that they are more conducive to promoting the ends than alternative traits—and counterfactualist—i.e., character traits are evaluated according to their conduciveness to promoting the ends in worlds sufficiently like the actual world.

49. Driver, *Uneasy Virtue*, 95–106.

50. Driver's emphasis is consistently on the social context of human flourishing, not the environmental context: "For human beings, of course, the 'habitat' or context in which they dwell is a socially constructed community. What we try to figure out is what character traits are conducive to human well-being within a community" (*Uneasy Virtue* 99).

51. For example, they differ with respect to the relationships among knowledge, virtue, and flourishing (Sandler, *Ignorance and Virtue*).

52. Driver, *Uneasy Virtue*, 71–73.

53. Hooker, *Ideal Code, Real World*.

54. This example is from Swanton, *Virtue Ethics: A Pluralistic View*, 83.

55. Pinker, *The Blank Slate: The Modern Denial of Human Nature*. As Swanton has put it, "A full theory of virtue is parasitic on a 'background' theory of human psychology and development" (*Virtue Ethics: A Pluralistic View* 60).

56. Spinoza, *Ethica*, Appendix I and Preface IV.

57. Spinoza called an individual's goal-orientedness, or striving in its characteristic way to persevere in its being, its "conatus" (*Ethica*, Book III).

58. Sober, "Philosophical Problems for Environmentalism," 153.

59. Taylor, *Respect for Nature: A Theory of Environmental Ethics*, 124.

60. The pluralistic teleological account also does not require the sort of metaphysics of essences and final causation that has been discredited in post-Darwin natural science. Contemporary population biology recognizes that genotypic and phenotypic variation within and across environments is a basic part of the biological landscape. There is a range of states that individuals of a particular species might accomplish, and none of them is metaphysically privileged as the "correct" one for an individual of the species. There is not some natural state that each living individual would accomplish were it not for interfering external forces. The pluralistic teleological account is consistent with this. It allows that there is a range of realizations of the ends among individuals of a given species, none of which is more natural than the others, and does not imply that there is anything unnatural in the failure of a particular individual to realize the ends toward which it is organized.

2. The Environment and Human Flourishing

1. Regan, *The Case for Animal Rights*.

2. Singer, *Animal Liberation*.

3. Taylor, *Respect for Nature: A Theory of Environmental Ethics*.

4. Kant, "Duties to Animals and Spirits."

5. These examples are intended to clarify what is meant by "basis of responsiveness" and "modes of responsiveness," as well as how these differ from virtue to virtue. They are not detailed, exhaustive accounts of the bases or modes of responsiveness for each of the virtues described. Nor do they fully indicate the complexities involved in providing such accounts. For a discussion of these complexities see Swanton, *Virtue Ethics: A Pluralistic View*, chs. 1–2, 5–6.

6. "Within an EV [ethics of virtue] it is not the theory of the virtues which is supposed to be primarily action guiding, but rather the virtues themselves.... [For example] it is not the theoretical account either of the point of the virtue of justice or of its role in the overall economy of practical

thought that is supposed to guide action, but rather the virtue of justice itself" (Solomon, "Internal Objections to Virtue Ethics," 439).

7. Van Wensveen, "Ecosystem Sustainability as a Criterion for Genuine Virtue," 227.

8. Van Wensveen, "Ecosystem Sustainability as a Criterion for Genuine Virtue," 232–33.

9. Van Wensveen, "Ecosystem Sustainability as a Criterion for Genuine Virtue," 233.

10. Cafaro calls this the "artificial alternatives argument: that when we have specified the good human life, we will find that it can be lived just as well in a largely artificial world: that we do not need wild nature" ("Thoreau, Leopold, and Carson: Toward an Environmental Virtue Ethics," 16–17).

11. Westra, *An Environmental Proposal for Ethics: The Principle of Integrity* and *Living in Integrity: A Global Ethic to Restore a Fragmented Earth.*

12. O'Neill, *Ecology, Policy, and Politics: Human Well-Being and the Natural World,* 33.

13. A few virtues of environmental activism, such as fortitude, cooperation, engagement and solidarity, do appear in the catalogue of environmental virtues complied by Wensveen (*Dirty Virtues,* Appendix A).

14. Expanding our understanding of environmental virtue beyond virtues of communion with nature to virtues of environmental activism requires a concomitant expansion of the pantheon of environmental role models to include not only renown activists such as Cesar Chavez, Wangari Maathai, and Ken Saro-Wiwa, but also local exemplars of environmental activism that are, as Jason Kawall has put it, "leading lives that their peers can identify as viable" ("Complacency, Apathy, and Resignation").

15. Emerson, "Art," 278.

16. Carson, *The Sense of Wonder,* 42–43.

17. "The lasting pleasures of contact with the natural world are not reserved for scientists but are available to anyone who will place himself under the influence of the earth, sea, sky and their amazing life," Carson, *The Sense of Wonder,* 93.

18. Carson, "Design for Nature Writing," 94. Several environmental ethicists have advocated, as Carson does, humility as an environmental virtue (Hill, "Ideals of Human Excellences and Preserving Natural Environments"; Chapman, "The Goat-Stag and the Sphinx: The Place of the Virtues in Environmental Ethics"; and Gerber, "Standing Humbly Before Nature").

19. For a detailed discussion of Carson's conception of wonder, see Moore, "The Truth of the Barnacles: Rachel Carson and the Moral Significance of Wonder."

20. Carson, *The Sense of Wonder*, 88.

21. For these reasons, Frasz has argued that sloth and laziness are environmental vices ("Benevolence as an Environmental Virtue") and that openness is an environmental virtue ("Environmental Virtue Ethics: A New Direction for Environmental Ethics").

22. Muir, *Our National Parks*, 56. "Everybody needs beauty as well as bread, places to play in and pray in, where nature may heal and give strength to body and soul" (Muir, *The Yosemite*, 256).

23. Opportunities for developing character traits and types of relationships that make these environmental goods possible are not equally or justly distributed. Among the virtues of environmental activism and the virtues of environmental stewardship (discussed below) are dispositions conducive to remedying those inequalities and promoting just distribution of environmental goods and opportunities.

24. For this reason, the importance of perception in moral development and environmental awareness is a central theme in the writings of Leopold (*A Sand County Almanac*), Thoreau (*Walden*), and Carson (*The Sense of Wonder*). Leopold's reflections on outdoor recreation are particularly compelling:

    The swoop of a hawk, for example, is perceived by one as the drama of evolution, by another as a threat to the full frying-pan.... To promote perception is the only truly creative part of recreational engineering. This fact is important, and its potential power for bettering "the good life" only dimly understood....

    The only true development in the American recreational resources is the development of the perceptive faculty in Americans. All of the other acts we grace by that name are, at best, attempts to retard or mask the process of dilution....

    It would appear, in short, that the rudimentary grades of outdoor recreation consume their resource-base; the higher grades, at least to a degree, create their own satisfactions with little or no attrition of the land or life. It is the expansion of transport without a corresponding growth of perception that threatens us with qualitative bankruptcy of the recreational process. Recreational development is a job not of building roads into lovely country, but of building receptivity into the still unlovely human mind (*A Sand County Almanac*, 173, 174, 176–77).

25. O'Neill, *Ecology, Policy, and Politics: Human Well-Being and the Natural World*, 24–25. Thomas Hill has made an analogous argument concerning moral development: "That *to value* certain natural phenomena *for their own sakes* and to recognise and respond appropriately *to the value they have*" is conducive to, if not essential for, developing the "human virtue that we might call 'appreciation of the good'" ("Finding Value in Nature" 333).

26. The passage from O'Neill suggests that they are superior. This is an over-statement. Art, artifacts, and interpersonal relationships can provide comparable realizations of many of these opportunities and benefits. Cafaro provides a more measured comparison (*Thoreau's Living Ethics*, 162–64).

27. An issue not addressed here is how these attitudes and dispositions can be fostered and encouraged. A common theme in the environmental ethics literature is that spending time and being active in nature is an effective and enjoyable way (Cafaro, "The Naturalist's Virtues," Light, "Restoration or Domination: A Reply to Katz"; O'Neill, *Ecology, Policy, and Politics: Human Well-Being and the Natural World*; Carson, *The Sense of Wonder*; and Leopold, *A Sand County Almanac*). There is also a substantial and growing psychology and social science literature on the development of ecological awareness and values. See, for example, Kahn, *The Human Relationship with Nature: Development and Culture* and Kahn and Kellert, *Children and Nature: Psychological, Sociocultural, and Evolutionary Investigations*.

28. For discussion of how these considerations support ecological rights see Westra, "Virtue Ethics as Foundational for a Global Ethic" and *Ecoviolence and the Law*.

29. "The Norwegian Nobel Committee has decided to award the Nobel Peace Prize for 2004 to Wangari Maathai for her contribution to sustainable development, democracy and peace. Peace on earth depends on our ability to secure our living environment. Maathai stands at the front of the fight to promote ecologically viable social, economic and cultural development in Kenya and in Africa. She has taken a holistic approach to sustainable development that embraces democracy, human rights and women's rights in particular" (The Norwegian Nobel Committee, "The Nobel Peace Prize 2004").

30. A Water Conflict Chronology appears in Gleick, *The World's Water: The Biennial Report on Freshwater Resources, 1998–1999*, 105–35. The chronology includes cases when water (or water availability) is used as a tool (military or political), cases when water degradation is used as a tool (military or political), and cases when water-related disputes are among the causes of conflict. A recent instance of water control being used as a military and political tool is Saddam Hussein's retribution against the Madan or "Marsh Arabs" who rose against him during the 1991 Gulf War. The marshes—between the Tigris and Euphrates rivers and formerly the largest aquatic system in the Middle East—were drained, displacing most of the people and killing much of the flora and fauna. There are currently reports coming from the Darfur region of Sudan that some militias are using environmental degradation, including water contamination, to dislocate entire villages.

31. Welchman, "The Virtues of Stewardship" and "Stewardship: Olmsted, Character, and Environmentalism." Welchman argues that recognition of virtues of environmental stewardship requires expanding the pantheon of environmental heroes to include people like Frederick Law Olmsted, who appreciated the value of nature as a public good and was a successful steward of it.

32. See also Wensveen, "Attunement: An Ecological Spin on the Virtue of Temperance"; Wenz, "Synergistic Environmental Virtues"; and Frasz, "Benevolence as an Environmental Virtue."

33. These findings do not imply that materialistic achievement, as opposed to materialistic orientation, is related negatively to well-being. At the lower end of the income scale, there is a strong relationship between income and happiness: "Findings from the World Values Survey, a set of surveys of life satisfaction in more than 65 countries conducted between 1990 and 2000, indicate that income and happiness tend to track well until about $13,000 of annual income per person (in 1995 purchasing power parity). After that, additional income appears to yield only modest additions in self-reported happiness" (The Worldwatch Institute, *State of the World 2004: Special Focus, The Consumer Society*, 166). Moreover, a 2005 poll found that in the United States, "People living in higher-income households are more likely than those in lower-income households to say they are very happy. The poll shows that 61% of Americans earning $50,000 per year or more are very happy. This compares with 46% of those earning between $30,000 and $50,000 per year, and 37% of those earning less than $30,000 per year" (Carroll, "Americans' Personal Satisfaction"). For a review of the empirical data on the relationship between wealth and well being see Diener and Seligman, "Beyond Money: Toward an Economy of Well-Being" and Bond, "The Pursuit of Happiness."

34. Kasser, *The High Price of Materialism*, 22. See also Kasser and Kanner, *Psychology and Consumer Culture: The Struggle for a Good Life in a Materialistic World* and De Graaf, Wann, Naylor, Horsey, and Simon, *Affluenza: The All-Consuming Epidemic*.

35. Kasser, *The High Price of Materialism*, 97.

36. Kasser, *The High Price of Materialism*, 23.

37. Kasser, *The High Price of Materialism*, 28. The relationship is more complicated than even this suggests. In a series of studies, Emily Solberg, Edward Diener, and Michael Robinson tested six hypotheses about the relationship between materialism and subjective well-being (SWB): 1) The scale causes the results; 2) People are most distant from their material goals; 3) Unhappy people become materialistic; 4) Thinking about materialist concerns leads to unhappiness; 5) Focusing on materialistic

goals conflicts with other goals; and 6) Materialistic goals are less enjoyable to work toward. Here is a summary of their findings: "The results of our studies suggest that materialism appears to be toxic to SWB and that this relation is multidetermined.... We found support for three of these hypotheses. Materialists' poorer social lives were related to lower levels of SWB. However, it could be the case that people with few friends or bad social skills tend to focus on material things to compensate. We also found evidence that working toward material goals is less rewarding in the moment than working toward other goals. We found support for the hypothesis that the gap between what people have and what they want in the material domain is larger than in other domains; therefore, valuing this domain highly is detrimental to well-being.... We found partial support for the hypothesis that unhappiness leads to the adoption of material values. Finally, we found little support for the hypotheses that simply thinking about financial goals and material objects leads to lower SWB, or that the materialism-SWB relation is spurious because of the relationship between materialism and neuroticism" ("Why Are Materialists Less Satisfied?" 45).

38. Solberg, Diener, and Robinson, "Why Are Materialists Less Satisfied?" 43–44.

39. Worldwatch Institute, *State of the World 2004*, 5–15.

40. The increase in average commute time in the United States between 1990 and 2000 was from 22.4 to 25.5 minutes one way (Goodman, Ansel, and Nakosteen, *Mass.commuting*).

41. Putnam, *Bowling Alone: The Collapse and Revival of American Community*, 223. Concerns about the drag that increases in consumption-related "demands" can have on interpersonal relationships and civic engagement in developed countries, including the United States, are also expressed in Healy and Cote, *The Well Being of Nations: The Role of Human and Social Capital*, Appendix E, 99–103 and Robin and Dominguez, *Your Money or Your Life*.

42. In 2000, the average size of new home construction in the United States was 2,265 square feet, up from 1,000 square feet in 1950 and 1,400 square feet in 1970 (National Association of Home Builders, *A Century of Progress: America's Housing 1900–2000*, 3). In the United States the percentage of sixth-graders with a television set in their bedroom increased from 6 percent to 77 percent between 1970 and 1999 (Putnam, *Bowling Alone*, 223). There are now more television sets than people in the United States (Bauder, "Average Home Has More TVs Than People").

43. In 2000, there were 221,475,000 motor vehicles registered in the United States, compared with 155,796,000 in 1980 (U.S. Census Bureau). Average

fuel efficiency of 2006 model year cars and trucks was 21.0 mpg, which is the same as the previous year and within the range (20.6–21.4 mpg) it had been for the last 15 years. The peak for average fuel efficiency was the 1987 and 1988 model years, when it reached 22.1 mpg. In 2006, 40 percent of the oil consumed in the United States was used for car and truck fuel (Heavenrich, *Light-Duty Automotive Technology and Fuel Economy Trends: 1975 Through 2006*).

Approximately half the sprawl in the United States is attributable to population growth and half is caused by consumption and land use choices, according to independent analyses of United States census data (Sprawl City, *Poor Land Use or Population Growth: Which Is Worse for Sprawl?*).

"Electricity generation in the U.S. increased by 10 percent between 1996 and 2000. Corresponding to this growth in generation, carbon dioxide and mercury emissions increased by more than 5 percent. During this time, regulatory measures resulted in the reduction of sulfur dioxide and nitrogen oxide emissions by approximately 15 percent" (EPA, *eGrid2002*). Between 1995 and 2005, energy used for transportation in the United States increased at an average annual rate of 1.6 percent (Davis and Diegel, *Transportation Energy Data Book: Edition 25–2006*, ch. 2).

44. In 2001, 85 percent of the energy produced in the United States was derived from fossil fuels (DOE, "Greenhouse Gases, Climate Change, and Energy"). In 2000, power plant emissions included: 2,652,901,442 tons of carbon dioxide, 11,513,033 tons of sulfur dioxide, 5,644,353 tons of nitrogen oxides, and 103,554 tons of mercury (EPA, *eGrid2002*). In 2000, the average passenger car in the United States emitted 77.1 pounds of hydrocarbons, 575 pounds of carbon monoxide, 38.2 pounds of nitrogen oxides, and 11,420 pounds of carbon dioxide. The average light truck emitted 108 pounds of hydrocarbons, 854 pounds of carbon monoxide, 55.8 pounds of nitrogen oxides, and 16,035 pounds of carbon dioxide (EPA, *Emission Facts: Average Annual Emissions and Fuel Consumption for Passenger Cars and Light Trucks*).

The links between particulate air pollution and lung disease, cancer, cardiovascular disease, cardiopulmonary disease, and asthma have been widely studied and established. See, for example, Brook, Franklin, Cascio, Hong, Howard, Lipsett, et al., "Air Pollution and Cardiovascular Disease: A Statement for Healthcare Professionals from the Expert Panel on Population and Prevention Science of the American Heart Association"; Samet, Dominici, Curriero, Coursac, and Zeger, "Fine Particulate Air Pollution and Mortality in 20 U.S. Cities, 1987–1994"; Pope III, Burnett, Thun, Calle, Krewski, Ito, et al., "Lung Cancer, Cardiopulmonary Mortality, and Long-Term Exposure to Fine Particulate Air Pollution"; Gauderman, Avol,

Gilliland, Vora, Thomas, Berhane, et al., "The Effect of Air Pollution on Lung Development from 10 to 18 Years of Age"; Pope III, Burnett, Thurston, Thun, Calle, Krewski, et al., "Cardiovascular Mortality and Long-Term Exposure to Particulate Air Pollution: Epidemiological Evidence of General Pathophysiological Pathways of Disease"; Bell, McDermott, Zegar, Samet, and Dominici, "Ozone and Short-Term Mortality in 95 US Urban Communities, 1987–2000."

The relationship between mercury contamination and developmental defects is sufficiently established that the EPA and the FDA have a standing advisory for women who might become pregnant, women who are pregnant, women who are breast feeding, and young children not to eat fish from waterways that have been contaminated by mercury pollution (EPA, "What You Need to Know About Mercury in Fish and Shellfish"). Mercury is the most prevalent cause of pollutant advisories for United States waterways (other pollutants include DDT, dioxins, PCBs, and chlordane). In 2003, 35 percent of the lake acreage (excluding the Great Lakes), 100 percent of the Great Lakes acreage, 24 percent of U.S. river mileage, and 65 percent of contiguous coastal waters (excluding Alaska) were under consumption advisories (EPA, "National Listing of Fish Advisories").

45. This is the finding of the Intergovernmental Panel on Climate Change (IPCC). The IPCC consists of several hundred climate scientists from United Nations member countries and prepares its reports of the basis of a comprehensive review of the climate science literature. The IPCC's third report on climate change was issued in 2001, and the fourth report is being released in 2007. Among the U.S. federal government agencies that have endorsed the IPCC's conclusion are EPA, NASA, NOAA, and DOE.

46. Eighty-two percent of U.S. greenhouse gas emissions come from burning fossil fuels. From 1990 to 2004, U.S. emissions of greenhouse gases increased 15.8 percent, an average rate of 1.1 percent annually. In 2004, 83.9 percent of greenhouse gas emissions in the United States was carbon dioxide, 9 percent was methane, 5 percent was nitrous oxide, and 2.2 percent was hydrofluorocarbons, perfluorocarbons, and sulfurhexafluoride. These percentages represent global warming potential of each gas, not absolute quantities. Not all greenhouse gases trap heat equally. Methane absorbs heat at a rate approximate 21 times that of carbon dioxide, nitrous oxide traps heat at 310 times the rate of carbon dioxide, hydrofluorocarbons and perfluorocarbons trap heat at 6,500 to 7,400 times the rate of carbon dioxide, and sulfurhexafluoride does so at 23,900 times the rate of carbon dioxide. The above percentages account for these differences. The United States is responsible for 25 percent of the world's carbon dioxide emissions (EPA, *Emission of Greenhouse Gases in the United States 2004*).

47. IPCC, *Third Assessment Report*.

48. Barlow and Clarke, *Blue Gold*, 5. See also Gleick, *The World's Water: The Biennial Report on Freshwater Resources, 2002–2003*; Pielou, *Fresh Water*; and United Nations Education, Scientific, and Cultural Organization (UNESCO), *United Nations World Water Development Report: Water for People, Water for Life*.

49. UNESCO, *United Nations World Water Development Report: Water for People, Water for Life*, 11.

50. UNESCO, *United Nations World Water Development Report: Water for People, Water for Life*, 228.

51. World Watch Institute, *State of the World 2004*, 54.

52. Barlow and Clarke, *Blue Gold*, 16. See also Glennon, *Water Follies: Groundwater Pumping and the Fate of America's Fresh Waters* and Ward, *Water Wars: Drought, Flood, Folly, and the Politics of Thirst*.

53. The U.S. Census Bureau estimates the current U.S. population to be 302,000,000 and the current world population to be 6,600,000,000. It projects a .9 percent increase in U.S. population and a 1.17 percent increase in world population in 2007.

54. Sixty-one percent of Americans were overweight or obese in 1999 (U.S. Surgeon General, "Overweight and Obesity: At a Glance"). In 1991, only 4 states reported adult obesity rates over 15 percent. In 2004, 42 states reported adult obesity rates above 15 percent, and 9 of those states reported rates above 25 percent (U.S. Center for Disease Control, "Overweight and Obesity: Obesity Trends: U.S. Obesity Trends 1985–2004"). The two primary causes for of this trend are increased caloric intake and decreased physical activity (U.S. Surgeon General, "The Surgeon General's Call to Action to Prevent and Decrease Overweight and Obesity 2001"). Increases in obesity rates are not confined to the United States or even to developed countries. The World Health Organization (WHO) has begun to track and address a "globesity" epidemic: "Paradoxically coexisting with undernutrition, an escalating global epidemic of overweight and obesity— 'globesity'—is taking over many parts of the world. If immediate action is not taken, millions will suffer from an array of serious health disorders. Obesity is a complex condition, one with serious social and psychological dimensions, that affects virtually all age and socioeconomic groups and threatens to overwhelm both developed and developing countries. In 1995, there were an estimated 200 million obese adults worldwide and another 18 million under-five children classified as overweight. As of 2000, the number of obese adults has increased to over 300 million. Contrary to conventional wisdom, the obesity epidemic is not restricted to industrialized societies; in developing countries, it is estimated that over

115 million people suffer from obesity-related problems" (WHO, "Controlling the Global Obesity Epidemic").

55. World Watch Institute, *State of the World 2004*, 5–15.

56. UNESCO, *United Nations World Water Development Report: Water for People, Water for Life*, 7–10.

57. Barlow and Clarke, *Blue Gold*; Gleick, *The World's Water: The Biennial Report on Freshwater Resources, 2002–2003* and *The World's Water: The Biennial Report on Freshwater Resources, 2004–2005*.

58. In response to this type of argument, advocates for consumerism sometimes appeal to the Environmental Kuznets Curve. According to the curve, increased wealth and income generated through a consumer economy leads (around the $5,000 per capita annual level) to environmental improvements. However, this claim is unsupported by the evidence. What has been found is that under some circumstances some environmental improvements (e.g., decreases in some pollutants) take place around a particular per capita income level in some countries. But there have been other environmental pollutants and other countries for which improvement has not occurred. Moreover, when improvements do occur, it is largely because a point of material comfort and security is reached where people are willing to trade further material gains for other goods, including environmental goods. So, far from implying that consumptive dispositions are good for the environment in the long run, nonconsumptive dispositions are crucial to bring about the curve (when there is a curve). For more on the difficulties with the Environmental Kuznets Curve argument, particularly as it pertains to neoliberal free trade issues, see Cox, "Golden Tropes and Democratic Betrayals: Prospects for Environmental Justice in Neoliberal 'Free Trade' Agreements."

3. The Environment Itself

1. In 1987, the United Nations World Commission on Environment and Development (WCED) issued a report, *Our Common Future*, in which it called for an updated charter that recognized more explicitly the connections among environment, poverty, education, health care, and development, and provided more detailed prescriptions for state and international behavior in support of environmental ends than does the World Charter. Many of the contributing organizations at UNCED had worked for the outcome of the conference to be such a charter.

2. The Earth Charter was not endorsed at the 2002 World Summit on Sustainable Development (WSSD), as had been hoped and worked for, although some of the language of the summit's final document, the "Johannesburg Declaration on Sustainable Development," was taken from it.

3. There is another sense of "respect" that has already been discussed: respect for environmental entities that have special significance in the way of life or culture of particular human communities. This sense of respect is derivative upon respect for the individuals who comprise those communities.

4. Taylor, *Respect for Nature: A Theory of Environmental Ethics*, 80.

5. Taylor, *Respect for Nature: A Theory of Environmental Ethics*, 81.

6. Taylor, *Respect for Nature: A Theory of Environmental Ethics*, 61.

7. Taylor, *Respect for Nature: A Theory of Environmental Ethics*, 75. Taylor does not attribute interests to every entity with a good of its own. He believes that it is too easy to conflate "having an interest" with "taking an interest." The latter requires consciousness, whereas the former does not. Nevertheless, I use the term "interest" to refer to what is in fact good for a particular teleological center of life, whether or not it is capable of "taking an interest" in its own interests.

8. Taylor, *Respect for Nature: A Theory of Environmental Ethics*, 81.

9. Taylor, *Respect for Nature: A Theory of Environmental Ethics*, 83.

10. Taylor, *Respect for Nature: A Theory of Environmental Ethics*, 90.

11. Taylor, *Respect for Nature: A Theory of Environmental Ethics*, 98.

12. Taylor, *Respect for Nature: A Theory of Environmental Ethics*, chs. 2 and 3.

13. Taylor, *Respect for Nature: A Theory of Environmental Ethics*, 99.

14. The five components that constitute this claim are: 1) like individuals of other species, we have biological and physical requirements for our survival and well-being; 2) like members of other species, we have a good of our own that is in part subject to factors that are beyond our control; 3) we have in common with individuals of other species a certain sense of freedom, being in a position to further one's own good; 4) we are a recent arrival on this planet and have a common origin (evolution) with other species; and 5) while we are dependent upon the good health of the earth's biosphere, its good health is not dependent upon us.

15. This formulation of the fourth belief is informed by James Sterba's interpretation of it in "A Biocentrist Fights Back" and *Three Challenges to Ethics: Environmentalism, Feminism, and Multiculturalism*, ch. 2.

16. Taylor, *Respect for Nature: A Theory of Environmental Ethics*, 121–24.

17. For discussion of some complications and shortcomings of this standard account of moral agency see Arpaly, *Unprincipled Virtue: An Inquiry Into Moral Agency*. None of those complications undermines the central point here: on any plausible account of the criteria for moral agency, nonhuman living organisms will not, with perhaps rare exceptions (e.g., psychologically complex primates), be moral agents to any substantial degree.

18. Taylor, *Respect for Nature: A Theory of Environmental Ethics*, 14–24.

19. Rachels, *Created from Animals*; Spinoza, *Ethica*.

20. Although we often evaluate people's intelligence, for example, and make decisions about them on that basis—e.g., as job candidates or potential partners—those evaluations, and others like them, are not assessments of people's relative inherent worth, but rather of their skills or suitability relative to particular roles or situations.

21. Carroll, *Endless Forms Most Beautiful: The New Science of Evo Devo and the Making of the Animal Kingdom*.

22. It is sometimes claimed that the greater inherent worth of humans is due to our capacity to adapt to and survive in different environments. The argument is that survival and adaptation are essential to any biological organism, so if we are superior to other biological organisms in those respects, then we are superior as a biological organism. However, human adaptability is for the most part the product of cultural accumulation, not individual innovation. If I were left by myself in the arctic, I would not quickly adapt, I would quickly die. The adaptive capacities of human culture need to be kept separate from the innovative capacities of individual humans, particularly in the context of discussions about the inherent worth of individual organisms.

23. "I propose the reasonableness of denying human superiority over other species on the ground that the whole notion of human superiority over other species does not fit coherently into the view of nature and life contained in the first three elements of the biocentric outlook. These elements taken together, I hold, would be found acceptable as a total world-perspective by any rational, informed person who has a developed capacity of reality-awareness regarding the lives of individual organisms.... My justification for the denial of human superiority, then, comes down to this. If we view the realm of nature and life from the perspective of the first three elements of the biocentric outlook, we will see ourselves as having a deep kinship with all other living things, sharing with them many common characteristics and being, like them, integral parts of one great whole encompassing the natural order of life on our planet. When we focus on the reality of their individual lives, we see each one to be in many ways like ourselves, responding in its particular manner to environmental circumstances and so pursuing the realization of its own good. It is within the framework of this conceptual system that the idea of human superiority is found to be unreasonable" (Taylor, *Respect for Nature: A Theory of Environmental Ethics*, 154–55).

24. Taylor, *Respect for Nature: A Theory of Environmental Ethics*, 155. Strictly speaking, what Taylor's arguments show is not that all teleological centers of life have inherent worth, but that there is no basis for regarding some of

them as having greater inherent worth than others. The gap between these two claims is bridged if at least some living things have inherent worth. As discussed previously, an assumption operative in this book (as in Taylor's) is that other people have a good of their own that there are reasons to care about for their own sake (i.e., they have inherent worth).

25. Schmidtz, "Are All Species Equal?" 59.

26. French, "Against Biospherical Egalitarianism"; Anderson, "Species Equality and the Foundations of Moral Theory"; Evans, *With Respect for Nature: Living as Part of the Natural World.*

27. Taylor, *Respect for Nature: A Theory of Environmental Ethics*, ch. 6.

28. Sterba, "A Biocentrist Fights Back," 54.

29. Evans, *With Respect for Nature: Living as Part of the Natural World*, 101, 125.

30. Davion, "Itch Scratching, Patio Building and Pesky Flies: Biocentric Individualism Revisited," 119.

31. Davion, "Itch Scratching, Patio Building and Pesky Flies: Biocentric Individualism Revisited," 126.

32. Schweitzer, *Civilization and Ethics*. For a critical discussion of Schweitzer's ethic in which these objections are emphasized, see Evans, *With Respect for Nature: Living as Part of the Natural World*, Part Two. Evans is also critical of Taylor's ethic on these grounds (Part Three). However, there is a basis in *Respect for Nature: A Theory of Environmental Ethics* for a more charitable interpretation of Taylor's ethic than Evans provides, one in which respect for nature, and thereby the demands of noninterference and nonmaleficence, is sensitive to our form of life (Sandler and Volkert, "Review of J. Claude Evans' *With Respect for Nature*").

33. Pluralism in the realization of virtue, including environmental virtue, allows that there are multiple ways to be disposed to meet well the demands of the world. Therefore, although character traits that are highly conducive to promoting the flourishing of living things but not conducive to their possessor's flourishing are virtues of respect for nature, they are not the only virtues of respect for nature or even the standard for such virtues.

34. For further discussion of what a conception of respect for nature that affirms human interconnectedness and interdependence with the natural world involves see Evans, *With Respect for Nature: Living as Part of the Natural World.*

35. Singer, *Animal Liberation.*

36. Sagoff, "Animal Liberation and Environmental Ethics: Bad Marriage, Quick Divorce."

37. Evans, *With Respect for Nature: Living as Part of the Natural World*; Taylor, *Respect for Nature: A Theory of Environmental Ethics*, 210–12.

38. For a virtue-oriented discussion of the treatment of domesticated animals, see Hursthouse, "Applying Virtue Ethics to Our Treatment of the Other Animals."

39. Taylor, *Respect for Nature: A Theory of Environmental Ethics*, 69.

40. Sterba, "A Biocentrist Fights Back," 30. John O'Neill also believes that ecosystems and species have a good of their own distinct from the good of the individuals that comprise or populate them (*Ecology, Policy, and Politics: Human Well-Being and the Natural World*, 20–22).

41. Johnson, *A Morally Deep World* and "Future Generations and Contemporary Ethics."

42. This is true even on Johnson's definition of life: "A living entity [is]...an ongoing process, occurring in a dissipative thermodynamically open system, organising and maintaining itself in near equilibrium with its environment by means of high levels of homeorhetic feedback sub-systems" ("Future Generations and Contemporary Ethics," 479).

43. O'Neill, *Ecology, Policy, and Politics: Human Well-Being and the Natural World*, 20–21.

44. An even more compelling example, provided by Johnson, is "colonies" of *Namonia cara*: "One individual takes the form of a gas-filled float, while other individuals join together in structures that ingest and distribute nutrients.... Yet other individuals serve to propel the colony by expelling tiny jets of water. Still other individuals form protective layers. Then, there are the sexual meduoids. These individuals carry the burden of the colony's reproductive function, freeing their genetically identical but physiologically very different partners to carry on with their own tasks. In fact, each colony arises from a single zygote, which, through a complex process, gives rise to a large number of individuals" (*A Morally Deep World*, 212–13). Given these examples, it is worth noting that there is no reason that environmental collectives with a good of their own must be monospecific.

45. Cahen, "Against the Moral Considerability of Ecosystems"; Sober, "Philosophical Problems for Environmentalism." According to Sober: "Darwinism...rejects the idea that species, communities and ecosystems have adaptations that exist for their own benefit. These higher-level entities are not conceptualized as goal-directed systems; what properties of organization they possess are viewed as artifacts of processes operating at lower level of organization" ("Philosophical Problems for Environmentalism," 153).

46. McShane, "Ecosystem Health."

47. Darwin, *The Origin of Species*; Crane, "On the Metaphysics of Species."

48. As discussed earlier, the end of continuance of the species must be understood in terms of propagating one's genetic material through future generations, rather than merely continuing the existence of the species.

49. Leopold, *A Sand County Almanac*; Callicott, "The Conceptual Foundations of the Land Ethic"; Westra, *Living in Integrity* and *An Environmental Proposal for Ethics*; Shaw, "A Virtue Ethics Approach to Aldo Leopold's Land Ethic."

50. Leopold, *A Sand County Almanac*, 203–4.

51. Leopold, *A Sand County Almanac*, Part III. This interpretation of the foundation of Leopold's Land Ethic largely follows Bryan Norton's in "The Constancy of Aldo Leopold's Land Ethic" and *Towards Unity Among Environmentalists*, ch. 3. For an alternative interpretation see Callicott, "The Conceptual Foundations of the Land Ethic."

52. "Conservation is getting nowhere because it is incompatible with our Abrahamic concept of land. We abuse land because we regard it as a commodity belonging to us. When we see land as a community to which we belong, we may begin to use it with love and respect," (Leopold, *A Sand County Almanac*, viii).

53. Leopold, *A Sand County Almanac*, 224–25.

54. Shaw, "A Virtue Ethics Perspective on Aldo Leopold's Land Ethic," 63.

55. Passmore, *Man's Responsibility for Nature*, 2nd ed., Appendix, 8, quoted in O'Neill, *Ecology, Policy and Politics: Human Well-Being and the Natural World*, 151.

4. Environmental Decision Making

1. Hursthouse, "Virtue Theory and Abortion," 219. In *On Virtue Ethics* she provides this formulation: "An action is right iff it is what a virtuous agent would characteristically (i.e., acting in character) do in the circumstances" (28).

2. Hursthouse, *On Virtue Ethics*, ch. 2, and "Virtue Theory and Abortion."

3. For this reason, Slote calls such views "agent-prior" (*Morals from Motives* 7).

4. Kant's formal account of virtue is the disposition of the will to act according to the demands of reason (i.e., the imperatives that constitute the moral law) and against inclinations to act otherwise. The substantive principles of morality are several—one must be benevolent, take care of oneself, and so on—so distinct substantive virtues are individuated by the formal account of virtue applied to particular moral imperatives (*Metaphysics of Morals*). For a discussion of this aspect of Kant's ethical system see Wood, *Kant's Ethical Thought*, 329–33.

Among utilitarians, virtue is standardly defined as dispositions the possession of which maximize utility. Here is Bentham's formulation of this utilitarian position: "If [the motives] are good or bad, it is only on account of their effects: good, on account of their tendency to produce pleasure, or avert pain: bad, on account of their tendency to produce pain, or avert pleasure" (*An Introduction to the Principles of Morals and Legislation* 102). Here is Sidgwick's formulation: "Finally, the doctrine that Universal Happiness is the ultimate *standard* must not be understood to imply that Universal Benevolence is the only right or always best *motive* of action. For... if experience shows that the general happiness will be more satisfactorily attained if men frequently act from other motives than pure universal philanthropy, it is obvious that these other motives are reasonably to be preferred on Utilitarian principles" (*Methods of Ethics* 413).

It is possible to construct a form of virtue utilitarianism that defines right action as action done from virtue, and defines virtue as dispositions the possession of which maximize utility (Adams, "Motive Utilitarianism" and Jamieson, "When Utilitarians Should be Virtue Theorists"). Dale Jamieson's version of virtue utilitarianism is particularly relevant here. He argues that "Utilitarianism is a universal emulator: it implies that we should lie, cheat, steal, even appropriate Aristotle, when that is what brings about the best outcomes. In some cases and in some worlds it is best for us to focus as precisely as possible on individual acts. In other cases and worlds it is best for us to be concerned with character traits.... When it comes to global environmental change, utilitarians should generally be inflexible, virtuous greens." This is because global environmental change is a large-scale collective action problem, and when faced with such problems, rather than "looking to moral mathematics for practical solutions...we should focus instead on non-calculative generators of behavior: character traits, dispositions, emotions, and what I shall call 'virtues.' When faced with global environmental change our general policy should be to try to reduce our contribution regardless of the behavior of others, and we are more likely to succeed in doing this by developing and inculcating the right virtues than by improving our calculative abilities. [Moreover,] focusing on the virtues helps to regulate and coordinate behavior, express and contribute to the constitution of community through space and time, and helps to create empathy, sympathy, and solidarity among agents" ("When Utilitarians Should Be Virtue Theorists" 27–28, 17–18, 9–10, 15). However, rather than implying that utilitarians should be virtue theorists locally for this issue, virtue-oriented ethical theory's capacity to respond to collective action problems, including those where an individual agent's actions are nearly inconsequential to causing or resolving the problem, favors it over utilitarianism generally (for beings like us in a world like ours). The considerations raised by Jamieson, as well as virtue-oriented ethical theory's emphases on the cumulative effects of patterns of behavior and flourishing as a good, also position it to respond effectively to the problem of future generations—i.e., how and why we ought to consider nonexistent, contingent future people who cannot be made worse off by us in decision making—in comparison with utilitarian and Kantian theories, and thereby also favor it over them generally (Sandler, "Why Should I Refrain from Contributing to Global Warming? (or) Why Environmental Ethicists Should Be Virtue Ethicists").

5. Johnson, "Virtue and Right," 834.

6. Kawall, "Virtue Theory and Ideal Observers."

7. Research in social psychology has found that situational factors can have considerably more influence on our actions than "folk psychology" tends to suppose. Some philosophers have argued that this research discredits the conception of character central in virtue-oriented ethics (i.e., stable dispositions that provide constancy in responsiveness to like considerations across situations), and that virtue-oriented ethics must therefore be given up (Doris, *Lack of Character*; Harmon, "Moral Philosophy Meets Social Psychology: Virtue Ethics and the Fundamental Attribution Error"). Others have argued, decisively I believe, that this "situationist" criticism is mistaken because the empirical data does not justify the situationist claims about character and, even if it did, those claims do not undermine the standard conception of character in virtue-oriented ethics (Sabini and Silver, "Lack of Character? Situationism Critiqued"; Kamtekar, "Situationism and Virtue Ethics on the Content of Our Character"; Montmarquet, "Moral Character and Social Science Research").

8. A virtue-oriented account of right action that in many respects resembles qualified agent principles is Slote's agent-based principle, according to which the "ethical status of acts [is] entirely derivative from independent and fundamental aretaic (as opposed to deontic) ethical characterizations of motives, character traits, or individuals.... They have to exhibit, express, or reflect such states or be such that they *would* exhibit, etc., such states if they occurred, in order to count as admirable or virtuous" (*Morals from Motives* 5, 17). Unlike Hursthouse, Slote does not define right action in terms of action done by a virtuous agent, so it is not, strictly speaking, a qualified agent account and is not subject to some of the problems discussed above. However, the account disallows several intuitively plausible and seemingly commonplace scenarios: that a person might do the right thing for the wrong reasons; that a less than virtuous person can act rightly; that a well-motivated person can bungle things badly and thereby act wrongly; and that character or motive evaluation and act evaluation can come apart. These and other problems with the view are discussed by Swanton (*Virtue Ethics: A Pluralistic View* ch. 11), Stohr and Wellman

("Recent Work on Virtue Ethics"), and Copp and Sobel ("Morality and Virtue: An Assessment of Some Recent Work in Virtue Ethics").

9. Kawall has defended such an account: "An action is right for an agent in a given set of circumstances if an unimpaired, fully-informed virtuous observer would deem the action to be right" ("Virtue Theory and Ideal Observers," 208).

10. A move of this sort is suggested by Copp and Sobel: "Imagine an agent to have a fully informed and fully virtuous counterpart. The good or right thing to do is what that counterpart would want the agent to do in the agent's actual circumstances" ("Morality and Virtue: An Assessment of Some Recent Work in Virtue Ethics," 546).

11. Swanton, *Virtue Ethics: A Pluralistic View*, 228.

12. Swanton, *Virtue Ethics: A Pluralistic View*, 233.

13. Swanton, *Virtue Ethics: A Pluralistic View*, 233.

14. Exceptions occur when having a certain motive is the target of a virtue, as may sometimes be the case for virtues concerned with character development.

15. Which virtues are operative in a particular situation also can differ among individuals. This is the case, for example, with many position- or relationship-specific virtues, as well as for virtues pertaining to character development.

16. This point is deemphasized in what follows. However, one reason it is important is that it largely forecloses the possibility that nonvirtuous character traits might enable a person to better or more reliably hit the target of virtue than the virtues themselves. For a discussion of what is involved in hitting the target of a virtue, and some complexities that arise, see Swanton, *Virtue Ethics: A Pluralistic View*, 233–38.

17. Swanton, *Virtue Ethics: A Pluralistic View*, 240.

18. Swanton, *Virtue Ethics: A Pluralistic View*, 241.

19. Swanton, *Virtue Ethics: A Pluralistic View*, 241.

20. Swanton attempts to address this difficulty (*Virtue Ethics: A Pluralistic View* 241).

21. This principle is compatible with a taxonomy of impermissible, permissible, obligatory, and supererogatory actions. Rightness is defined along a continuum. An action is right to the extent that it hits the target of the virtues and is wrong to the extent that it fails to do so. Therefore, it allows a permissible-obligatory distinction and an obligatory-supererogatory distinction to be made along the continuum. The principle is neutral on where along the continuum the distinctions are located. It is not neutral, however, on the terms in which those thresholds are defined. They will be formulated in terms of the targets of the operative virtues, rather than in terms of consequences or types of contradictions in universalization, for example.

22. There is convergence in decision-making method with ideal observer accounts and, to a considerable extent, with qualified agent accounts as well.
23. Hursthouse, "Normative Virtue Ethics"; Solomon, "Virtue Ethics: Radical or Routine?"
24. Hooker, *Ideal Code, Real World.*
25. I suggested earlier that ethical naturalism favors evaluating character traits rather than rules. If this is correct, then a properly formulated rule-consequentialism would collapse into this virtue-oriented ethical theory. Brad Hooker has argued that the collapse goes the other way—that virtue ethics (when properly formulated) collapses into rule-consequentialism ("The Collapse of Virtue Ethics").
26. Cafaro, "The Ethics of ORV Use on America's Public Lands"; Orton, "Off-Highway Vehicles and Deep Ecology: Cultural Clash and Alienation from the Natural World."

5. The Virtue-Oriented Approach and Environmental Ethics

1. Callicott, "The Case Against Moral Pluralism."
2. Wenz, "Minimal, Moderate, and Extreme Pluralism," 222.
3. Wenz, "Minimal, Moderate, and Extreme Pluralism," 224.
4. Ross, *The Right and the Good,* 19–24.
5. Callicott, "On Norton and the Failure of Monistic Inherentism" and "Silencing the Philosophers: Minteer and the Foundations of Anti-foundationalism"; Westra, "Why Norton's Approach Is Insufficient for Environmental Ethics"; Rolston III, "Saving Nature, Feeding People, and the Foundations of Ethics."
6. Norton, "Why I Am Not a Nonanthropocentrist" and *Towards Unity Among Environmentalists*; Minteer, "No Experience Necessary?" and "Intrinsic Value for Pragmatists"; Callicott, "The Pragmatic Power and Promise of Theoretical Environmental Ethics"; Harmon, "Notions of Self-Interest: Reflections on the Intersection Between Contingency and Applied Environmental Ethics"; Welchman, "The Virtues of Stewardship"; Light and Katz, "Environmental Pragmatism and Environmental Ethics as Contested Terrain."
7. Hill, "Ideals of Human Excellences and Preserving Natural Environments"; Frasz, "What Is Environmental Virtue Ethics That We Should Be Mindful of It?" and "Environmental Virtue Ethics: A New Direction for Environmental Ethics"; Sterba, "Comments on a Morally Defensible Aristotelian Environmental Ethics"; Elliot, "Normative Ethics."
8. For responses to these concerns see Solomon ("Internal Objections to Virtue Ethics"), Hursthouse (*On Virtue Ethics*), Annas (*The Morality of Happiness*), and Swanton (*Virtue Ethics: A Pluralistic View*).

9. Rolston III, "Environmental Virtue Ethics: Half the Truth but Dangerous as a Whole," 69. Rolston has been the most prominent champion of the intrinsic value of nature and wilderness (*Philosophy Gone Wild*). My view is that nature's intrinsic value is the material and creative contribution that it makes in the production of all the sorts of environmental goods and values (including inherent worth) already discussed. The essential contribution that the natural environment makes to the production of aesthetic value, biological and human flourishing, recreational value, and so on, constitutes its intrinsic value. To recognize and appreciate that contribution is to acknowledge the intrinsic value of nature. There is no "intrinsic value" beyond or behind this. For this reason, the intrinsic value of nature is not an additional human-independent value that grounds a distinct end in the pluralistic teleological account of what makes a character trait a virtue. However, if it turns out that this is mistaken, or other human-independent values in nature are identified, the pluralistic teleological account can be easily modified to accommodate them.

10. For a similar response to Rolston, see James, "Human Virtues and Natural Values."

11. Routley, "Is There a Need for a New, an Environmental, Ethic?".

12. Vogel, "Environmental Philosophy After the End of Nature" and "The Silence of Nature."

13. The relationship between virtue and human dependence and vulnerability is discussed by Macintyre, *Dependent Rational Animals: Why Human Beings Need the Virtues*, and Geach, *The Virtues*.

14. In a 2005 poll, 65 percent of Americans surveyed reported worrying a "great deal" or "fair amount" about the environment, up from 62 percent in 2004, but down from 68 percent in 2003 (Lyons, "Daily Concerns Overshadow Environmental Worries").

15. In a 2006 poll, U.S. citizens were asked, "Thinking specifically about the environmental movement, do you think of yourself as: (1) an active participant in the environmental movement, (2) sympathetic toward the movement, but not active, (3) neutral, or (4) unsympathetic toward the environmental movement?" Fourteen percent of respondents described themselves as active, 48 percent as sympathetic but not active, 29 percent as neutral, and 7 percent and unsympathetic (Gallup, "Environment"). When the same question was asked of citizens of the United States, Great Britain, and Canada in 2004, 47 percent of respondents in the U.S. described themselves as sympathetic but inactive, compared with 59 percent in Great Britain and 48 percent in Canada (Winseman, "Environmental Situations in U.S., Britain, Canada").

16. Many "theories" in the family are also located within or informed by the American pragmatist tradition. This set of themes was developed from the following sources: Barrett and Grizzle, "A Holistic Approach to Sustainability Based on Pluralism Stewardship"; Castle, "A Pluralistic, Pragmatic, Evolutionary Approach to Natural Resource Management"; Hickman, "Nature as Culture: John Dewey's Pragmatic Naturalism"; Holden, "Phenomenology versus Pragmatism"; Light, "Environmental Pragmatism as Philosophy or Metaphilosophy? On the Weston-Katz Debate"; Light and Katz, "Environmental Pragmatism and Environmental Ethics as Contested Terrain"; McDonald, *John Dewey and Environmental Philosophy*; Minteer, "No Experience Necessary" and "Intrinsic Value for Pragmatists?"; Norton, "Why I Am Not a Nonanthropocentrist: Callicott and the Failure of Monistic Inherentism," *Towards Unity Among Environmentalists*, and "Integration or Reduction: Two Approaches to Environmental Values"; Parker, "Pragmatism and Environmental Thought" and "The Ecofeminist Pragmatism of Charlotte Perkins Gilman"; Rosenthal and Buckholz, "How Pragmatism *Is* an Environmental Ethic"; Santas, "The Environmental Value in G. H. Mead's Cosmology"; Thompson, "Pragmatism and Policy: The Case for Water"; Weston, "Before Environmental Ethics," "Beyond Intrinsic Value: Pragmatism in Environmental Ethics," and "Unfair to Swamps: A Reply to Katz"; and Wenz, "Environmental Synergism."

17. Parker, "Pragmatism and Environmental Thought," 26.

18. Parker, "Pragmatism and Environmental Thought," 33.

19. Weston, "Beyond Intrinsic Value," 285.

20. Thompson, "Pragmatism and Policy: The Case for Water," 187. There is also a weaker version of this procedural commitment according to which "Pragmatism sees individuals as the sources of genuine insight into what is needed, and accordingly tries to maximize participation in governing" (Parker, "Pragmatism and Environmental Thought," 31).

21. Minteer, "Intrinsic Value for Pragmatists?" 70.

22. Swanton describes this as a qualified dialogue account of rightness (*Virtue Ethics: A Pluralistic View*, 266–67). It has been a favorite target for critics of environmental pragmatism. Here, for example, is Rolston III: "Minteer will reply that he wants to take account of a pluralism of values in human experiences. He wants a democratic debate among contesting parties. I think he is left in a muddle. Talk about a debate that is a 'non-starter'! In this one there are no grounds (a.k.a. 'foundations') for argument; the outcome will be only the result of a power struggle, which may be disguised as 'pragmatic'" ("Saving Nature, Feeding People, and the Foundations of Ethics" 356).

6. A Virtue-Oriented Assessment of Genetically Modified Crops

1. United Nations Food and Agriculture Organization (FAO), *The State of Food and Agriculture, Agricultural Biotechnology: Meeting the Needs of the Poor?*, 35–39.
2. U.S. Department of Agriculture Economic Research Service, "Adoption of Genetically Engineered Crops in the U.S."
3. This represents an 11 percent increase from 2004. Total market value of all crops in 2005 was $34 billion (James, *Executive Summary of Global Status of Commercialized Biotech/GM Crops: 2005*). The area of land cultivated with genetically modified crops worldwide—categorized by year, nation, and type of crop—can be found at the International Service for the Acquisition of Agri-biotech Applications (ISAAA) Web site, http://www.isaaa.org/.
4. For an accessible overview of agricultural biotechnology in general and GM crops in particular, see FAO, *The State of Food and Agriculture, Agricultural Biotechnology: Meting the Needs of the Poor?*, ch. 2. The primary focus of this chapter is genetically engineered food crops, although at points I discuss agricultural biotechnology more broadly.
5. Ho, "The Unholy Alliance"; Bailey, "Dr. Strangelunch: Why We Should Learn to Love Genetically Modified Food"; Borlaug, "Are We Going Mad?".
6. There is a related issue that has significant regulatory importance in the United States. According to the Food and Drug Administration's "substantial equivalence" policy, a new variety of food crop is permitted to enter the market without full bureaucratic review provided that it is substantially equivalent to an existing food crop. Substantial equivalence has typically been judged on the basis of the intrinsic properties of food crops, not the processes by which the crop varieties are created or cultivated. Proponents of genetically modified crops have, therefore, argued that whether a certain crop is genetically modified is irrelevant to the issue of substantial equivalence. For discussion of this regulatory issue, see Lappe, "A Perspective on Anti-Biotechnology Convictions," and Ruse and Castle, *Genetically Modified Foods: Debating Biotechnology*, Part Six.
7. Bailey, "Dr. Strangelunch: Why we Should Learn to Love Genetically Modified Foods"; Borlaug, "Are We Going Mad?"; Wambugu, "Why Africa Needs Agricultural Biotech."
8. Lappe, "A Perspective on Anti-Biotechnology Convictions"; Bailey and Lappe, *Against the Grain: Biotechnology and the Corporate Takeover of Your Food*; Rossett, "Taking Seriously the Claim That Genetic Engineering Could End Hunger: A Critical Analysis"; Shiva, "Genetic Engineering and Food Security"; Lappe and Bailey, "Biotechnology's Negative Impact on World Agriculture"; GeneWatch, "Genetic Engineering: Can It Feed the World?".

9. Ellstrand, "When Transgenes Wander, Should We Worry?"; GeneWatch, "Genetically Engineered Oilseed Rape: Agricultural Saviour or New Form of Pollution?".

10. Lappe, "A Perspective on Anti-Biotechnology Convictions"; Union of Concerned Scientists, "Gone to Seed: Transgenic Contaminants of the Traditional Food Supply."

11. Rossett, "Taking Seriously the Claim That Genetic Engineering Could End Hunger: A Critical Analysis."

12. According to the FAO, there have been more than 11,000 field trials of GM crops (*The State of Food and Agriculture, Agricultural Biotechnology: Meeting the Needs of the Poor?*, 34). However, few of these have been independent field studies that test the environmental impacts of GM crops, particularly in tropical or nontemperate regions. Those that have been conducted on environmental impacts have provided mixed results. For example, a study by the British Department for Environment, Food, and Rural Affairs (DEFRA) on the effects of GM crops on biodiversity completed in 2005 found that there was little difference in the effects on wildlife between growing conventional winter rape and growing GM herbicide-tolerant winter rape, but that growing conventional beets and spring rape was better for many groups of wildlife than growing GM herbicide-tolerant beets and spring rape, whereas growing herbicide-tolerant maize was better for many groups of wildlife than growing conventional maize (DEFRA, *Managing GM Crops with Herbicides: Effects on Wildlife*). According to a 2005 report by the U.S. Department of Agriculture (USDA) Office of Inspector General, since 1986 the USDA has approved over 10,600 applications for more than 49,300 field sites to test GM crops. However, the Office of Inspector General found that there has been inadequate oversight of those tests, including: inadequate knowledge about exactly where they are taking place; inadequate review of the containment protocols of those conducting them; inadequate oversight of final disposition of the crops at the conclusion of the test; and inadequate follow-up at testing sites to monitor for regrowth. This was found to be the case not only with food crops but also with pharmaceutical crops (USDA Office of Inspector General, *Animal and Plant Health Inspection Service Controls Over Issuance of Genetically Engineered Organism Release Permits*).

13. Shiva, "Genetic Engineering and Food Security"; Ho, "The Unholy Alliance"; Johnson and Hope, "GM Crops and Equivocal Environmental Benefits"; Comstock, *Vexing Nature? On the Ethical Case Against Agricultural Biotechnology*.

14. Ellstrand, "When Transgenes Wander, Should We Worry?"; GeneWatch, "Genetically Engineered Oilseed Rape: Agricultural Saviour or New Form of Pollution?".

15. Union of Concerned Scientists, "Gone to Seed: Transgenic Contaminants of the Traditional Food Supply"; DEFRA, *Managing GM Crops with Herbicides: Effects on Wildlife*; Watrud, Lee, Fairbrother, Burdick, Reichman, Bollman, et al., "Evidence for Landscape-Level, Pollen-Mediated Gene Flow from Genetically Modified Creeping Bentgrass with CP4 EPSPS as a Marker"; Reichman, Watrud, Lee, Burdick, Bollman, Storm, et al., "Establishment of Transgenic Herbicide-Resistant Creeping Bentgrass (*Agrostis stolonifera* L.) in Nonagronomic Habitats."

16. Heimlich, Fernandez-Cornejo, McBride, Klotz-Ingram, Jans, and Brooks, "Genetically Engineered Crops: Has Adoption Reduced Pesticide Use?".

17. World Health Organization, "Vitamin A."

18. UNICEF, *The State of the World's Children 2006: Excluded and Invisible*, 29.

19. Micronutrient Initiative and UNICEF, *Vitamin and Mineral Deficiency: A Global Progress Report*, 3.

20. UNICEF, *The State of the World's Children 1998*, 12–13.

21. Ye, Al-Babili, Kloti, Zhang, Lucca, Beyer, et al., "Engineering the Provitamin A (Beta-Carotene) Biosynthetic Pathway Into (Carotenoid-Free) Rice Endosperm."

22. Potrykus, "Golden Rice and the Greenpeace Dilemma"; Conway, "Open Letter to Greenpeace."

23. Detractors of golden rice have argued: 1) that it will not be able itself to deliver the recommended daily amount of vitamin A; 2) that it will promote chemically intensive monocultural agriculture; 3) that it will provide a foothold from which transnational corporations will be able to take control of rice production in developing countries; and 4) that it does not address the root causes of vitamin A deficiency: poverty and displacement of traditional diverse diets (Shiva, "Golden Rice Is a Hoax: When Public Relations Replace Science"; Greenpeace, "Genetically Engineered 'Golden Rice' is Fools Gold"). Each of these concerns has been addressed above.

24. This has been found to be the case with *B.t.* cotton cultivated in the United States (Heimlich, Fernandez-Cornejo, McBride, Klotz-Ingram, Jans, and Brooks, "Genetically Engineered Crops: Has Adoption Reduced Pesticide Use?"), which is one of the primary reasons, along with the economic effects in developing countries, that the FAO considers GM cotton to be an example of how GM crops can help meet the needs of the poor (*The State of Food and Agriculture, Agricultural Biotechnology: Meeting the Needs of the Poor?*, 43–57).

25. McKibben, *Enough*; Raffensperger, "Learning to Speak Ethics in Technological Debates"; Rifkin, *Algeny*. These claims are critically discussed in Gould, "On the Origin of Specious Critics," Comstock, *Vexing Nature?: On the Ethical Case Against Agricultural Biotechnology*, and Gifford, "Biotechnology."

26. McKibben, *The End of Nature*, 94.

27. McKibben, *The End of Nature*, 96.

28. He provides with apparent approval the following quotation from David Donigan of the Natural Resources Defense Council: "The only thing objectively good about the current atmosphere and climate is that they are the ones we are used to... Life and civilization are adapted to this environment: change necessarily will be disruptive" (*The End of Nature* 100).

29. McKibben, *The End of Nature*, 150.

30. McKibben, *The End of Nature*, 204.

31. Katz, "The Big Lie," 85–86.

32. Val Plumwood, *Environmental Culture: The Ecological Crisis of Reason*, 6. Plumwood, like Katz and McKibben, considers this attitude a type of arrogance: "The logic of Othering suggests that it is not the primitiveness and unworthiness of the Other but our own species' arrogance that is the main barrier to forming ethical and responsive relationships with earth others" (*Environmental Culture: The Ecological Crisis of Reason* 167).

33. Carson, *Silent Spring*, 118. Wendell Berry is another eloquent critic of environmentally related hubris: "Thus, deeply implicated in the very definition of this gift [the land] is a specific warning against *hubris*, which is the great ecological sin, just as it is the great sin of politics. People are not gods. They must not act like gods or assume godly authority. If they do, terrible retributions are in store. In this warning we have the root of the idea of propriety, of *proper* human purposes and ends. We must not use the world as though we created it ourselves" (*The Gift of Good Land* 270).

34. Raffensperger, "Learning to Speak Ethics in Technological Debates," 133.

35. Bailey, "Dr. Strangelunch: Why We Should Learn to Love Genetically Modified Food"; Borlaug, "Are We Going Mad?"; Conway, "Open Letter to Greenpeace"; Potrykus, "Golden Rice and the Greenpeace Dilemma"; Trewavas, "GM Food Is the Best Option We Have" and "The Population/Diversity Paradox: Agricultural Efficiency to Save Wilderness"; Wambugu, "Why Africa Needs Agricultural Biotech."

36. Plumwood, *Environmental Culture: The Ecological Crisis of Reason*, 6.

37. A similar point holds with respect to donating food to those who are starving. Merely donating food creates a donation treadmill, analogous to a pesticide treadmill, that is likely to be ultimately unsustainable (i.e., we cannot reasonably expect to perpetually produce a next green revolution) and has undesirable unintended consequences (e.g., reduced fresh water availability). Garret Hardin identifies the attitude that we could continue in this way as "hubris": "We can, of course, increase carrying capacity somewhat. But only hubris leads us to think that our ability to do so is without limit. Despite all of our technological accomplishments—and

there are many—there is a potent germ of truth in the saying of Horace (5–8 B.C.): *Naturam expelles furca, tamen usque recurret.* 'Drive nature off with a pitchfork, nevertheless she will return with a rush.' This is the message of Rachel Carson, which has been corroborated by many others" ("Lifeboat Ethics: The Case Against Helping the Poor" 66). It does not follow from this that donating food is wrong, or even not obligatory. What it implies is that merely giving food—i.e., donating in the absence of an integrated approach that addresses the social, political, economic, and ecological factors that lead to extreme poverty and food shortages—is the sort of targeted approach that, like magic bullet approaches in agriculture and medicine, is inadequate and likely to fail to hit the target of the operative virtues, including environmental virtues (Carter, "Feeding People and Saving Nature"; Rolston III, "Saving Nature, Feeding People, and the Foundations of Ethics").

38. Scott, "The Magic Bullet Criticism of Agricultural Biotechnology."

39. "By challenging the myths of biotechnology, we expose genetic engineering for what it really is; another 'technological fix' or magic bullet aimed at circumventing the environmental problems of agriculture (which themselves are the outcome of an earlier round of technological fixes) without questioning the flawed assumptions that gave rise to the problems in the first place" (Altieri, "The Myths of Agricultural Biotechnology").

40. FAO, *The State of Food and Agriculture, Agricultural Biotechnology: Meeting the Needs of the Poor?*

41. The principle of commensurate burdens and benefits operative here—that, all other things being equal, those who derive benefits should sustain the burdens associated with those benefits—is defended by Wenz ("Just Garbage").

42. Comstock, *Vexing Nature?*, ch. 1.

43. Shiva, *Biopiracy: The Plunder of Nature and Knowledge.*

44. Delivery of golden rice has been slowed by intellectual property and patent issues. There are 72 patents, held by 40 organizations, on the technology involved in its production. Therefore, one way to support golden rice (and other acceptable GM crops) would be to support those organizations (such as Public Intellectual Property Resource for Agriculture and African Agricultural Technology Foundation) who are trying to get access to the technology for those who would benefit from it. This could be done, for example, by implementing humanitarian exemptions on food technology patents or developing open-source and freedom-to-operate technology databases.

45. Other GM crops being developed or in the field that might be acceptable upon evaluation include rice with the capacity to fix nitrogen, cassava (a

staple food in much of Africa) with resistance to the cassava mosaic virus, corn with resistance to the stem borer (which takes about 15 percent of Kenya's corn crop each year), crops with high salinity tolerance, and potatoes, canola, bananas, sorghum, and cassava with nutritional (e.g., protein, vitamin, or mineral) enhancement. The most prominent supporter of the development of agricultural biotechnologies that would help the world's worst-off without compromising the quality of the environment has been the William and Melinda Gates foundation, through its $450 million Grand Challenges in Global Health grant program.

46. New Zealand Ministry for the Environment, *Genetic Modification: The New Zealand Approach*; United Kingdom, Department for Environment, Food, and Rural Affairs, "Margaret Beckett [Secretary of State for Environment, Food, and Rural Affairs] Outlines Precautionary Approach to GM Crops." A study by the Australian Bureau of Rural Sciences (BRS) on the issue of gene flow from genetically modified crops similarly concludes: "The actual amount of gene flow from GM crops and its consequences will depend on the crop, the transgene, the trait encoded, the particular environment and the risk management practices adopted" (Glover, *Gene Flow Study: Implications for the Release of Genetically Modified Crops in Australia*, vii).

47. Among the challenges that attend this "middle way" is establishing a framework for regulatory assessment that does not make development and approval costs so prohibitive that only technologies with the potential for significant commercial success—i.e., those that are most attractive to large chemically intensive and monocultural farming operations—will be viable. This issue is connected to several others concerning research funding, research priorities, technology control and accountability, intellectual property, and regulatory capacity. Other factors relevant to the success of the middle way include access to technology and resources, agricultural subsidies, international trade agreements, and market and other distribution mechanisms (for both seed and produce). For discussion of several of these issues, see FAO, *The State of Food and Agriculture, Agricultural Biotechnology: Meeting the Needs of the Poor?*.

BIBLIOGRAPHY

Adams, R. 1976. "Motive Utilitarianism." *Journal of Philosophy* 73:467–81.

Altieri, M. 2000. "The Myths of Agricultural Biotechnology." http://www.cnr.berkeley.edu/~agroeco3/the_myths.html (accessed August 11, 2006).

Anderson, J. 1993. "Species Equality and the Foundations of Moral Theory." *Environmental Values* 2 (4): 347–65.

Annas, J. 1993. *The Morality of Happiness.* Oxford: Oxford University Press.

Aristotle. 1985. *Nicomachean Ethics.* Trans. T. Irwin. Indianapolis, IN: Hackett.

Arpaly, N. 2003. *Unprincipled Virtue: An Inquiry Into Moral Agency.* Oxford: Oxford University Press.

Bailey, B. and M. Lappe. 1998. *Against the Grain: Biotechnology and the Corporate Takeover of Your Food.* Monroe, ME: Common Courage.

Bailey, R. 2002. "Dr. Strangelunch: Why We Should Learn to Love Genetically Modified Food." In G. Pence, ed., *The Ethics of Food,* 100–15. Lanham, MD: Rowman and Littlefield.

Barlow, M. and T. Clarke. 2002. *Blue Gold.* New York: The New Press.

Barrett, C. B. and R. Grizzle. 1999. "A Holistic Approach to Sustainability Based on Pluralism Stewardship." *Environmental Ethics* 21 (1): 23–42.

Bauder, D. 2006. "Average Home Has More TVs Than People." *Associated Press,* September 21.

Becker, L. 1998. *A New Stoicism.* Princeton: Princeton University Press.

Bell, M., A. McDermitt, S. L. Zeger, J. M. Samet, and F. Dominici. 2004. "Ozone and Short-Term Mortality in 95 US Urban Communities, 1987–2000." *Journal of the American Medical Association* 292 (19): 2372–2378.

Bentham, J. 1961. *An Introduction to the Principles of Morals and Legislation.* New York: Hafner.

Berry, W. 1977. *The Unsettling of America: Culture and Agriculture.* San Francisco: Sierra Club Books.

——. 1982. *The Gift of Good Land.* San Francisco: North Point Press.

Bond, M. 2003. "The Pursuit of Happiness." *New Scientist* (October 4):40–47.

Borlaug, N. 2002. "Are We Going Mad?" In G. Pence, ed., *The Ethics of Food,* 74–79. Lanham, MD: Rowman and Littlefield.

Bradley, B. 2005. "Virtue Consequentialism." *Utilitas* 17 (3): 282–98.

Brook, R. D., B. Franklin, W. Cascio, Y. Hong, G. Howard, M. Lipsett, et al. 2004. "Air Pollution and Cardiovascular Disease: A Statement for Healthcare Professionals from the Expert Panel on Population and Prevention Science of the American Heart Association." *Circulation* 109 (21): 2655–2671.

Cafaro, P. 2001. "The Naturalist's Virtues." *Philosophy in the Contemporary World* 8 (2): 85–99.

———. 2001. "Thoreau, Leopold, and Carson: Toward an Environmental Virtue Ethic." *Environmental Ethics* 23 (1): 3–17.

———. 2004. *Thoreau's Living Ethics: Walden and the Pursuit of Virtue.* Athens: University of Georgia Press.

———. In press. "The Ethics of ORV Use on America's Public Lands." In G. Wuerthner, ed., *Off-Road Rage: The Motorized Destruction of Nature.* Washington, DC: Island Press.

Cahen, H. 1988. "Against the Moral Considerability of Ecosystems." *Environmental Ethics* 10 (3): 196–216.

Callicott, B. 1987. "The Conceptual Foundations of the Land Ethic." In B. Callicott, ed., *Companion to* A Sand County Almanac: *Interpretive and Critical Essays,* 186–217. Madison: University of Wisconsin Press.

———. 1990. "The Case Against Moral Pluralism." *Environmental Ethics* 12 (2): 99–124.

———. 1996. "On Norton and the Failure of Monistic Inherentism." *Environmental Ethics* 18 (2): 219–21.

———. 1999. "Silencing the Philosophers: Minteer and the Foundations of Antifoundationalism." *Environmental Values* 8 (4): 499–516.

———. 2002. "The Pragmatic Power and Promise of Theoretical Environmental Ethics." *Environmental Values* 11 (1): 3–25.

Carroll, J. 2005. "Americans' Personal Satisfaction." http://poll.gallup.com/content/default.aspx?ci = 14506andpg = 2 (accessed August 10, 2006).

Carroll, S. B. 2005. *Endless Forms Most Beautiful: The New Science of Evo Devo and the Making of the Animal Kingdom.* New York: Norton.

Carson, R. 1956. *The Sense of Wonder.* New York: Harper and Row.

———. 1962. *Silent Spring.* New York: Fawcett World Library.

———. 1999. "Design for Nature Writing." In L. Lear, ed., *Lost Woods: The Discovered Writings of Rachel Carson,* 93–97. Boston: Beacon.

Carter, A. 2004. "Saving Nature and Feeding People." *Environmental Ethics* 26 (4): 339–60.

Castle, E. N. 1996. "A Pluralistic, Pragmatic, Evolutionary Approach to Natural Resource Management." In A. Light and E. Katz, eds., *Environmental Pragmatism*, 231–50. New York: Routledge.

Chapman, R. 2002. "The Goat-Stag and the Sphinx: The Place of the Virtues in Environmental Ethics." *Environmental Values* 11 (2): 129–44.

Comstock, G. 2000. *Vexing Nature?: On the Ethical Case Against Agricultural Biotechnology*. Boston: Kluwer.

Conway, G. 2002. "Open Letter to Greenpeace." In M. Ruse and D. Castle, eds., *Genetically Modified Foods: Debating Biotechnology*, 63–64. Amherst, NY: Prometheus.

Copp, D. and D. Sobel. 2004. "Morality and Virtue: An Assessment of Some Recent Work in Virtue Ethics." *Ethics* 114 (3): 514–54.

Cox, J. R. 2007. "Golden Tropes and Democratic Betrayals: Prospects for Environmental Justice in Neoliberal 'Free Trade' Agreements." In R. Sandler and P. Pezzullo, eds., *Environmental Justice and Environmentalism: The Social Justice Challenge to the Environmental Movement*. 225–280. Cambridge, MA: MIT Press.

Crane, J. 2004. "On the Metaphysics of Species." *Philosophy of Science* 71 (2): 156–73.

Darwin, C. 1999/1859. *The Origin of Species*. New York: Bantam.

Davion, V. 2006. "Itch Scratching, Patio Building and Pesky Flies: Biocentric Individualism Revisited." *Environmental Ethics* 28 (2): 115–28.

Davis, S. C. and S. W. Diegel. 2006. *Transportation Energy Data Book: Edition 25–2006*. Oak Ridge, TN: Oak Ridge National Laboratory.

De Graff, J., D. Wann, and T. H. Naylor. 2002. *Affluenza: The All-Consuming Epidemic*. San Francisco: Berrett-Koehler.

Diener, E. and M. Seligman. 2004. "Beyond Money: Toward an Economy of Well-Being." *Psychological Science in the Public Interest* 5 (1): 1–31.

Doris, J. M. 2002. *Lack of Character: Personality and Moral Behavior*. Cambridge: Cambridge University Press.

Driver, J. 2001. *Uneasy Virtue*. Cambridge: Cambridge University Press.

Earth Charter International. 2000. "The Earth Charter." http://www.earthcharter. org (accessed August 14, 2006).

Ehrlich, P. 2002. *Human Natures: Genes, Cultures, and the Human Prospect*. New York: Penguin.

Elliot, R. 2001. "Normative Ethics." In D. Jamieson, ed., *A Companion to Environmental Philosophy*, 177–91. Oxford: Blackwell.

Ellstrand, N. 2002. "When Transgenes Wander, Should We Worry?" In M. Ruse and D. Castle, eds., *Genetically Modified Foods: Debating Biotechnology*, 325–30. Amherst, NY: Prometheus.

Emerson, R. W. 2000. "Art." In B. Atkinson, ed., *The Essential Writings of Ralph Waldo Emerson*, 274–83. New York: Modern Library.

Evans, J. C. 2005. *With Respect for Nature: Living as Part of the Natural World*. Albany: State University of New York Press.

Foot, P. 2001. *Natural Goodness*. Oxford: Oxford University Press.

Frasz, G. 1993. "Environmental Virtue Ethics: A New Direction for Environmental Ethics." *Environmental Ethics* 15 (3): 259–74.

——. 2001. "What Is Environmental Virtue Ethics That We Should Be Mindful of It?" *Philosophy in the Contemporary World* 8 (2): 5–14.

——. 2004. "Benevolence as an Environmental Virtue." In R. Sandler and P. Cafaro, eds., *Environmental Virtue Ethics*, 121–34. Lanham, MD: Rowman and Littlefield.

French, W. 1995. "Against Biospherical Egalitarianism." *Environmental Ethics* 17 (1): 39–57.

Gallup. 2006. "Environment." http://poll.gallup.com/content/default.aspx?ci = 1615 (accessed August 10, 2006).

Gauderman, W. J., E. Avol, F. Gilliland, H. Vora, D. Thomas, K. Berhane, et al. 2004. "The Effect of Air Pollution on Lung Development from 10 to 18 Years of Age." *The New England Journal of Medicine* 351 (11): 1–11.

Geach, P. T. 1977. *The Virtues*. Cambridge: Cambridge University Press.

GeneWatch. 1998. "Genetic Engineering: Can It Feed the World?" http://www.genewatch.org/uploads/f03c6d66a9b354535738483c1c3d49e4/Brief3_A3.pdf (accessed August 14, 2006).

——. 1998. "Genetically Engineered Oilseed Rape: Agricultural Saviour or New Form of Pollution?" http://www.genewatch.org/uploads/f03c6d66a9 b354535738483c1c3d49e4/brief2.pdf (accessed August 14, 2006).

Gerber, L. 2002. "Standing Humbly Before Nature." *Ethics and the Environment* 7 (1): 39–53.

Gifford, F. 2002. "Biotechnology." In G. Comstock, ed., *Life Science Ethics*, 191–224. Iowa City: Iowa State University Press.

Gleick, P. 1998. *The World's Water: The Biennial Report on Freshwater Resources, 1998–1999*. Washington, DC: Island Press.

——. 2002. *The World's Water: The Biennial Report on Freshwater Resources, 2002–2003*. Washington, DC: Island Press.

——. 2004. *The World's Water: The Biennial Report on Freshwater Resources, 2004–2005*. Washington, DC: Island Press.

Glennon, R. 2004. *Water Follies: Groundwater Pumping and the Fate of America's Fresh Waters*. Washington, DC: Island Press.

Glover, J. 2002. *Gene Flow Study: Implications for the Release of Genetically Modified Crops in Australia*. Canberra: Australia Bureau of Rural Sciences.

Goodman, M., D. Ansel, and R. Nakosteen. 2004. *Mass.commuting*. Boston: MassINC.

Gould, S. J. 1985. "On the Origin of Specious Critics." *Discover* (January):34–42.

Greenpeace. 2002. "Genetically Engineered 'Golden Rice' Is Fools Gold." In M. Ruse and D. Castle, eds., *Genetically Modified Foods: Debating Biotechnology*, 52–54. Amherst, NY: Prometheus.

Hardin, G. 2002. "Lifeboat Ethics: The Case Against Helping the Poor." In G. Pence, ed., *The Ethics of Food*, 54–70. Lanham, MD: Rowman and Littlefield.

Harmon, G. 1999. "Moral Philosophy Meets Social Psychology." *Proceedings of the Aristotelian Society* 99 (3): 315–31.

Harmon, J. 2001. "Notions of Self-Interest: Reflections on the Intersection Between Contingency and Applied Environmental Ethics." *Environmental Ethics* 23 (4): 377–89.

Healy, T. and S. Cote. 2001. *The Well-being of Nations: The Role of Human and Social Capital*. Paris: OECD Publishing.

Heavenrich, R. M. 2006. *Light-Duty Automotive Technology and Fuel Economy Trends: 1975 Through 2006*. Washington, DC: Environmental Protection Agency.

Heimlich, R., J. Fernandez-Cornejo, W. McBride, K.-I. Cassandra, J. Sharon, and B. Nora. 2000. "Genetically Engineered Crops: Has Adoption Reduced Pesticide Use?" *Agricultural Outlook*, 13–17.

Hickman, L. 1996. "Nature as Culture: John Dewey's Pragmatic Naturalism." In A. Light and E. Katz, eds., *Environmental Pragmatism*, 50–72. New York: Routledge.

Hill, T. 1983. "Ideals of Human Excellences and Preserving Natural Environments." *Environmental Ethics* 5 (3): 211–24.

——. 2006. "Finding Value in Nature." *Environmental Values* 15 (3): 331–41.

Ho, M.-W. 2002. "The Unholy Alliance." In G. Pence, ed., *The Ethics of Food*, 80–95. Lanham, MD: Rowman and Littlefield.

Holden, M. 2001. "Phenomenology versus Pragmatism." *Environmental Ethics* 23 (1): 37–56.

Hooker, B. 2000. *Ideal Code, Real World*. Oxford: Oxford University Press.

——. 2002. "The Collapse of Virtue Ethics." *Utilitas* 14 (1): 22–40.

Hume, D. 1966/1751. *An Enquiry Concerning the Principles of Morals*. La Salle, IL: Open Court.

Hursthouse, R. 1996. "Normative Virtue Ethics." In R. Crisp, ed., *How Should One Live?: Essays on the Virtues*, 19–36. Oxford: Oxford University Press.

——. 1997. "Virtue Theory and Abortion." In R. Crisp and M. Slote, eds., *Virtue Ethics*, 217–38. Oxford: Oxford University Press.

——. 1999. *On Virtue Ethics*. Oxford: Oxford University Press.

———. 1999. "Virtue Ethics and Human Nature." *Hume Studies* XXV (1–2): 67–82.

———. 2002. "Virtue Ethics vs Rule-Consequentialism: A Reply to Brad Hooker." *Utilitas* 14 (1): 41–53.

———. 2006. "Applying Virtue Ethics to Our Treatment of the Other Animals." In J. Welchman, ed., *The Practice of Virtue: Classic and Contemporary Readings in Virtue Ethics*, 136–54. Indianapolis: Hackett.

Intergovernmental Panel on Climate Change. 2001. *Third Assessment Report*. Cambridge: Cambridge University Press.

James, C. 2005. *Executive Summary of Global Status of Commercialized Biotech/GM Crops: 2005*. Ithaca, NY: International Service for the Acquisition of Agri-biotech Applications (ISAAA).

James, S. 2006. "Human Virtues and Natural Values." *Environmental Ethics* 28 (4): 339–53.

James, W. 1948. *Essays in Pragmatism*. New York: Hafner.

Jamieson, D. In press. "When Utilitarians Should Be Virtue Theorists." *Utilitas*. http://www.utilitas.org.uk/pdfs/jamieson.pdf (accessed January 3, 2007).

Johnson, B. and A. Hope. 2002. "GM Crops and Equivocal Environmental Benefits." In M. Ruse and D. Castle, eds., *Genetically Modified Foods: Debating Biotechnology*, 331–34. Amherst, NY: Prometheus.

Johnson, L. 1991. *A Morally Deep World*. Cambridge: Cambridge University Press.

———. 2003. "Future Generations and Contemporary Ethics." *Environmental Values* 12 (4): 471–87.

Johnson, R. 2003. "Virtue and Right." *Ethics* 113 (4): 810–34.

Kahn, P. 1999. *The Human Relationship with Nature: Development and Culture*. Cambridge, MA: MIT Press.

Kahn, P. and S. R. Kellert, eds. 1999. *Children and Nature: Psychological, Sociocultural, and Evolutionary Investigations*. Cambridge, MA: MIT Press.

Kahneman, D. 1980. "Human Engineering Decisions." In M. Kranzberg, ed., *Ethics in the Age of Pervasive Technology*, 190–92. Boulder: Westview.

Kamtekar, R. 2004. "Situationism and Virtue Ethics on the Content of Our Character." *Ethics* 114 (3): 458–91.

Kant, I. 1994. *The Metaphysics of Morals*. Trans. J. Ellington. 2nd ed. Indianapolis, IN: Hackett.

Kant, I. 1997. "Duties to Animals and Spirits." Trans. P. Heath. In P. Heath and J. B. Schneewind, eds., *Lectures on Ethics*, 212–13. Cambridge: Cambridge University Press.

———. 1997. *Groundwork for the Metaphysics of Morals*. Trans. M. Gregor. Cambridge: Cambridge University Press.

Kasser, T. 2002. *The High Price of Materialism*. Cambridge, MA: MIT Press.

Kasser, T. and A. D. Kanner, eds. 2004. *Psychology and Consumer Culture: The Struggle for a Good Life in a Materialistic World*. Washington, DC: American Psychological Association.

Katz, E. 2000. "The Big Lie." In W. Throop, ed., *Environmental Restoration*, 83–93. Amherst, NY: Humanity.

Kawall, J. 2002. "Virtue Theory and Ideal Observers." *Philosophical Studies* 109 (3): 197–222.

——. 2005. "Complacency, Apathy, and Resignation." Presented at the International Society for Environmental Ethics, Eastern Division Meeting of the American Philosophical Association, New York.

Kurzweil, R. 2005. *The Singularity Is Near: When Humans Transcend Biology*. New York: Viking.

Lappe, M. 2002. "A Perspective on Anti-Biotechnology Convictions." In B. Bailey and M. Lappe, eds., *Engineering the Farm: Ethical and Social Aspects of Agricultural Biotechnology*, 135–56. Washington, DC: Island Press.

Lappe, M. and B. Bailey. 2002. "Biotechnology's Negative Impact on World Agriculture." In G. Pence, ed., *The Ethics of Food*, 156–67. Lanham, MD: Rowman and Littlefield.

Leopold, A. 1968. *A Sand Country Almanac*. Oxford: Oxford University Press.

——. 1986. *Game Management*. Madison: University of Wisconsin Press.

Lewis, C. S. 2001. *Mere Christianity*. New York: HarperCollins.

Light, A. 1996. "Compatibilism in Political Ecology." In A. Light and E. Katz, eds., *Environmental Pragmatism*, 161–84. New York: Routledge.

——. 1996. "Environmental Pragmatism as Philosophy or Metaphilosophy? On the Weston-Katz Debate." In A. Light and E. Katz, eds., *Environmental Pragmatism*, 325–36. New York: Routledge.

——. 2000. "Restoration or Domination? A Reply to Katz." In W. Throop, ed., *Environmental Restoration*, 95–111. Amherst, NY: Humanity.

Light, A., and Katz, E. 1996. "Environmental Pragmatism and Environmental Ethics as Contested Terrain." In A. Light and E. Katz, eds., *Environmental Pragmatism*, 1–18. New York: Routledge.

Lyons, L. 2005. "Daily Concerns Overshadow Environmental Worries" (April 19). http://poll.gallup.com/content/default.aspx?ci = 15925 (accessed August 10, 2006)

Macintyre, A. 1999. *Dependent Rational Animals: Why Human Beings Need the Virtues*. Chicago: Open Court.

McDonald, H. 2004. *John Dewey and Environmental Philosophy*. Albany: State University of New York Press.

McDowell, J. 1980. "The Role of *Eudaimonia* in Aristotle's Ethics." In A. O. Rorty, ed., *Essays on Aristotle's Ethics*, 359–76. Berkeley: University of California Press.

McKibben, B. 1999. *The End of Nature*. 2nd ed. New York: Anchor.

——. 2003. *Enough: Staying Human in an Engineered Age*. New York: Times Books.

McShane, K. 2004. "Ecosystem Health." *Environmental Ethics* 26 (3): 227–45.

Metz, T. 2002. "Recent Work on the Meaning of Life." *Ethics* 112 (4): 781–814.

Micronutrient Initiative, and United Nations Children's Fund. 2004. *Vitamin and Mineral Deficiency: A Global Progress Report*. Ottawa, New York: Micronutrient Initiative and UNICEF.

Minteer, B. 1998. "No Experience Necessary? Foundationalism and the Retreat from Culture in Environmental Ethics." *Environmental Values* 7 (3): 333–48.

——. 2001. "Intrinsic Value for Pragmatists?" *Environmental Ethics* 23 (1): 57–75.

Montmarquet, J. 2003. "Moral Character and Social Science Research." *Philosophy* 78:355–68.

Moore, K. D. 2005. "The Truth of the Barnacles: Rachel Carson and the Moral Significance of Wonder." *Environmental Ethics* 27 (3): 265–77.

Muir, J. 1875. "Wild Wool." *Overland Monthly*, 14 (April): 361–66.

——. 1901. *Our National Parks*. Cambridge, MA: Riverside Press.

——. 1912. *The Yosemite*. New York: Century.

National Association of Home Builders. 2000. *A Century of Progress: America's Housing 1900–2000*. Washington, DC: National Association of Home Builders.

New Zealand Ministry for the Environment. 2004. *Genetic Modification: The New Zealand Approach*. Wellington, NZ: New Zealand Ministry for the Environment.

Nielsen, K. 1990. *Ethics Without God*. Rev. ed. Amherst, New York: Prometheus.

Norton, B. 1991. *Toward Unity Among Environmentalists*. New York: Oxford University Press.

——. 1995. "Why I Am Not a Nonanthropocentrist: Callicott and the Failure of Monistic Inherentism." *Environmental Ethics* 17 (4): 341–58.

——. 1996. "The Constancy of Aldo Leopold's Land Ethic." In A. Light and E. Katz, eds., *Environmental Pragmatism*, 84–102. New York: Routledge.

——. 1996. "Integration or Reduction: Two Approaches to Environmental Values." In A. Light and E. Katz, eds., *Environmental Pragmatism*, 105–38. New York: Routledge.

The Norwegian Nobel Committee. 2004. "The Nobel Peace Prize 2004." http://nobelprize.org/peace/laureates/2004/press.html (accessed August 14, 2006).

Nussbaum, M. C. 1986. *Fragility of Goodness*. Cambridge: Cambridge University Press.

——. 2000. *Women and Human Development: The Capabilities Approach*. Cambridge: Cambridge University Press.

——. 1994. *The Therapy of Desire: Theory and Practice in Hellenistic Ethics*. Princeton: Princeton University Press.

O'Neill, J. 1993. *Ecology, Policy, and Politics: Human Well-Being and the Natural World*. London: Routledge.

Orton, D. 2004. "Off-Highway Vehicles and Deep Ecology: Cultural Clash and Alienation from the Natural World." *Green Web Bulletin* 75. http://home. ca.inter.net/~greenweb/OHV-DE.html (accessed December 29, 2006).

Parker, K. 1996. "Pragmatism and Environmental Thought." In A. Light and E. Katz, eds., *Environmental Pragmatism*, 21–37. New York: Routledge.

Parker, K. 2001. "The Ecofeminist Pragmatism of Charlotte Perkins Gilman." *Environmental Ethics* 23 (1): 19–36.

Passmore, J. 1974. *Man's Responsibility for Nature: Ecological Problems and Western Traditions*. New York: Scribner.

——. 1980. *Man's Responsibility for Nature: Ecological Problems and Western Traditions*. 2nd ed. London: Duckworth.

Pielou, E. C. 1998. *Fresh Water*. Chicago: University of Chicago Press.

Pincoffs, E. L. 1986. *Quandaries and Virtues: Against Reductivism in Ethics*. Lawrence: University of Kansas Press.

Pinker, S. 2002. *The Blank Slate: The Modern Denial of Human Nature*. New York: Viking.

Plumwood, V. 2002. *Environmental Culture and the Ecological Crisis of Reason*. London: Routledge.

Pope III, C. A., R. T. Burnett, M. J. Thun, E. E. Calle, D. Krewski, K. Ito, et al. 2002. "Lung Cancer, Cardiopulmonary Mortality, and Long-Term Exposure to Fine Particulate Air Pollution." *Journal of the American Medical Association* 287 (9): 1132–1141.

Pope III, C. A., R. T. Burnett, G. D. Thurston, M. J. Thun, E. E. Calle, D. Krewski, et al. 2004. "Cardiovascular Mortality and Long-Term Exposure to Particulate Air Pollution: Epidemiological Evidence of General Pathophysiological Pathways of Disease." *Circulation* 109 (1): 71–77.

Potrykus, I. 2002. "Golden Rice and the Greenpeace Dilemma." In M. Ruse and D. Castle, eds., *Genetically Modified Foods: Debating Biotechnology*, 55–57. Amherst, NY: Prometheus.

Putnam, R. D. 2000. *Bowling Alone: The Collapse and Revival of American Community*. New York: Simon and Schuster.

Rachels, J. 1990. *Created from Animals*. Oxford: Oxford University Press.

Raffensperger, C. 2002. "Learning to Speak Ethics in Technological Debates." In B. Bailey and M. Lappe, eds., *Engineering the Farm: Ethical and*

Social Aspects of Agricultural Biotechnology, 125–33. Washington, DC: Island Press.

Regan, T. 1983. *The Case for Animal Rights*. Berkeley: University of California Press.

Reichman, J., L. S. Watrud, E. H. Lee, C. A. Burdick, M. A. Bollman, M. J. Storm, et al. In press. "Establishment of Transgenic Herbicide-Resistant Creeping Bentgrass (*Agrostis stolonifera* L.) in Non-Agronomic Habitats." *Molecular Ecology*.

Richerson, P. J. and R. Boyd. 2005. *Not by Genes Alone: How Culture Transformed Human Evolution*. Chicago: University of Chicago Press.

Rifkin, J. 1983. *Algeny*. New York: Viking.

Robin, V. and J. Dominguez. 1992. *Your Money or Your Life*. New York: Penguin.

Roco, M. 2004. "Science and Technology Integration for Increased Human Potential and Societal Outcomes." In M. Roco and C. Montemagno, eds., *The Coevolution of Human Potential and Converging Technologies*, 1–16. New York: The New York Academy of Sciences.

Roco, M. and W. S. Bainbridge, eds. 2002. *Converging Technologies for Improving Human Performance: Nanotechnology, Biotechnology, Information Technology and Cognitive Science* (NBIC). Arlington, VA: NSF/DOC.

Roco, M. and W. S. Bainbridge. 2002. "Overview." In M. Roco and W. S. Bainbridge, eds., *Converging Technologies for Improving Human Performance: Nanotechnology, Biotechnology, Information Technology and Cognitive Science (NBIC)*, 1–27. Arlington, VA: NSF/DOC.

Roco, M. and C. Montemagno. 2004. "Preface." In M. Roco and C. Montemagno, eds., *The Coevolution of Human Potential and Converging Technologies*, vii–viii. New York: The New York Academy of Sciences.

Rolston III, H. 1989. *Philosophy Gone Wild*. Amherst, NY: Prometheus.

——. 1998. "Saving Nature, Feeding People, and the Foundations of Ethics." *Environmental Values* 7 (3): 349–57.

——. 2005. "Environmental Virtue Ethics: Half the Truth but Dangerous as a Whole." In R. Sandler and P. Cafaro, eds., *Environmental Virtue Ethics*, 61–78. Lanham, MD: Rowman and Littlefield.

Rosenthal, S. B. and R. A. Buckholtz. 1996. "How Pragmatism *Is* an Environmental Ethic." In A. Light and E. Katz, eds., *Environmental Pragmatism*, 38–49. New York: Routledge.

Ross, W. D. 2002. *The Right and the Good*. Oxford: Oxford University Press.

Rossett, P. 2002. "Taking Seriously the Claim That Genetic Engineering Could End Hunger: A Critical Analysis." In B. Bailey and M. Lappe, eds., *Engineering the Farm: Ethical and Social Aspects of Agricultural Biotechnology*, 81–93. Washington, DC: Island Press.

Routley, R. 2003. "Is There a Need for a New, an Environmental, Ethic?" In A. Light and H. Rolston III, eds., *Environmental Ethics: An Anthology*, 47–52. Oxford: Blackwell.

Ruse, M. and D. Castle, eds. 2002. *Genetically Modified Foods: Debating Biotechnology*. Amherst, NY: Prometheus.

Sabini, J. and M. Silver. 2005. "Lack of Character? Situationism Critiqued." *Ethics* 115 (3): 535–62.

Sagoff, M. 1984. "Animal Liberation and Environmental Ethics: Bad Marriage, Quick Divorce." *Osgoode Hall Law Journal* 22 (2): 297–307.

Samet, J.M., F. Dominici, F. C. Curriero, I. Coursac, and S. L. Zeger. 2000. "Fine Particulate Air Pollution and Mortality in 20 U.S. Cities, 1987–1994." *The New England Journal of Medicine* 343:1742–1749.

Sandler, R. 2005. "Ignorance and Virtue." *Philosophical Papers* 34 (2): 261–72.

——. In press. "Nanotechnology and Human Flourishing: Toward a Framework for Assessing Human Enhancements." In F. Jotterand, ed., *Nanotechnology: Framing the Field*. Dordrecht: Kluwer.

——. N.d. "Why Should I Refrain from Contributing to Global Warming (or) Why Environmental Ethicists Should Be Virtue Ethicists."

Sandler, R. and E. Volkert. 2006. "Review of J. Claude Evans' *With Respect for Nature*." *Environmental Values* 15 (4): 536–38.

Santas, A. 1996. "The Environmental Value in G. H. Mead's Cosmology." In A. Light and E. Katz, eds., *Environmental Pragmatism*, 73–83. New York: Routledge.

Schmidtz, D. 1998. "Are All Species Created Equal?" *Journal of Applied Philosophy* 15 (1): 57–67.

Schweitzer, A. 1923. *Civilization and Ethics*. Trans. J.P. Naish. London: A. and C. Black.

Scott, D. 2005. "The Magic Bullet Criticism of Agricultural Biotechnology." *Agricultural and Environmental Ethics* 18 (3): 259–67.

Shaw, B. 1997. "A Virtue Ethics Approach to Aldo Leopold's Land Ethic." *Environmental Ethics* 19 (2): 53–67.

Shiva, V. 1997. *Biopiracy: The Plunder of Nature and Knowledge*. Cambridge, MA: South End Press.

——. 2002. "Genetic Engineering and Food Security." In G. Pence, ed., *The Ethics of Food*, 130–47. Lanham, MD: Rowman and Littlefield.

——. 2002. "Golden Rice Hoax: When Public Relations Replace Science. "In M. Ruse and D. Castle, eds., *Genetically Modified Foods: Debating Biotechnology*, 58–62. Amherst, NY: Prometheus.

Sidgwick, H. 1981/1874. *The Methods of Ethics*. Indianapolis, IN: Hackett.

Singer, P. 1975. *Animal Liberation*. New York: The New York Review.

Slote, M. 2001. *Morals from Motives*. Oxford: Oxford University Press.

Sober, E. 2002. "Philosophical Problems for Environmentalism." In D. Schmidtz and E. Willott, eds., *Environmental Ethics: What Really Matters, What Really Works*, 145–57. Oxford: Oxford University Press.

Solberg, E., E. Diener, and M. Robinson. 2004. "Why Are Materialists Less Satisfied?" In T. Kasser and A. D. Kanner, eds., *Psychology and Consumer Culture: The Struggle for a Good Life in a Materialistic World*, 29–48. Washington, DC: American Psychological Association.

Solomon, D. 1988. "Internal Objections to Virtue Ethics." In P. French, T. Uehling, and H. Wettstein, eds., *Ethical Theory: Character and Virtue*, 428–41. Notre Dame, IN: University of Notre Dame Press.

——. 2003. "Virtue Ethics: Radical or Routine?" In M. DePaul and L. Zagzebski, eds., *Intellectual Virtue: Perspectives from Ethics and Epistemology*, 57–80. Oxford: Oxford University Press.

Spinoza, B. 1972. *Ethica*. In C. Gebhardt, ed., *Spinoza, Opera, Vol. II*, 45–308. Heidelberg: Carl Winters Universitaetsbuchhandlung.

Sprawl City. 2000. "Poor Land Use or Population Growth: Which Is Worse for Sprawl?" http://www.sprawlcity.org/cgpg/index.html (accessed September 4, 2006).

Sterba, J. 1995. "A Biocentrist Fights Back." *Environmental Ethics* 17 (4): 361–76.

——. 2001. "Comments on a Morally Defensible Aristotelian Environmental Ethics." *Philosophy in the Contemporary World* 8 (2): 63–66.

——. 2001. *Three Challenges to Ethics: Environmentalism, Feminism, and Multiculturalism*. Oxford: Oxford University Press.

Stohr, K. and C. H. Wellman. 1992. "Recent Work on Virtue Ethics." *American Philosophical Quarterly* 39 (1): 49–72.

Sullivan, R. 2005. "Gates Says Technology Will One Day Allow Computer Implants—But Hardwiring's Not for Him." *Associated Press*, July 1.

Swanton, C. 2003. *Virtue Ethics: A Pluralistic View*. Oxford: Oxford University Press.

Taylor, P. 1986. *Respect for Nature: A Theory of Environmental Ethics*. Princeton: Princeton University Press.

Thompson, P. 1996. "Pragmatism and Policy: The Case of Water." In A. Light and E. Katz, eds., *Environmental Pragmatism*, 187–208. New York: Routledge.

Thoreau, H. D. 1951. *Walden*. New York: Bramhall House.

Trewavas, A. 2002. "GM Food Is the Best Option We Have." In G. Pence, ed., *The Ethics of Food*, 148–55. Lanham, MD: Rowman and Littlefield.

——. 2002. "The Population/Diversity Paradox: Agricultural Efficiency to Save Wilderness." In G. Pence, ed., *The Ethics of Food*, 168–79. Lanham, MD: Rowman and Littlefield.

The Union of Concerned Scientists. 2004. "Gone to Seed: Transgenic Contaminants of the Traditional Food Supply." http://www.ucsusa.org/food_and_environment/genetic_engineering/gone-to-seed.html (accessed August 14, 2006).

United Kingdom Department for Environment, Food, and Rural Affairs. 2004. "Margaret Beckett [Secretary of State for Environment, Food, and Rural Affairs] Outlines Precautionary Approach to GM Crops." http://www.defra.gov.uk/news/2004/040309a.htm (accessed August 11, 2006)

——. 2005. *Managing GM Crops with Herbicides: Effects on Wildlife.* London: United Kingdom Department for Environment, Food, and Rural Affairs.

United Nations. 1982. "World Charter for Nature" (October 28). http://www.un.org/documents/ga/res/37/a37r007.htm (accessed August 14, 2006).

——. 1992. "Rio Declaration on Environment and Development" (August 12). http://www.un.org/documents/ga/confi51/aconfi5126–1annex1.htm (accessed August 14, 2006).

United Nations Children's Fund. 1998. *The State of the World's Children 1998.* New York: UNICEF.

——. 2006. *The State of the World's Children 2006: Excluded and Invisible.* New York: UNICEF.

United Nations Educational, Scientific, and Cultural Organization. 2003. *United Nations World Water Development Report: Water for People, Water for Life.* Paris, New York, Oxford: United Nations.

United Nations Food and Agriculture Organization. 2004. *The State of Food and Agriculture, Agricultural Biotechnology: Meeting the Needs of the Poor?* Rome: United Nations Food and Agriculture Organization.

United Nations World Commission on Environment and Development. 1987. *Our Common Future.* Oxford: Oxford University Press.

United Nations World Summit on Sustainable Development. 2003. "Johannesburg Declaration on Sustainable Development." http://www.un.org/esa/sustdev/documents/WSSD_POI_PD/English/POI_PD.htm (accessed August 14, 2006).

United States Centers for Disease Control and Prevention. 2006. "Overweight and Obesity: Obesity Trends: U.S. Obesity Trends 1985–2004." http://www.cdc.gov/nccdphp/dnpa/obesity/trend/maps/ (accessed September 4, 2006).

United States Department of Defense, Defense Armed Research Projects Agency. 2006. "Darpa Programs." http://www.darpa.mil/index.html (accessed December 27, 2006).

United States Department of Agriculture, Economic Research Service. 2006. "Adoption of Genetically Engineered Crops in the U.S." http://www.ers.usda.gov/Data/BiotechCrops/ (accessed August 10, 2006).

United States Department of Agriculture, Office of Inspector General, Southwest Region. 2005. *Animal and Plant Health Inspection Service Controls Over Issuance of Genetically Engineered Organism Release Permits*. Washington, DC: United States Department of Agriculture, Office of Inspector General.

United States Department of Energy, Energy Information Administration. 2001. "Greenhouse Gases, Climate Change, and Energy." http://www.eia. doe.gov/oiaf/1605/ggccebro/chapter1.html (accessed September 4, 2006).

United States Environmental Protection Agency. 2000. *Emission Facts: Average Annual Emissions and Fuel Consumption for Passenger Cars and Light Trucks*. Washington, DC: Environmental Protection Agency.

——. 2002. *eGrid2002*. Washington, DC: Environmental Protection Agency.

——. 2004. "National Listing of Fish Advisories." http://epa.gov/waterscience/fish/advisories/ (accessed September 4, 2006).

United States Environmental Protection Agency, and United States Food and Drug Administration. 2004. "What You Need to Know About Mercury in Fish and Shellfish." http://www.epa.gov/waterscience/fishadvice/advice. html (accessed September 4, 2006).

United States Surgeon General. 2001. "The Surgeon General's Call to Action to Prevent and Decrease Overweight and Obesity." http://www.surgeon-general.gov/topics/obesity/calltoaction/toc.htm (accessed September 4, 2006).

——. 2005. "Overweight and Obesity: At a Glance." http://www.surgeon-general.gov/topics/obesity/calltoaction/fact_glance.htm (accessed September 4, 2006).

Van Wensveen, L. 2000. *Dirty Virtues: The Emergence of Ecological Virtue Ethics*. Amherst, NY: Humanity.

——. 2001. "Attunement: An Ecological Spin on the Virtue of Temperance." *Philosophy in the Contemporary World* 8 (2), 67–78.

——. 2001. "Ecosystem Sustainability as a Criterion for Genuine Virtue." *Environmental Ethics* 23 (3): 227–41.

Vogel, S. 2002. "Environmental Philosophy After the End of Nature." *Environmental Ethics* 24 (1): 23–39.

——. 2006. "The Silence of Nature." *Environmental Values* 15 (2): 145–71.

Wambugu, F. 2002. "Why Africa Needs Agricultural Biotech." In M. Ruse and D. Castle, eds., *Genetically Modified Foods: Debating Biotechnology*, 304–308. Amherst, NY: Prometheus.

Ward, D. R. 2003. *Water Wars: Drought, Flood, Folly, and the Politics of Thirst*. New York: Riverhead.

Watrud, L. S., E. H. Lee, A. Fairbrother, C. Burdick, J. R. Reichman, M. Bollman, et al. 2004. "Evidence for Landscape-Level, Pollen-Mediated Gene Flow from Genetically Modified Creeping Bentgrass with CP4 EPSPS as a Marker." *Proceedings of the National Academy of Sciences* 101 (40): 14533–14538.

Welchman, J. 1999. "The Virtues of Stewardship." *Environmental Ethics* 21 (4): 411–23.

———. 2005. "Stewardship: Olmsted, Character, and Environmentalism." Presented at the International Society for Environmental Ethics, Eastern Division Meeting of the American Philosophical Association, New York.

Wenz, P. 2001. "Just Garbage." In L. Westra and B. Lawson, eds., *Faces of Environmental Racism: Confronting Issues of Global Justice,* 2nd ed., 57–71. Lanham, MD: Rowman and Littlefield.

———. 2002. "Environmental Synergism." *Environmental Ethics* 24 (4): 389–408.

———. 2003. "Minimal, Moderate, and Extreme Moral Pluralism." In A. Light and H. Rolston III, eds., *Environmental Ethics: An Anthology,* 220–28. Oxford: Blackwell

———. 2004. "Synergistic Environmental Virtues." In R. Sandler and P. Cafaro, eds., *Environmental Virtue Ethics,* 197–213. Lanham, MD: Rowman and Littlefield.

Weston, A. 1996. "Before Environmental Ethics." In A. Light and E. Katz, eds., *Environmental Pragmatism,* 139–60. New York: Routledge.

———. 1996. "Beyond Intrinsic Value: Pragmatism in Environmental Ethics." In A. Light and E. Katz, eds., *Environmental Pragmatism,* 285–306. New York: Routledge.

———. 1996. "Unfair to Swamps: A Reply to Katz." In A. Light and E. Katz, eds., *Environmental Pragmatism,* 319–22. New York: Routledge.

Westra, L. 1994. *An Environmental Proposal for Ethics: The Principle of Integrity.* Lanham, MD: Rowman and Littlefield.

———. 1997. "Why Norton's Approach Is Insufficient for Environmental Ethics." *Environmental Values* 19 (3): 279–97.

———. 1998. *Living in Integrity: A Global Ethic to Restore a Fragmented World.* Lanham, MD: Rowman and Littlefield.

———. 2004. *Ecoviolence and the Law: Supranational Normative Foundations of Ecocrime.* Ardsley, NY: Transnational Publishers.

———. 2005. "Virtue Ethics as Foundation for a Global Ethic." In R. Sandler and P. Cafaro, eds., *Environmental Virtue Ethics,* 79–91. Lanham, MD: Rowman and Littlefield.

Winseman, A. 2004. "Environmental Situations in U.S., Britain, Canada" (June 1). http://poll.gallup.com/content/default.aspx?ci = 11839 (accessed August 10, 2006).

Wood, A. W. 1999. *Kant's Ethical Thought.* Cambridge: Cambridge University Press.

World Health Organization. 2006. "Controlling the Global Obesity Epidemic." http://www.who.int/nutrition/topics/obesity/en/ (accessed September 4, 2006).

——. 2006. "Vitamin A." http://www.who.int/vaccines-diseases/en/vitamina/science/sci02.shtml (accessed August 20, 2006).

World Watch Institute. 2004. *State of the World 2004: Special Focus, The Consumer Society*. New York: Norton.

Ye, X., S. Al-Babili, A. Kloti, J. Zhang, P. Lucca, P. Beyer, et al. 2000. "Engineering the Provitamin A (Beta-Carotene) Biosynthetic Pathway Into (Carotenoid-Free) Rice Endosperm." *Science* 287:303–305.

INDEX

DATE DUE

Demco, Inc. 38-293